Lecture Notes in Artificial Intelligence   1599

Subseries of Lecture Notes in Computer Science
Edited by J. G. Carbonell and J. Siekmann

Lecture Notes in Computer Science

Edited by G. Goos, J. Hartmanis and J. van Leeuwen

Springer
Berlin
Heidelberg
New York
Barcelona
Hong Kong
London
Milan
Paris
Singapore
Tokyo

Toru Ishida (Ed.)

Multiagent Platforms

First Pacific Rim International Workshop
on Multi-Agents, PRIMA'98
Singapore, November 23, 1998
Selected Papers

 Springer

Series Editors

Jaime G. Carbonell, Carnegie Mellon University, Pittsburgh, PA, USA
Jörg Siekmann, University of Saarland, Saarbrücken, Germany

Volume Editor

Toru Ishida
Kyoto University, Department of Social Informatics
606-8501 Kyoto, Japan
E-mail: ishida@i.kyoto-u.ac.jp

Cataloging-in-Publication data applied for

Die Deutsche Bibliothek - CIP-Einheitsaufnahme

Multiagent platforms : selected papers / First Pacific Rim International
Workshop, PRIMA '98, Singapore, November 23, 1998. Toru Ishida (ed.). - Berlin
; Heidelberg ; New York ; Barcelona ; Hong Kong ; London ; Milan ; Paris ;
Singapore ; Tokyo : Springer, 1999
  (Lecture notes in computer science ; 1599 : Lecture notes in artificial
  intelligence)
  ISBN 3-540-65967-6

CR Subject Classification (1998): I.2.11, C.2, I.2, H.3, H.4

ISBN 3-540-65967-6 Springer-Verlag Berlin Heidelberg New York

© Springer-Verlag Berlin Heidelberg 1999
Printed in Germany

Typesetting: Camera-ready by author
SPIN 10704753   06/3142 – 5 4 3 2 1 0   Printed on acid-free paper

Preface

Autonomous agents and multiagent systems are computational systems in which several (semi-)autonomous agents interact with each other or work together to perform some set of tasks or satisfy some set of goals. These systems may involve computational agents that are homogeneous or heterogeneous, they may involve activities on the part of agents having common or distinct goals, and they may involve participation on the part of humans and intelligent agents. The increase of agent research activities can be observed in the ICMAS (International Conference of Multi-Agent Systems) series. Two hundred and nine participants attended ICMAS'95. At ICMAS'96, the number increased to 282, and at ICMAS'98, there were 552 participants. Though we already have several workshops in Asia Pacific countries, such as MACC (Multiagent Systems and Cooperative Computation) in Japan from 1991 and the Australian Workshop on Distributed Artificial Intelligence from 1995, there is not enough interaction so far among the countries compared to Europe and the Americas.

PRIMA'98 is the First Pacific Rim International Workshop related to autonomous agents and multiagent systems. The aim of this workshop is to encourage activities in this field, and to bring together Pacific Rim researchers concerned with agents and multiagent issues. Unlike usual conferences, however, since this is the first agent-related international workshop in Asia Pacific countries, participation is by invitation only and is limited to professionals who have made significant contributions to the topics of the workshop. The contributions include technical presentations, progress reports and so on. We have received a reasonable number of papers in a short period: twenty-one papers including three invited presentations from nine countries, i.e., Australia, China, France, Japan, Korea, Singapore, Taiwan, Thailand and the United States. The workshop also included discussion on future workshops: PRIMA'99 will be held in Japan, and PRIMA'00 in Australia.

This workshop would not have been possible without the contributions of a great many people. We wish to thank Hiroshi Motoda (PRICAI'98 Program Co-Chair), Jane Hsu (PRICAI'98 Workshop Chair) for their warm support, and Xiao Feng Wang, Jung Jin Lee and Makoto Takema for their young energy and contributions to the workshop.

Workshop Chair: Toru Ishida (Kyoto University, Japan)
Marzuki Bin Khalid (Universiti Teknologi Malaysia, Malaysia)
Kwok-Yan Lam (National University of Singapore, Singapore)
Jaeho Lee (The University of Seoul, Korea)
Hideyuki Nakashima (ETL, Japan)
Ramakoti Sadananda (Asian Institute of Technology, Thailand)
Zhongzhi Shi (Chinese Academy of Sciences, China)
Soe-Tsyr Yuan (Fu-Jen University, Taiwan)
Chengqi Zhang (The University of New England, Australia)

Table of Contents

MAS Building Environments with Product-Line-Architecture Awareness

Soe-Tsyr Yuan

Information Management Department, Fu-Jen University
Taipei, Taiwan, R.O.C.
E-mail: yuans@tpts1.seed.net.tw

Abstract: A multiagent system, conceptually, is often explained in terms of a collection of agents, each of which is loosely connected with each other via Internet/Intranet and possesses the capabilities claimed such as autonomy, adaptation, and cooperation using speech acts like KQML. The agent-view of software is indeed very powerful and will keep attracting more and more people into this fantasy. But years from now, an alternative view of multiagent-based software must be developed in order to raise the quality, productivity, and scalability as well as to reduce the complexity and delivery time. Accordingly, the building environments in support of such an alternative view should be developed. This papers first illustrates the new view of next generation multiagent-based software, product-line architectures, and then presents a building environment towards such an alternative view of multiagent-based software.

1. Introduction

Intelligent agents are a new paradigm for developing software application. Agent-based computing has been recognized as a *new revolution in software* [1] and it has been predicted that agents will be pervasive in every market by year 2000 [2]. The essence of intelligent agents comprises *autonomy, adaptation, and cooperation* that are beyond the object-oriented (OO) technologies. Autonomy and adaptation basically could be realized at individual agents; however, cooperation should be investigated at multiagent systems[1]. Multi-agent systems are computational systems in which several agents interact for their own goal and for the good of the overall system. As in human world, sophisticated and huge jobs are usually performed by several individuals because individual capabilities are, after all, to some limited extent. Consequently, miming the human world, individual agents in the multi-agent system communicate, coordinate, and negotiate with one another in order to achieve greater jobs. Currently, multiagent system are being used in an increasingly wide variety of application areas, ranging from operational support and diagnosis, electronic commerce, manufacturing, information finding and filtering, planning and resource allocation, process control,

---

[1] Most of current muliagent systems still lack of the adaptation capability from the perspective of the whole system.

and service integration [3]. In the near future, we might live in a universe of agent-based software.

A multiagent system, conceptually, is often explained in terms of a collection of agents, each of which is loosely connected with each other via Internet/Intranet and possesses the capabilities claimed such as autonomy, adaptation, and cooperation using speech acts like KQML[6][2]. The agent-view of software is indeed very powerful and will keep attracting more and more people into this fantasy. But years from now, *will we have an alternative view of multiagent-based software? What will be the abstractions of agents and speech–act interactions? How will we produce and specify multiaegnt-based software?* Our clairvoyance is guided by negating some obvious contemporary "truths" and seeing if a consistent alternative view remains in the future universe of agent-based software.

As follows show the contemporary truths:
- Multiagent-based software is aiming at producing one-of-a-kind application.
- System designs are expressed in terms of agents and hard-wired interaction protocols at agents.
- Developers manually code the implementations given such designs.

It is not difficult to envision the necessary future changes to each of these points. First, future multiagent design methodologies will not focus on unique application but rather on families of related applications called product-line architectures (PLA) [4]. Designs of multiagent-based PLA will not be expressed purely in terms of agents and hard-wired interaction protocols, but rather in terms of interrelated agents or protocols. Finally, system development will exploit the concept of system infrastructure – the ability to assemble /disassemble systems of a product-line quickly and cheaply through agent component composition with less code writing.

In Section 2, we detail the rationale behind these necessary changes and shows alternative view of future multiagent-based software and the abstractions of agents and interaction protocols. Section 3 then presents a building environment implemented at our institution that is out initial step towards next generation of multiagent-base software production. Finally, a discussion and the conclusion are conducted in Section 4 and Section 5 respectively.

2. Next-Generation Multiagent-Based software

This section mainly further clarifies the necessary changes to the contemporary "truth" mentioned in Section 1. These clarification then leads to the alternative view of multiagent-based software. Various factors as shown in Fig. 1, that affect next-generation multiagent-based software, will be described in the following subsections.

---

[2] This paper only considers linguistic coordination using KQML-like speech acts, and does not consider algorithmic coordination.

2.1 Product-line Architectures

Future multiagent design methodologies will not focus on unique application because this is not rational from the economic viewpoint from past rich set of lessons [4]:

- Ad-hoc designs do not work for large-scale reuse or multiagent-generators.
- Conventional one-of-a-kind system design needs a lot of repeated efforts on communication and cooperation to configuration between agents.
- Ad-hoc designs are not suitable for assembling families of related multiagent systems.

Instead, future multiagent design methodologies should focus on families of related multiagent systems in order to enable automatic/non-automatic large-scale reuse. And the generation of a family of systems requires definition of architectures called product-line architectures (PLA). Don Batory [4] defines a PLA to be a blue-print for creating families of related applications. PLAs are appropriate for domains that are well understood and have known standard processes. Though the concept of PLAs in that paper were only concerning to conventional software like object-oriented applications. However, we think the concept should also applies to multiagent-based software. The importance of PLAs is two-fold: multiagent system complexity is greater then conventional software and keeps growing and the costs of system development and maintenance must be restrained. PLAs enable companies to amortized the effort of software design and development over multiple products within their families, substantially reducing costs at companies.

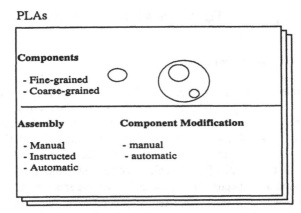

Fig. 1. Various factors that affect next-generation multiagent-based software.

2.2 Product-Line Components

Building multiagent systems from components is the ultimate goal of PLA concept. A component can be described at two levels: the fine-grained level of a single agent or a protocol; the coarse-grained level of a suite of interrelated agents and the involved interaction protocols or a set of protocols. The purpose of the coarse-level components is to scale the unit of multiagent design and system construction from an individual agent or a protocol to a multiagent framework or a protocol package, enabling large-scale reuse and abstractions of agents and speech–act interactions. Since a PLA is only concerning to a family of related multiagent systems, the scope of necessary components is easily confined and justified so that companies can fully focus on their to-be-produced components and even collaborate with other companies for a given PLA. Also the components will be written by domain experts with best-practice approaches so that the components will offer substantial increases in software productivity, performance, reliability, and quality.

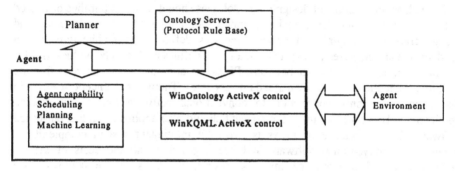

Fig. 2. Empowered Agent Structure.

2.3 Product-Line Assembly

Given a collection of PLA components, building of multiagent systems then reduced to a task of assembling suitable components to solve the problem at hands. Assembly also can be realized at three levels: manual integration of components (assembly components under designers' will), instructed manual integration of components (assembly components under the instructions of building environments), and use of generators that automatically assemble systems from either the problem specification or the component specification (assembly components by just giving the system goals). Each way of assembly is exercising component reuse. In component reuse, it is often the case that manual modification of components would result in a major loss in productivity, but sometime component modification is unavoidable. Therefore, there are two ways of exercising component reuse: manual customized modification of components or automatically customized modification of components (with or without hands-on modification inside components in order to make the integration of components workable).

3. Towards Next-Generation Multiagent Building Environment

Seeing various characteristics of next-generation multiagent-based software, it is obvious that any multiagent building environment would depend on the characteristics the multiagent software intends to possess This section presents a building environment called Eureka that is our initial step towards building next-generation multiagent-based software. The tool aims to build PLA-view multiagent-based software with fine-grained components (The extension to coarse-grained components is also underway.), manual assembly of components, and minor manual customized modification in component reuse (Currently, we are working on automatically customized modification in component reuse and expect it will be completed at the end of this year). As shown in Fig. 2, the tool also provides a communication component, WinKQML, that enable agents to communicate with each other, and has two bulit-in component, Protocol Package (Server) that enable agents to know how to cooperate with each other and Planner that enables easy invocation of constructed multiagent systems by users.

3.1 The Basic Concepts in Eureka

As we mentioned Section 1, the magic of multiagent system is in the autonomous and adaptive capabilities of individual agents and the cooperative capability among individual agents. Each individual agent is like a IC-chip (a PLA fine-grained component) which might be designed by the multiagent system designing team, purchased from other companies, or attained from your inventory of used stuff. Each of them has its own heterogeneous capability of autonomous or adaptive type. No matter the nature of their intelligence is user-programmed, created by traditional knowledge-based AI techniques, or learning from the users [10], there is a common capability existing among them, that is, knowing how to communicate with each other and thus cooperate with each other in order to achieve some common goal. *Eureka's intended missions are providing a panel for facilitating the assembly of agents, making them work together, and installing a switch-like handle for future users of the multiagent system who are able to initiate the working of the whole multiagent system. In other words, a panel filled with the assembled architecture of component agents constitutes a fielded real-world problem processing software that employs the multi-agent technology.* As follows are more detailed descriptions of Eureka's missions:

- Provide a graphical configuration panel for developers to create or modify their own configuration of individual agents (PLA fine-grained component) that are attained from varying sources. (Details are in Section 3.2.2)
- Endow each activated individual agent the communicative and coordinative capability so that the agent could work with other agents for achieving the common goal of the multiagent system. (Details are in Section 3.1.1, 3.2.2, 3.2.3)
- Offer a planning mechanism on the top of all individual agents of multiagent system. As a result, given the common goal of the whole multiagent system as well as the capabilities of individual agents, the multiagent system then autonomously knows how to initiate the high level cooperation between some agents.

Accordingly, the detail-level cooperation between agents, that involves agent communication and interaction, is in progress, fulfilling the intended goal of the multiagent system. (Details are in Section 3.2.4)

3.1.1 Built-in PLA Component – Protocol Package

This section describe a coarse-grained component provided by Eureka, which consists of a suited of interrelated interaction protocols and enables large-scale reuse of cooperation knowledge at agents. The illustration goes break as follows: first the concept and then core elements of linguistic agent cooperation.

Individual agents of multiagent system operate in a distributed environment, cooperating with each other. Therefore, agents require mechanisms that allow them to communicate with other, including human agent. When agents cooperate, they engage in conversations or protocols that can be represented in speech acts, and languages have been developed to support this. KQML is a language for simple communication among individual agents, which is currently becoming a defacto standard agent communication language.

As we mentioned above, the common capability among individual agents is to know how to communicate and then cooperate with other agents, including human agents. Eureka presumes each individual agent knows and uses the KQML language as the communication language among individual agents. As for cooperation, the nature of cooperation intelligence could be user-programmed, created by traditional knowledge-based AI techniques, or by learning from the users. Jenning [11] considered cooperation intelligence could be captured as another form of knowledge, social level knowledge, above the general domain problem-solving level knowledge within agents as in Fig. 3.

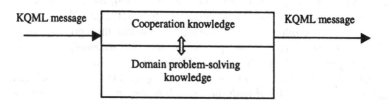

Fig. 3. Simple agent knowledge architecture.

Jennings claimed such social level knowledge provides an abstract framework for comparing and analyzing all types of multiagent system. It peels away the consideration of implementation and application specific details so that the core of whole system could be investigated more easily. Also, it provides a high-level model, which can assist in the development of future multiagent system, there is an increasingly greater need of design methodologies and tools for the social knowledge level.[3] Eureka is just playing such role of social knowledge level tool, at which

---

[3] Just like there are now many domain knowledge level methodologies and tools [11].

various social level design methodologies, such as organizational design [5,6] and market-based design [7,8], can be easily employed and played.

In general, there is some common and popular cooperation knowledge, which are currently heavily used by a lot of multiagent system. For example, a commonly used cooperation protocol, Contract Net Protocol (CNP) [12], is used in many multiagent system like [7]. CNP is a type of market-based social level design methodology. With CNP, a Manager has a task and broadcasts a Task Announcement message to other agents. If the agent that receives the message has the ability to execute the task, it sends a Bid message to the Manager. If the Manager sends an Award message, the agent that receives it becomes a Contractor of the Manager. Another example of a popular cooperation protocol is the Facilitator Protocol (FP) [6]. FP is a type of organizational social level design. With FP, a single agent termed a facilitator is used to help one agent communicate with another agent, possibly unknown to it, to help the first agent solve its problem. The possible helps the facilitator offer can vary. Here are a variety of possibilities, taken from [6]: subscribe, recruit, recommend, and broker.

This common social level knowledge could be duplicated at each individual agent as in [13]. However, our opinion is that there is no need of incorporating such cooperation knowledge at each individual agent within multiagent system. The reasons are three-fold:

- Each individual agent may play different role in a cooperation protocol and thus their social behaviors subsequently might not be the same. For example, with CNP protocol, the Manager's behavior is different from the contractor's.
- On the other hand, an individual agent might involve in multiple cooperation protocols at the same time and thus play different roles in different protocols. For example, an agent plays the Manger role in a CNP protocol dealing with some members of the multiagent system, and plays a service-provider role in a FP protocol dealing with some other members of the multiagent system.
- In case there is a change in some cooperation protocol, the duplication method then might incur the problems of heavy overhead of updating the cooperation knowledge and inconsistency of cooperation knowledge at those individual agents.

As a result, putting the social level knowledge in a centralized place and facilitating the different usages of such knowledge at different moments of cooperations is the rest we should investigate. Such a centralized place constitutes a PLA coarse-grained component, Protocol Package, which is built in Eureka. The way we propose will be described in Section 3.2.3. People might criticize this with the communication overhead. However, if the members of multiagent system are distributed within a local intranet, then such communication overhead should be negletable. When the members of multiagent system distributed scatteringly over a very large scope on the Internet, we could sector them into a few territories and duplicate the social level knowledge in each territory where the local agents still utilize their centralized social level knowledge. Even though the problem of inconsistency might occur here, the sources of this problem will be reduced to the minimal level. In this paper, we investigate the former situation where the agents of multiagent system inhabit within some easily reachable cyberspace.

3.1.2 Built-in PLA Component – Planner

Eureka currently only supports those multiagent systems where the component agents commit themselves to coordinate their strategies for the common goal of the whole coalition. The users of these developed multiagent systems should have an interface to invoke the operation of the multiagent system. We call such interface the handle to the multiagent system. Such handle should be as simple as possible. Otherwise, chances are the users, who are supposed to have far less technical background than multiagent system developers, reluctantly use the multiagent system at their fields. For example, asking those users to write some special scripts in order to invoke the processing of a multiagent system is almost infeasible at many fields. In most cases, the handle is the step of initiating the starting component of the system, which subsequently invokes the necessary speech-act cooperation between components. However, for complicated MAS, the handle might involve initiating many different starting components synchronously/asynchronously. Eureka thus bears the responsibilities of lessening the load to the greatest extent in behalf of users as possibly as it can. What the users need to do is only specify a common goal, and the subsequent detailed invocation would be handled by Eureka. The details will be described in Section 3.2.4.

3.2. The Design of Eureka

In this section, descriptions of the internal architecture of Eureka and its components are provided. We also explain how Eureka's mission is reached via such architecture.

3.2.1 The Internal Architecture

Fig. 4 shows the internal architecture of Eureka. System developers first register each participating agent with the agent name server with its name, IP address, and port number. The graphical agent configuration panel then is the graphical configuration place for system developers to create or modify their own configuration of individual agents. Whenever system developers drop an agent icon into the panel, the panel would ask for the name of that agent, which is running at its dedicated place in the cyber space. Whenever system developers drop an arc between agents, the panel would ask for the name of the communication protocol used by the agents. Each individual agent inside the panel has the power of communication and cooperation through some ActiveX controls provided by Eureka. The communication capability of agents is offered by the KQML ActiveX controls. The cooperation capability of agents is offered by the ontology server and ontology ActiveX controls. The ontology server is the centralized place where the common social level knowledge of agents resides. The ontology server facilitates the different usages of these common social level knowledge at different moments of cooperation. The planner aims to simply the multiagent system handle on the behalf of multiagent system users.

3.3 Graphical Agent Configuration Panel

The panel aims to *provide a place to configure real-world agents graphically and make them into workable multiagent system revealing the agent capabilities of autonomy, adaptation, and cooperation.* As shown in Fig. 4, each smiling node represents a real-world agent and may play different roles at different communication protocols. The addition of such a smiling node requires the steps as follows:
1. The specification of where the real-world agent is at or its name with the help of the agent name server.
2. The specification of the actions (functionalities) when it comes to starting components.

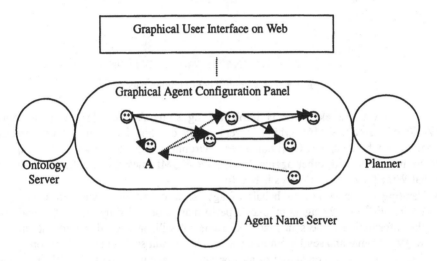

Fig. 4. Architecture of Eureka.

The addition of an arc between agent nodes specifies the relationship between agents within a particular protocol indicated by those particular styled arc lines. For example, in Fig. 4, the smiling agent A plays a bidder role in a CNP protocol indicated by solid lines, but plays the facilitator role in a facilitator protocol indicated by dash lines. All these setups are done very easily via graphical editing panel. In other words, *a system developer is able to designate the component agents of multiagent system, and arrange them abiding by a given PLA.* The look of the panel is shown in Fig. 5 .

The rest of this section then explains how each agent inside the panel has the power of communication via some ActiveX controls provided by Eureka. As to the power of cooperation among agents will be explained in section 3.2.3.

Agent communication language KQML has been heavily used as the inter-communication language among agents. There are some available KQML packages such as Lockheed [14], which provided KQML APIs for agent developers to incorporate into their systems so that they could communicate with each other with KQML informatives. They have two drawbacks. First, the process of the incorporation of these KQML API, in fact, is still bothersome and becomes an obstacle on the road paved for easy configuration of multiagent systems. Second, current KQML API packages are only available for Unix workstation users and only compatible with C language implementations, and thus personal computer users have no easy way to incorporate such defacto communication standard. Accordingly, Eureka bears the responsibilities of lessening the load of incorporating KQML communication capability at each agent, and making these communication empowered agents, which are implemented with various languages, workable over personal computers.

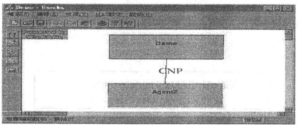

Fig. 5. The graphical configuration panel.

The way Eureka does is implementing some ActiveX [15] control called WinKQML ActiveX [16], which is very easily combined into agents on personal computers where support OLE container environment [15], and enables those agents to communicate with other agents through the KQML messages as shown in Fig. 2. What WinKQML ActiveX does is two-folds:

- Sending out messages on behalf of agents: when an agent want to send some information out, the agent invokes a performative provided by the control and gets the information to be sent ready. The control will package this information into KQML format and send it out in a way of Data Gram socket communication.
- Receiving message on behalf of agents: when an agent receives a KQML message, the control will unpackage the KQML message and extract the information content for the agent's subsequent processing.

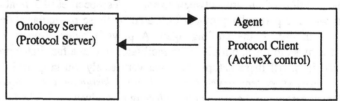

Fig. 6. Cooperation mechanism based on client-server model.

3.2.3 Ontology Server

The ontology server is a centralized place where the common social level knowledge of agents resides, and facilitates the different usages of these common social level knowledge at different moments of cooperation in behalf of agents. As mentioned in section 3.2.1, each agent inside the panel has the power of cooperation. This power is provided by the combination of the Ontology ActiveX control at agents' side (client side) and the ontology server of Eureka (server side) as shown in Fig. 6. The rest of this section then describes the cooperation mechanisms based on client-server model.

On agent client-side, Eureka provides Ontology ActiveX control called WinOntology ActiveX [17], which is very easily combined into agents on personal

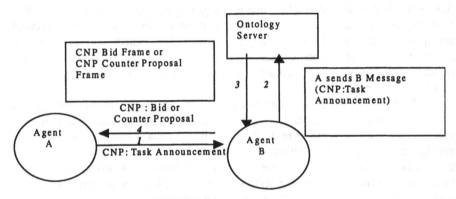

Fig. 7. Detailed cooperation mechanism.

computers where support OLE container environment, and enables those agents to know how to cooperate with other agents. What WinOntology ActiveX does is two-fold, taking the Fig. 7 as the example:

- When agent B receives a CNP Task Announcement from agent A, what agent B is supposed to response is attained by the control sending a request to the ontology server for appropriate response frames in correspondence to the CNP Task announcement message, as in the second step of Fig. 7
- The control receives the response frames (the third step of Fig. 7), such as bid frame or counter proposal frame, and presents them to agent B so that agent B, based on its capability, determines the frame, fills in relevant information, and sends the frame to agent A, as in the fourth step of Fig. 7.

On the server side, the ontology server is a rule-based system, which aims to produce appropriate response frames in correspondence to the incoming request of protocol and performative.

3.2.4 Planner

The planner aims to automate the reasoning of the necessary high level cooperation between some agents and thus much simplifies the handle of the multiagent system for users. The planner Eureka uses is UCPOP [18], which is a partial-ordered causal planner and has been prevalent in recent years.

As mentioned in Section 3.2.1, the starting components in the panel are associated with its actions (functionalities). These actions, specified by its preconditions and postconditions, are then made to be known to the planner. Accordingly, an input of the multiagent system, a user's goal, could be realized by the causal reasoning of the preconditions and postconditions of actions of agents, and thus the high level cooperation between some agents autonomously takes place. That is, a fielded real-world problem solving process is coming alive.

3.3 Application of Eureka

This section briefly describes a financial multiagent system as shown in Fig. 8, which is configured at Eureka and is currently running on the Internet. For detailed descriptions, please refer [19]. The basic objective of this financial multiagent system is to provide the performance prediction on high-technology stocks according to the internal reasoning of the multiagent system on past and most current stock information and news.

The agents of the architecture fall into three categories. The first category is information agents, whose task is the automatic gathering and integration of information such as stock news on Web, subscribed e-mails of economic indexes, and real-time stock market information. The second category is task agents, whose jobs are processing and reasoning those gathered information for stock performance prediction. The third category is interface agent, whose jobs are accepting investors' inputs of stock ticker names. These agents communicate and cooperate with each other, using WinKQML performative as well as some conversation protocol like CNP and FP.

For example, information agent manager for HTTP takes charge of regularly gathering stock news or data on Web, which might be available from multiple agents such as HTTP agent1 and HTTP agent2. These three agents are related in a CNP protocol, in which the information agent manager for HTTP plays the Manager role, and HTTP agent1 and HTTP agent2 play the bidder role. That is, in a situation where the sources of information are not predetermined and might not be stable, the job is still performed without depending on specific sources of information. Same thing applies to the information agent manager for POP3 that takes charge of regularly gathering economic indexes from subscribed e-mail.

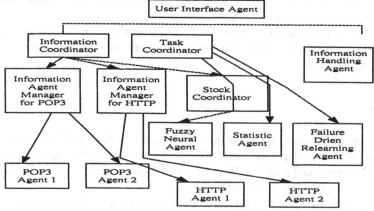

Fig. 8. Financial multi-agent architecture.

The Stock coordinator is responsible for daily collection of stock data from some web sites or Systex company, a stock information vendor licensed by official Taiwan Stock Exchange Center. This shows the flexibility on the choice of stock information resources.

The information coordinator plays a facilitator role in a facilitator protocol, in which the information agent manager for HTTP, information agent manager for POP3, and the stock coordinator get the answer from the information coordinator regarding where their gathered information are supposed to be placed and stored. Accordingly, these information agent managers and the stock agent could send their information gathered as well as its type to the information handling agent to store. The type of coordination allows minimal managerial efforts for future system growth in terms of data-storage expansion and change.

The information handling agent basically takes charge of the management of different types of information, comprising the storage, retrieval, and updating of news, indexes, and stock data from various information agent mangers and the stock coordinator.

The task coordinator takes charge of coordinating different agents, the fuzzy neural agent, the statistic agent, the failure driven relearning agent, and the information handling agent, in order to obtain a performance prediction for high-technology stocks. The task coordinator does is also play a facilitator role. The fuzzy neural agent, communicating with the information handling agent and receiving stock information via the task coordinator, regularly learns prediction models of high-technology stocks. The failure driven relearning agent refines prediction model by obtaining more appropriate representation space of the fuzzy neural agent and by relearning the prediction model when the original prediction model's performance is poor to a point where it exceeds a failure-threshold point. That is, both the fuzzy neural agent and failure driven relearning agent autonomously trigger further data collection and extraction due to their own need at run time. The statistic agents produce a variety of stock charts or plots in correspondence to users' requests.

4. Discussion

In this section, we would state the experience of developing multiagent systems using Eureka, discuss its further strength other than PLA view of multiagent-based software mentioned in section 2 and section 3 and its further future improvements.

The initial motivations behind Eureka are simply smaller agent-reuse effort, easier multi-agent configuration, simple human-computer interaction, prevailing multiagent enabling environment, and raised quality in mutltiagent systems. Accordingly, Eureka ends up having simple agent reuse, graphical assembly style of configuration, agent cooperation facilitated by high-level planning and low-level protocol sharing, simple user interaction with multiagent systems, and window-based multiagent enabling environment. In other words, Eureka reduces the complexity, the delivery time, the amount of reinvention in the context of multiagent system design.

With Eureka, with all stand-alone components being available, what developers should do are simply do things as follows:

- Drop the WinKQML ActiveX control and the ontology ActiveX control into each component agent when these controls are not yet there. Subsequently, only minor modification is needed within agents in order to reuse them.
- Configure the component agents within the Graphic Agent Configuration Panel binding the social relationships between agents. With the reported functions of the starting agents, the planner of Eureka invokes the execution of the Task Coordinator and thus detail-level cooperation between agents are then in progress fulfilling user's goal.

Table 1 further shows Eureka's strength over other current existing tools mentioned in section 2.

	Current tools	Eureka
•Agent reuse effort	medium-heavy	small
•Agent configuration	No	Yes
•Agent communication/ Agent interoperability	Unix-KQML	Win-KQML
•Agent cooperation effort	medium-heavy	small
• Platform	Unix	Window
• User-interaction	medium-hard	easy

Table 1. Eureka's strength analysis.

Below are further comparison between Eureka and other most relevant tools with regards to social cooperation knowledge management within agents:

- COOL: an extension to KQML and with it agents can make proposals and counterproposals, accept and reject goals, and notify other agents of goal cancellation, satisfaction, or failure. *COOL is a language with which multiagent system developers could build the cooperation knowledge inside agents.* The strength of COOL is its flexibility of specifying cooperation knowledge. However, its weakness is 'high entrance barrier' of using COOL and thus hard to be promoted among public. Also reuse of cooperation knowledge is not considered here.
- AgentTalk: another specification language of cooperation knowledge within agents and with it new protocols could be defined as extensions of predefined ones. Its strength and weakness are the same as COOL.
- MASCOOF: a platform in which the cooperation between agents is driven by cooperation protocols specified by the language COOPLAS[22] and stored in a library duplicated inside each agent. Its strength is stepping a big jump than before by reusing interaction protocols. Its weakness mainly lies in the problems of duplicating, such as overhead of duplicating and inconsistency as mentioned in section 3.2, and its still-hard-to-use nature.
- KAoS: a tool that provides a communicative language with semantics and a way of defining social cooperation knowledge based on an alternative form of state-transition diagrams. Basically, agents' social protocols are self-implemented. As a

result, the same strength and weakness as COOL and AgentTalk also apply to KAoS here.

In summary, Eureka is an attempt in making the development of multiagent system as possibly easy as it can. Therefore, issues of human-computer interaction, ease of communication, reuse of interaction protocols, facilitation of cooperation are all taken into account. As a result, Eureka stands in a global view assisting multiagent system configuration. This contrasts with the other tools that depend on careful deployment of interaction at each agent made by multiagent developers.

In advancing the merits of Eureka, naturally comes scalability, that enables graceful resolve of the development complexity of large scale multiagent systems. As we have mentioned in the beginning of the paper, component reuse, regardless of fine-grained reuse or coarse-grained reuse, is very important at the issue of how to attack the complexity and scalability of large systems. Eureka beats other existing tools by originally providing the assembly/disassembly infrastructure for fine-grained components. It then comes naturally that Eureka has the extensibility of having assembly/disassembly infrastructure for coarse-grained components.

After mentioning the strength of Eureka, we think there are still plenty of rooms for its future further improvements as shown below:

- Allow self-defined protocols: Eureka does not have the flexibility of specifying arbitrary interaction protocols as developer's wish. Our future research is to devise a protocol specification language with which multiagent system developers could define their own protocols. Subsequently, the newly defined protocols would be automatically translated into new social-level knowledge stored at the ontology server and reused by their multiagent systems.

- Enable automatically customized modification of agents in reuse: As so far minor modification within agents is still necessary before their reuse, as opposed to free modification within agents for their reuse. Now we are in a process of devising and implementing such a mechanism, and that seems very promising.

- Instructed assembly of agents: Currently, the assembly of agents is a manual configuration process, in which system developers are responsible for the social relationship between agents, as opposed to a semi-automatic configuration process, in which developers are guided at determining the social relationships between agents.

- Provide better management of multiagent systems: In addition to offering a multi-agents assembly/disassembly workplace, the Panel has the great potential of doing more things like monitoring the status of all individual agents of the workplace, tallying some statistics of the multiagent system such as service through-put in low net traffic and high net traffic.

- Put into practice the assembly/disassembly infrastructure for coarse-grained components: Add minor extension to Eureka and experience it with a large scale and complex problems.

5. Conclusion

As Internet/WWW has brought human world more closer, the scope of human's job is becoming broader and more sophisticated. Multiagent system research then plays increasingly important role at helping out human's job because of cooperation automation between autonomous or adaptive agents. However, the bigger scope of a system it is, the greater need its building environments should embrace the concept of the product line architecture, because these environments determine the success of the resulting systems. Therefore, PLA-aware building environments are worth of everybody's attention and effort.

Eureka is an attempt at becoming such a PLA-aware building environment for system developers. The main contributions Eureka are the first attempt in making the development of multiagent system as easily as chip assembly of personal computers. With such attempt in mind, Eureka greatly simplifies the configuration of agents, the endowment of communication capability as well as cooperation capability at agents, and fielded problem solving. Hence, Eureka reduces the complexity, delivery time, reinvention in the context of multiagent system design, and furthermore, it has the extensibility of larger scale reuse within agents.

Reference:

1. Ovum Report: Intelligent Agents: the New Revolution in Software (1994)
2. P.C. Janc: Pragmatic Application of Information Agents. BIS Strategic Report (1995)
3. The Practical Application Company: Proceedings of the Second International Conference on the Practical Application of Intelligent and Multi-Agent Technology (1997)
4. D. Batory: Product Line Architectures. Small Talk an Java in Industry and Practical Training, Germany (1998).
5. S-T Yuan: A Decentralized Multy Virtual Mall. PAAM (1997)
6. T. Finin and R. Fritzson: KQML as an Agent Communication Language. Proceedings of the Third International Conference on Information and Knowledge Management (1994)
7. Isoo Ueno, Sen Yoshida, and Kazuhiro Kuwabara: A Multi-Agent Approach to Service Integration. PAAM (1997)
8. J.A Rodriguez. P. Noriega, C. Sierra, and J. Padget: FM96.5 a Java-Based Electronic Auction House. PAAM (1997)
9. B. Chaib-draa: Interaction between Agents in Routine, Familiar, and Unfamiliar Situations. Department d'informatique, Faculte des Science, Universite Laval, Canada (1997)
10. Pattie Maes: Software Agents.   Media Lab, MIT (1997)
11. N.R. Jennings and J.R. Campos: Towards a Social Level Characterization of Socially Responsible Agents.   IEEE Proceedings on Software Eengineering (1997)
12. R.G. Smith: The Contract Nnet Protocol: High-Level Communication and Control in a Distributed Problem Solver.   IEEE Transaction on Computing (1980)
13. Omar Belakhdar: Using Ontology-Sharing to Designing Automated Cooperation in Protocol-Driven Multi-Agent Systems.   PAAM (1997)
14. Lockheed Martin C2 Integration Systems: Lockheed Martin/UMBC Implementation of KQML. http://www.paoli.atm.lmco.com/kqml (1995)
15. Microsoft: http://www.microsoft.com/ (1996)

16. AI Lab of Fu-Jen: WinKQML ActiveX Control. Information Management Department, Fu-Jen University, Taipei, Taiwan (1997)

17. AI Lab of Fu-Jen: WinOntology ActiveX Control. Information Management Department, Fu-Jen University, Taipei, Taiwan (1997)

18. UCPOP: Computer Science Department, University of Washington, USA (1995)

19. S-T Yuan: Multi-agent Approach as a Catalyst to a Financial KDD Process. Third International Symposium on Data Engineering and Learning, Hong Kong (1998)

20. M. Barbuceanu and M.S. Fox: COOL: a Language for Describing Coordination in Multi-Agent Systems. First International Conference on Multi-Agent Systems (1995)

21. K. Kuwabara, T. Ishida, and N. Osata: AgentTalk: Describing Multiagent Coordination Protocols with Inheritance. Proceedings of Tools for Artificial Intelligence (1995)

22. Belakhdar and J. Ayel: COOPLAS - Cooperation Protocols Specification Language. First International Workshop on Decentralized Intelligent and MultiAgent Systems (1995)

23. JATlite: Stanford University, http://java.stanford.edu/java_agent/html/

24. Odyssey: General Magic, http://www.genmagic.com/agents/odyssey.html (1997)

25. DMARS: Australian Artificial Intelligence Institute Ltd., http://www.aaii.oz.au/proj/dMARS-prod-brief.html (1997)

26. H. J. Mueller: (Multi-) Agent Engineering. International Journal on Data and Knowledge Engineering, Special Issue on Distributed Expertise, 23 (1997)

27. F.v. Martial: Coordinating Plans of Autonomous Agents. Springer LNCS 610 (1992)

28. Jeffrey M. Bradshaw: KaoS - an Open Agent Architecture – Supporting Reuse, Interoperability, and Extensibility. KAW'96 (1996)

29. ABE: IBM T. J. Watso Aglets, IBM Japan, http://www.trl.ibm.co.jp/aglets/ (1997)

30. Research Lab: http://www.networking.ibm.com/iag/iagwatsn.htm (1996)

ADIPS Framework for Flexible Distributed Systems

Tetsuo Kinoshita[1]   and   Kenji Sugawara[2]

[1] Research Institute of Electrical Communication, Tohoku University,
2-1-1 Katahira Aoba-ku, Sendai 980-8577, Japan
kino@riec.tohoku.ac.jp
[2] Dep. of Network Science, Chiba Institute of Technology,
2-17-1 Tsudanuma, Narashino 275-0016, Japan
suga@suga.cs.it-chiba.ac.jp

Abstract.   A next generation distributed system is expected to be flexible in the sense that the system is able to deal with various changes of both the users' requirements and the operational conditions of system's environment. The aim of our research is to establish a new design methodology of the flexible distributed systems based on agent-based computing technology. To do so, we propose an agent-based distributed information processing system (ADIPS) as a design model of flexible distributed systems. Furthermore, we have developed an agent-based computing framework called ADIPS Framework which supports the design and implementation of flexible distributed systems. In this paper, we discuss the architecture and functions of ADIPS Framework together with the applications realized by using ADIPS framework.

1   Introduction

The next generation distributed systems have to provide various services for the users living in the networked information spaces realized on the large-scale distributed systems. In the real world, the distributed systems confront with various perturbations of their functions which are caused by the changes of both the users' requirements and operational conditions of the system's environment. As a result, the quality of service of such systems is changed and degraded along with these changes of the systems.

Recently, the studies aiming this problem have been started in the fields such as the advanced information networks [2,7,9,10] and the distributed mullet-media application systems [1,8,14,15]. In order to provide the user-oriented, intelligent and stable services for users, a distributed system should have a mechanism to maintain the quality of service against various changes observed in the system's operational environment. With this mechanism, a distributed system has a capability to deal with the fluctuating operational environment, and we call such a distributed system a flexible distributed system.

The essential functions of flexible distributed system are defined from a view point of changes of both the users' requirements and the operational conditions of the systems' environment. To design and implement a flexible distributed system with new functions, we adopt the agent-based computing technology as one of the promising technologies. Although many kinds of architecture and mechanisms of agent-based systems have been proposed and implemented, the effective methodology and tools have not been provided for designers and developers of agent-based systems. Hence, we have proposed and implemented an agent-based computing framework for developing the agent-based flexible distributed systems.

In section 2, we propose a notion of a flexible distributed system (FDS), and discuss the essential functions of FDS. In section 3, an agent-based distributed information processing system (ADIPS) is introduced as a design model of FDS. Then, the ADIPS framework is proposed as a new framework to design and implementation of the agent-based flexible distributed systems based on the ADIPS model. Next, in section 4, we explain the several applications of FDS to show the ability of the ADIPS Framework. Finally, we conclude our work and future problems in section 5.

2   Flexible Distributed System

2.1   Notion of Flexible Distributed System

A distributed system consists of various distributed computer systems and the information networks which are called a platform of the distributed system. According to the requests given by users, the services of distributed system are realized by using functions of the platform and provided for users. From a view point of the configuration of the services of distributed system, the following changes have to be considered at the run time of the system.

• variation of the required services: many kinds of services have to be realized in accordance with various user's requests in which the quality of the required services (the required QoS) are specified.

• change of the quality of service (QoS) of a platform: due to the growth of the communication traffic or the computational load of the platform, the QoS provided for users are degraded as the computational resources of the platform are decreased.

• change of the users' requirements: due to change of both the required services and the provided QoS of the platform, the users' requirements can easily be shifted to another one.

A notion of flexibility is expressed as a system's capability to deal with these changes, i.e., the flexibility of a distributed system is that the system can modify its structure and functions against various changes of the system's operational environment observed at the run time [8]. In this sense, a flexible distributed system (FDS) has to have the following functional characteristics.

• *User-oriented*:   a FDS accepts a user's request at any time and tries to realize the services which maximally satisfy the request from a view points of the user.

• *Homeostatic*: a FDS can modify its structure and functions temporally to maintain the required QoS against various temporal changes observed at the run.

• *Evolution*: a FDS can change its structure and functions permanently to adapt the drastic and permanent changes of both the users' requirements and the system's operational environment.

A distributed system in which the above three characteristics have been reflected harmonically, is called a Flexible Distributed System (FDS).

2.2   Essential Functions of Flexible Distributed System

A distributed system, in general, consists of various functional components located on a platform. In the design of a FDS, we assume that the FDS consists of a distributed system (DS), a component repository (CR) which holds and manages the components to be used in the DS, and the following five functions.

(F1) *Request Acquisition Function (RAF)* receives and analyses the user's requests to detect the changes of the user's requirements.

(F2) *Platform Sensor Function (PSF)* monitors the operational conditions of a platform and sends the reports to other functions.

(F3) *Parameter Tuning Function (PTF)* receives the reports on the changes from RAF and PSF, makes a plan to find a component of DS to be tuned, and modifies the parameters of the selected component.

(F4) *Component Replacement Function (CRF)* receives the reports from RAF and PSF, and makes and executes a plan to exchange a component of DS with a new component selected by CR.

(F5) *DS Reconstruction Function (DRF)* is a function to deal with a drastic change of the system. As same as CRF, receiving the reports from RAF and PSF, DRF determines a subsystem to be redesigned and makes a plan to build a new subsystem. According to the plan, DRF selects the components from CR, combines them into a new subsystem in order to reorganize the whole system.

To realize these functions, it is convenient to treat the functional components of the distributed systems as high level modules that can be combined each other and organized as the subsystems of the FDS. Hence, the functional components will be realized as intelligent agents using knowledge of respective components.

3   Agent-based Computing Framework for FDS

3.1   ADIPS Model

To realize the FDS, the functional components of a distributed system are design and implemented as the agents of FDS which work cooperatively to realize the users' requirements based on knowledge of both the structure and functions (services) of respective agents. To do so, we propose a design model of *an agent-based distributed information processing system (ADIPS)* and a design support environment called *ADIPS Framework*[3,4,5].

The features of the ADIPS model can be summarized as follows;

(1) *Agentification of components*: the functional components of distributed systems have been designed and implemented as the computational processes called base processes in this paper, that run on the platforms of distributed systems. Acquiring knowledge of a design of a base process, the functions to manage and control the base process as an agent are defined and combined with the base process. In the ADIPS model, this kind of agent is called *primitive agent*. An operation to define a primitive agent is called *agentification* of a base process. The ADIPS agent architecture provides an agentification mechanism for designers.

(2) *Requirements-driven design*: according to the users' requirements, the primitive agents can be combined each other to make an organization of agents which provides the requested services for users. In an organization of agents, there exists an agent which is responsible to manage and control an organization and its members. This kind of agent is called *organizational agent*. The hierarchical construction of services can easily be designed by defining an organizational agent which holds several organizational agents as its members. Hence, the design of distributed system is reformed into the design of the agents and the organization of agents based on the users' requirements.

(3) *Reuse of assets*: it is useful to provide the existing sets of both organizational agents and primitive agents for designers in advance, because the designers can select suitable agents which have the required services and functions, and also reuse these agents to construct the target distributed system. The reuse-based design is one of effective methods to develop the design object in an efficient and systematic way. Using agentification operation, the existing useful base processes can be defined as the primitive agents. The organizational agents can also be defined to reuse the design cases of services/functions of distributed systems. Accumulating and reusing the assets based on the ADIPS model, the reuse-based design of distributed system can be promoted.

Under the ADIPS model, an ADIPS is designed as an organization of agents which consists of both the primitive agents and the organizational agents. The organization of agents can work as an intelligent software robot which provides the required services for users. Moreover, an ADIPS can cooperate with the other ADIPS to deal with the complex tasks. Such an organization of ADIPS can be considered as a society of intelligent software robots.

3.2 ADIPS Agent Architecture

An ADIPS agent architecture depicted in Fig.1 is introduced to design and implement the primitive and organizational agents. An agentification mechanism consists of three functional modules, i.e., 1) *Cooperation Mechanism* (CM), 2) *Task Processing Mechanism* (TPM), and 3) *Domain Knowledge base* (DK).

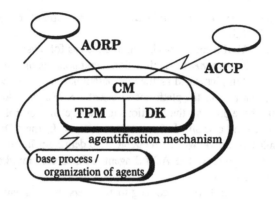

Fig. 1. ADIPS Agent Architecture

The CM provides the communication functions not only to exchange information between agents but also to construct/reconstruct the organization of agents. The CM uses two kinds of communication protocols, i.e., *ADIPS organization/reorganization protocol (AORP)* and *ADIPS communication/cooperation protocol (ACCP)*. The details of the protocols are explained in the next section.

The TPM is responsible to execute and control a task assigned to an agent via the communication between CM and DK. A TPM of a primitive agent is responsible to manage the task execution done by its base process. In an organizational agent, a TPM is responsible to manage and control the execution of subtasks assigned to the members of its organization.

The DK holds knowledge and knowledge processing mechanisms to control whole behavior of an agent. As shown in Fig.2, a message analyzer receives and classifies the message of both CM and TPM, and selects a suitable message processor to deal with this message. A message processor is a knowledge processing mechanism that has knowledge to deal with a task specified by the received messages.

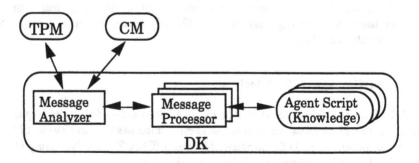

Fig. 2. Structure of DK of ADIPS agent

To realize the essential functions of flexible distributed systems, various knowledge have to be represented and stored in the agents. For instance, the functional specifications of base processes, the heuristic to control the base processes and the organization of agents, the strategies to cooperate with other agents and so on, are acquired and represented as the agent scripts by using *ADIPS/L script language*. Moreover, many kinds of knowledge processing mechanisms can be defined and utilized as the message processors to make an agent intelligent. Depend upon the capabilities of the DK, the designers can develop various agents from deliberative type to reactive type.

3.3   ADIPS Framework

The ADIPS Framework is an agent-based computing environment to implement and execute the ADIPSs based on various users' requirements. The ADIPS framework consists of three subsystems as shown in Fig.3. 1) *ADIPS Workspace* (AWS) is an agent operational environment. 2) *ADIPS Repository* (ARS) is a mechanism to manage and utilize the reusable agents. 3) *ADIPS Design Support* (ASP) provides the facilities for designers to design and implement various agents based on ADIPS model.

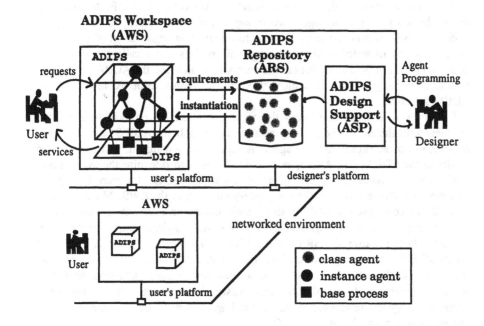

Fig. 3 . ADIPS Framework

From a viewpoint of implementation of the ADIPS Framework, the agents are classified to two types of agents, i.e., class agent and instance agent. An agent stored in the ARS is called a *class agent* that is designed as a primitive/organizational agent and managed as a reusable component of ADIPS in the functional class hierarchies. On the other hand, an agent run on the AWS is called an *instance agent* that is generated as an instance of a class agent in the ARS to realize an executable component of ADIPS.

An AWS is allocated as an agent operational environment on a distributed platform. According to the structure and functions of an ADIPS to be designed, a lot of AWSs can be installed on many platforms.

The instance agents of an ADIPS are created from the class agents into ARS by using the ADIPS organization/reorganization protocol (AORP). For instance, a user sends a message for requiring a new service to a secretary agent in AWS. The secretary agent sends a message for creating the requested service into an ARS run on the other platform. Responding to the message, the ARS creates the suitable instance agents on the designated AWS. Activating the instance agents, the requested service is provided for the user. Due to the requests of the instance agents or the users, the AWS can also remove the useless instance agents using the AORP.

The instance agents run on the AWSs can communicate with each other by using the ADIPS communication/cooperation protocol (ACCP) which has a set of the customized performatives of the agent communication protocol of KQML.

The ARS and AWS work together cooperatively based on the AORP. As explained above, the AWS sends a message of requesting a service to the ARS. In the ARS, the received message is sent to the class agents to construct an organization of agents that can provide the requested service. Although this process is basically the same of a task-announcement-bidding process of the contract net protocol, the AORP is defined as a unique inter-agent communication protocol for construction/reconstruction of ADIPS's agents.

For instance, it is different from the original contract net protocol to await the awarding until the all members of organization are fixed. In the ADIPS Framework, the construction of an organization of agents is regarded as a design task of the required service of the ADIPS. The ARS is responsible not only to determine the whole structure of organization of agents that can provide the required service for users, but also to generate the instance agents of the designed organization in the AWS. Moreover, it is required to reconfigure the ADIPSs to maintain the required services against various changes of both the users' requirements and the system environment, as explained in section 2. In such a case, the ARS and the AWS work cooperatively to reconstruct the organization of instance agents based on the AORP. For example, when an organizational agent in the AWS detects the irregular situations and issues a message to replace some of members of its organization, this message is sent to the ARS. In the ARS, several class agents are selected and instantiated again to reconstruct the corresponding organization of agents based on the AORP.

As explained above, the AORP takes the most important role to realize the essential functions of flexible distributed systems such as the component replacement function and the DS reconstruction function explained in section 2. An example of performatives of the AORP and the ACCP is shown in Fig.4.

AORP performatives

task-announcement	inform a task to be done
bid	response to task-announcement
award	allocate a task
directed-award	allocate a task directly
report	send result to a manager agent
initialize	setup instance agents
release	remove useless instance agents
dissolution	report remove-operation

ACCP performatives

Ask	send a question
Tell	send an answer to a question
request-information	require information
information	response to request-information
request	send a request
acceptance	accept a request
refusal	refuse a request
direction	require an action of agent

Fig. 4 . Example of Performatives used in AORP and ACCP

The ASP is responsible to help various activities of ADIPS designers. At present, the ASP provides the design support facilities to specify the class agents in the ARS and monitor the behavior of instance agents in the AWS. To support the design of class agents, an *ARS-browser* supports the designers to retrieve, inspect and modify the agent scripts based on ADIPS/L. Since it is difficult for designers to specify knowledge of an new class agent, the standard description formats of agent scripts called *knowledge templates*, are defined and provided for designers. On the other hand, to support the on-line debugging of knowledge and behavior of agents, an *ADIPS-agent-monitor* is designed and implemented to visualize the real time behavior of both the class agents in the ARS and the instance agents in the AWS.

For several years, the prototypes of the ADIPS Framework have been designed and implemented by using different kinds of programming languages. The first generation prototypes was designed in Smalltalk environment, and the second generation proto-types was implemented by using C++ and Tcl/Tk programming languages. The third generation prototype is now implemented in Java environment. The AWS, ARS and ASP are realized on the distributed platforms such as UNIX workstations and Win-dows-based personal computers with the TCP/IP-based network environment.

4 FDS Application Experience

Several applications of flexible distributed systems have been designed and implemented using the ADIPS Framework. In this section, we explain the following three applications briefly to show the capability of the ADIPS Framework.

4.1 Flexible Videoconference System

According to the growth and spread of networked environment, various distributed real-time multimedia applications such as videoconference system have been developed and utilized, e.g., CU-SeeMe, VdeoPhone, NetVideo, INRIA Videoconference system. However, it is difficult for naive users to utilize such a videoconference system, because (i) users cannot express their request correctly in detail to get the services, (ii) users cannot select or combine the suitable communication services which require the complex operations for users, (iii) users feel a lot of inconvenience to coordinate and accomplish their ongoing tasks when the quality of the required service is degraded due to the changes of operational conditions of videoconference systems. To solve these problems, a *flexible videoconference system (FVCS)* [11,12] is proposed and implemented based on the ADIPS Framework.

An agent-based architecture of a FVCS is depicted in Fig.5. The FVCS consists of FVCS modules on the respective distributed platforms. Each FVCS module is designed as an organization of FVCS agents such as service agents, sensor agents and user agents, as shown in Fig.5. There exist two kinds of the service agents, i.e., *service primitive agent* and *service manager agent*.

A service primitive agent is defined as a primitive agent that has knowledge to monitor and control a base process of multimedia communication. We can utilize the existing software modules as the base processes, for instance, the vic, the nv and the Vtalk for real-time video services, the Vat for audio service, and the wb for shared text-editing service. A service primitive agent can tune the parameters of a base process to maintain the required QoS under the observed conditions.

A service manager agent is defined as an organizational agents that has knowledge to create and manage the organization of service primitive agents. For instance, a video-conferencing Manager-agent-A in Fig.5, holds knowledge of the real-time communication services and selects a vic-service-agent as a video communication service agent which can provide the most suitable service for users under the operational situations at that time. A service manager agent can make the contracts with a user agent, the sensor agents and the other service manager agents to exchange information of changes of both the users' requirements and the system's operational situations.

A user agent communicates with its user, accepts the user's requests, and transforms the requests into the descriptions of users' requirements. Furthermore, several kinds of sensor agents are defined as the primitive agents to monitor the static/dynamic operational conditions and detect the changes occurred in the system environment. For instance, a CPU-sensor agent uses a sar-command of UNIX to monitor the current CPU-utilization-rate and a Net-sensor agent also monitors the current status of available bandwidth of communication between platforms by using netperf-command.

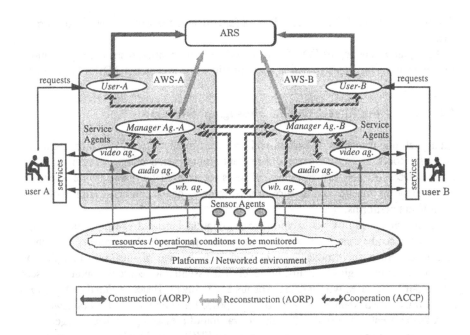

Fig. 5 . An architecture of FVCS

We have developed a prototype of FVCS using the ADIPS Framework/C++ version and confirmed that the following functions can be realized.

a) *Automatic composition of services*: Using the AORP of ADIPS Framework, the organizations of instance agents of FVCS are generated onto the AWSs and a session of videoconference with the suitable QoS parameters are started by the autonomous operations of FVCS agents. This composition process took about 30 seconds.

b) *Autonomous control of the required QoS*: due to the changes of the system environment, the operational conditions of the FVCS have been changed and the required QoS is fluctuated. For instance, when the CPU load of user's platform go down under 50% at the run time of the FVCS, the manager agents try to reduce the resolution QoS parameters of the video-service agents based on the ACCP. As a result, the FVCS can get the excess CPU resource to maintain the required QoS of the videoconference session. Moreover, we have confirmed that the users can specify the new requests on QoS freely during a videoconferencing session in order to tune the FVCS by manual.

c) *Autonomous reconfiguration of services*: when some kinds of changes that cannot be handled by the tuning operations of service agents, the manager agents decide to change the organization of FVCS at that time. Using AORP and ACCP, the manager agents negotiate with each other to replace and reconfigure some of members of organization of the FVCS agents. Instantiating the new FVCS agents using the ARS, the videoconferencing session can be continued by the renewed FVCS. Such a reconfiguration operation took about 50 seconds. It is faster than the manual operations of human users.

As explained above, the FDS for the real-time (synchronous) distributed applications can be designed and implemented in a systematic way based on the ADIPS Framework.

4.2 Flexible Asynchronous Messaging System

An asynchronous messaging system such as electric mail systems, is appreciated as one of useful tools to communicate and exchange information among people reside in distant places. Although many kinds of tools are utilized by many people, they get confused by the functional difference or heterogeneity of the communication tools run on different platforms.

For instance, due to a lack of message cancellation functions of recipients' messaging tools, a sender cannot remove the wrong messages before the recipients open their mailboxes. Such an inconvenience of users may be one of intrinsic properties of asynchronous messaging systems, however, it is essential to reduce the burden of users for handling messages within heterogeneous environment. Hence, a *Flexible Asynchronous Messaging System (FAMES)* [6] is proposed based on the ADIPS Framework.

A key concept of the FAMES is the abstraction of messaging services by agentification of conventional mail hosts. As same as the FVCS, the FAMES is composed of the FAMES agents, i.e., *mailing task agent* and *manager agent*, as shown in Fig.6.

A Message Manager Agent (MMA) is a top-level organizational agent in a *personal messaging environment* (PE). A Secretary Agent (SA) mediates a human user and the MMA to specify the requests using the user's personal information. According to the requests of both the user and the other MMA of another PE, the MMA controls behavior of organization of the mailing task agents which are managed by a Flow Control Manager Agent (FCMA), a Message Transfer Manager Agent (MTMA) and a User Interface Manager Agent (UIMA), respectively.

A FCMA organizes and manages a set of Flow Control Agents (FCAs) and a FCA executes a message flow control task such as circulation, cancellation, prioritized message delivery and so on. The FCMA is responsible to create and control of instances of FCAs based on the cooperation with the ARS.

A MTMA manages the Message Transfer Agents (MTAs) in the PE. A MTA is an instance agent which performs a message delivery task together with another MTA of the other PE. The FCA provides a receiver's address for the MTA. The spooling of received messages is also done by the MTA.

A UIMA manages the instance agents of both the Mail Client Agent (MCA) and the User Interface Agent (UIA). A MCA is an agent realized by the agentification of conventional e-mail client software. The MCA holds knowledge of the user's e-mail client to decide whether the required messaging service can deal with the e-mail client or not. When a new messaging service is required, the FCMA creates a new instance of suitable FCA together with a new UIA that provides a user interface of the created FCA.

A prototype of the FCMA is implemented by using the ADIPS Framework/Java version.

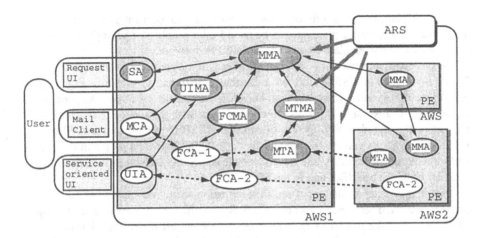

Fig. 6 . An architecture of FAMES

In the prototype, the mail hosts such as EudraPro, InternatMail, and OutlookExpress, have been agentified and utilized as members of organization of FAMES agents of the users' personal messaging environment, and the following functions can be provided for users.

a) *User-adaptive service customization*: when a user gives a request to utilize a messaging service which cannot be supported by a mail host at that time, the FAMES analyze the required service, select and organize an organization of messaging service agents in the user's personal messaging environment. In our prototype, this process terminates in a few seconds, and the users can utilize the new service together with the existing services of the mail hosts that the users get familiar.

b) *Requirements-driven service configuration*: a mail host of a user has to prepare a new messaging function to deal with the requests of the other users. Facing such an unexpected request of the users, the manager negotiate with each other to establish a cooperative group to process the required messaging tasks.

We verified that the tasks such as circulation and cancellation of delivered mails, are easily realized and attached in the FAMES. It remains a future work to provide a support facility to agentify the existing software assets for designers.

Under the ADIPS Framework, various functions for realizing the intelligent messaging services can easily be defined and added as the messaging service agents to enhance the capabilities of the FAMES.

4.3   CyberOffice

Recently, an information space over the global networked environment provides a new work place for people so called cyberspace based on the web-technology. To make such a new work place useful and fruitful, various functions to augment and enhance the *digital reality* of the work place have to be provided for people. A *CyberOffice* [13] is proposed as a new work place based on the ADIPS Framework.

The CyberOffice consists of a *CyberOffice-unit* in a *Symbiotic Space* (SS) and a *Symbiotic Space Base* (SSB) built on a distributed platform, as shown in Fig.7. A cyber office unit is defined based on both knowledge and models of work/tasks done by people in the real world. A SS is an information space with the *social reality* which is one part of the digital reality. On the other hand, a SSB is realized by the AWSs in which various agents execute the tasks of the CyberOffice-unit. The people in the real world and the agents in the AWSs can collaborate and cooperate with each other as the members of the CyberOffice-unit in the SS.

People in the real world cannot see an information space over the networked environment directly. Therefore, a cyber office unit has an office room view presented using the VRML, and the *perceptual reality* which is another part of the digital reality is enhanced to make people easy to access and collaborate with members reside in the SS. In the CyberOffice, people can recognize the other people and various agents as the human-like avatars which move around the office rooms.

A prototype of the CyberOffice is developed using the ADIPS Framework/Java version. Several stationary member of CyberOffice such as personal secretary agents, information retrieval agents and librarian agents, have been implemented in advance.

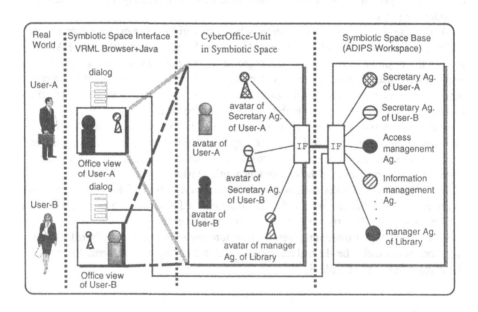

Fig. 7 . An architecture of CyberOffice

According to a service request of a member in a CyberOffice-unit, the organization of agents is generated in the SSB, and the required service is provided for the member.

For instance, a human member asks a secretary agent to get information from a library. The secretary agent sends an information-retrieval request to a manager agent of the library to retrieve the required information. The manager agent sends the request to suitable librarian agents or creates a new organization of librarian agents based on the ARS to deal with the request. Then, the librarian agent sends the retrieved information to the secretary agent and the human member.

A prototype of CyberOffice can deal with several simple tasks of office work. The digital reality of this prototype is also weak at present. However, the prototype provides a easy-to-use information space for naive users based on the office room metaphor. Moreover, we confirmed that the digital reality is one of essential properties of an information space over the networked environment in which people and agents can communicate and collaborate with each other to accomplish meaningful work/tasks in the real world.

5   Conclusion

In order to realize the next generation distributed systems, we introduce a notion of flexibility of distributed system and propose a design model of flexible distributed systems called agent-based distributed information processing system (ADIPS) and its design support environment called ADIPS Framework, in this paper. Various agents can be designed and implemented using knowledge embedded in respective agents together with the agentification mechanisms and the agent execution mechanisms of the ADIPS Framework. Furthermore, several examples of applications based on the ADIPS Framework are explained to demonstrate the capabilities of the ADIPS Framework. At present, many problems remain as our future work, e.g., a ease-of-use knowledge representation and manipulation mechanisms for intelligent agent, the design support functions, an effective design method of agent-based system, and so on. However, we confirm that the ADIPS Framework is useful to make a conventional distributed system flexible in order to deal with the changes of both the users' requirements and the system environment through the experiment of prototypical applications.

References

1. Campbell, A., Coulson, G. and Hutchison, D., "A Quality of Service Architecture", Computer Communication Review 24(2), ACM SIGCOM (1994) 6-27.
2. Feldhoffer, M., "Model for Flexible Configuration of Application-oriented Communication Services", Comp. Commun, 18(2), (1995) 69-78.
3. Fujita, S., Sugawara, K., Kinoshita, T. and Shiratori, N., "Agent-based Architecture of Distributed Information Processing Systems", Trans. IPSJ 37(5), (1996) 840-852.

4. Fujita S., Sugawara K., Kinoshita T., Shiratori N., "An Approach to Developing Human-Agent Symbiotic Space", Proc. Second Joint Conf. on Knowledge-based Software Engineering, JSAI&RAS, (1996) 11-18.

5. Kinoshita, T., Sugawara, K., Shiratori, N., "Agent-based Framework for Developing Distributed Systems", Proc. CIKM'95 Workshop on Intelligent Information Agent, ACM-SIGART (1995).

6. Sekiba J., Kitagata G., Suganuma T., Kinoshita T., Okada K. and Shiratori N., "FAMES: Design and Implementation of Flexible Asynchronous Messageing System", Proc. Int. Conf. on Software in Telecommunications and Computer Networks (SoftCOM'98), IEEE COMSOC (1998) 125-134.

7. Magedanz T., et al, "Intelligent Agents: An Emerging Technology for Next Generation Telecommunications?", Proc. INFOCOM'96, (1996) 1-9.

8. Nahrstedt, K. and Smith, J.M., "The QoS Broker", Multimedia Mag. 2(1), IEEE (1995) 53-67.

9. Shiratori, N., Sugawara, K., Kinoshita, T., Chakraborty, G., "Flexible Networks: Basic concepts and Architecture", Trans. Comm. E77-B(11), IEICE (1994) 1287-1294.

10. Sugawara, K., Suganuma, T., Chakraborty, G., Moser, M., Kinoshita, T. and Shiratori, N., "Agent-oriented Architecture for Flexible Networks", Proc. the Second International Symposium on Autonomous Decentralized Systems, (1995) 135-141.

11. Suganuma T., Fujita S., Sugawara K., Kinoshita T., Shiratori N., "Flexible Videoconference System based on Muliagent-based Architecture", Trans. IPSJ 38(6), IPSJ (1997) 1214-1224.

12. Suganuma T., Kinoshita T., Sugawara K., Shiratori N., "Flexible Videoconference System based on ADIPS Framework", Proc. Third Int. Conf. on Practical Application of Intelligent Agent and Multi-agent Technology (PAAM98), (1998) 83-98.

13. Saga T., Sugawara K., Kinoshita T., Shiratori N., "An Approach to Developing CyberOffices based on Multiagent System", Tech. Rep. AI96-11, IEICE (1996) 23-30.

14. Turletti, T. and Huitema, C., "Videoconferencing on the Internet", IEEE/ACM Trans. on Networking 4(3), IEEE (1996) 340-351.

15. Vogel, A., Kerherve, B., Bochmann, G. and Gecsei, J., "Distributed Multimedia and QoS: A Survey", Multimedia Mag. 2(2), IEEE (1995) 10-19.

A Conceptual "Role-Centered" Model for Design of Multi-Agents Systems

Jean-Dany Vally and Rémy Courdier

MAS² IREMIA, Université de la Réunion
15 Avenue René Cassin - BP 7151
97715 Saint-Denis messag cedex 9
La Réunion, FRANCE
[jdvally][courdier]@univ-reunion.fr

Abstract. In this paper, we present a conceptual model and the associated framework that can be used to model and implement MASs simulation based on a core concept: the Role. We especially assume that collective agent structures, such as groups and organizations gain to be represented through the concept of Role. We first provide a formal specification of the role concept. Then we show how this concept can be used favorably to consider collective organizations. The resulting model supports dynamic knowledge changes such as organization emergence, disappearance and transformation. It also provides an interesting issue to allow the definition of macroscopic simulation levels, by not considering the underlying agents' organization composing some given collective organizations. To illustrate our purposes, a simulation system in ecological phenomena simulation realized in cooperation with the CIRAD[1] has been investigated. An implementation has been realized into the Geamas platform with the Java language.

1 Introduction

The multi-agent paradigm has been successfully applied to the development of simulation environments. We obtained our first promising results with MASs for geophysical natural phenomena developed with agent technologies [MGG96] [LGMG96]. Our background is then in supporting multi-agent systems which have been classified as being reactive. We then propose a generic simulation platform called Geamas [MG98] (GEneric Architecture for Multi-Agent Simulation) designed to support specific considerations of non linear complex systems as defined in [BG96]. Our aim is now to extend the scope of applications supported by Geamas by accepting application classified to be either reactive or cognitive and to propose methodology principles to guide the process of the system design [CM98].

We realized that relevant distinctions between both types of applications are:

---

[1] International Agronomic Research Center for the Development

- The number of agents that constitute an application [JBM97]: It is a consequence of the abstraction level considered in the modeling process, which produces a large number of finely grained agents.
- The multitude of situations in which an agent can be considered during its life cycle. During its existence, an agent can handle successively or asynchronously several roles: handling a role is dependent on several factors (existing resources in the environment, organizational structures in the MASs, etc...). The valid services handled by an agent depends on roles handled by the agent at a given time. Such a complexity does not exist in reactive applications.

In this paper, we describe how the concept of role is introduced in our framework to complete the Geamas generic meta-model in order to support cognitive applications. Moreover, the paper focuses on an interesting use of this concept of role: the description of collective organizations.

Other attempts to include the concept of role in multi-agent meta-models occur in particular in the use of team plans for collaborative action [Tam96] [SV98], and in the work of J. Ferber [FG98] in his Aalaadin model. The definition proposed in our work is quite closed to Ferber's one. Some knowledge representation variants can be noted in the meta-model description. Differences are specially related to the Geamas objective which is dedicated to simulation systems. We consider works related to the knowledge representation for collective organizations in MASs. Most common approaches are (i) defining a new type of agent which represent group of agents [FBC98] ; (ii) describing group of agents through a computational organization (which is not an agent) and which is dedicated to manage an organization in the MASs [FG98] [Fis98]. In the paper, we propose a new original approach where a group can be considered as a role: the "group's role", throw a very simple, flexible and powerful issue.

This paper is organized in 5 sections. The first one describes the new meta-model proposal for Geamas V4.0 which intend to become the new operational version of the Geamas platform. Following this description, we focus on the concept of role, in particular by providing a formal definition of this notion in the context of MASs simulation. In a second time we concentrate on the representation of collective organization and argue benefits and contributions of our proposal. At this stage, we briefly describe the Biomas application which proposes a good pragmatic example of role use in a cognitive system. In conclusion, we present the current state of the platform implementation and discuss future working lines.

2 Agent and Multi-agents System

The conceptual model relies on the hierarchical organization of Geamas V3 [MG98] and extends the Multi-agent System definition by considering the new above definition:

Let Mas be a multi-agent system.

$$Mas = \langle Organization, Roles, Messages, Objects \rangle, \; S \; a \; Mas$$
$$Organization = \langle Agents, Integer^{Agent} \rangle, \; O \; an \; Organization \quad (1)$$

The general architecture of the system S describes an organization O containing agents a_i and defining a level function l. For simplicity we will say that $a_i \in O$. Any agent of a given level l is created by a agent of a higher level l' which manage its cycle of life (the agent of higher level becomes the "supervisor" of created agent). The "isSupervisor" relation is a transitive relation. It should be noticed that for a given agent, it is not any agent of a higher level which manages its cycle of life.

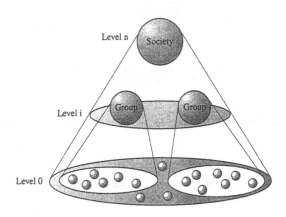

Fig. 1. The general organization of a hierarchical multi-agents system

$$\forall a_i \in O, \forall a_j \in O$$
$$isSupervisor(a_j, a_i) \Rightarrow l(a_j) > l(a_i)$$
$$\forall a_i \in O, \forall a_j \in O, \forall a_k \in O \quad (2)$$
$$(isSupervisor(a_k, a_j) \wedge isSupervisor(a_j, a_i)) \Rightarrow isSupervisor(a_k, a_i)$$

First, we define a generic agent architecture.

2.1 The Agent

An agent $a_i \in O$ is an active and communicative identified entity composed of a list of attributes at_i and faculties f_i.

$$Agent = \langle Id, Attributes, Faculties \rangle; \; Agents = \{Agent\} \quad (3)$$

where Id is an agent's property that distinguishes it from other agents (like [KC86] definition for object identifier). Knowing that an attribute is information which qualifies the agent, each attribute can take a value in a given domain of definition.

The interest of our agent model relies in the way the different faculties are defined.

Faculties We distinguish primarily three faculties as presented in the above figure.

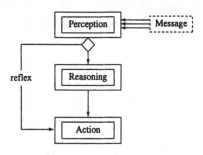

Fig. 2. The three faculties of an agent: functional mechanism

$$Faculties = \langle Perception, Reasoning, Action \rangle \qquad (4)$$

Perception It is a mechanism which allows, according to the signal, to start behaviors in a direct (reflex type) or indirect way, by subjecting this signal to the reasoning. The agent partially controls this mechanism. It can, by learning, acquire reflexes with the reception of signals which before were analyzed during the reasoning phase. This mechanism allows, for example, to match behaviors in a reactive way to certain types of events coming from the environment. Such events can be actually undergone by the agent. Their effects can be analyzed during the reasoning phase

$$Perception = (Reasoning, Action)^{Message} \qquad (5)$$

Example: Case of a person receiving a shock on his arm, the arm automatically moves and the pain (signal coming from his arm) arrives at the reasoning process which starts other movements.

Reasoning It represents faculties of analysis, evaluation and decision for an agent. For a given type of agent a type of reasoning is defined. It also allows, thanks to learning mechanisms, to create, modify, and remove behaviors.

$$Reasoning = \langle AttributesChanges, BehaviorsChanges, Action \rangle^{Message} \qquad (6)$$

Action The Action corresponds to how agent's behaviors are activated. Those behaviors are defined inside the roles the agent plays. For example, an activation can be done parallel to other active behaviors or require to suspend other behaviors. This task can also be delegated to an agent which synchronizes actions.

$$Action = \langle AttributesChanges, StatesChanges, MessagesSending \rangle^{Behavior} \tag{7}$$

We described the system's and agents' architectures. Now, we concentrate on the concept of role.

3 The Role, Central Feature of the System

Now, we define the concept of role. This concept does not have completely the same semantics as the one defined in the Aalaadin model.

3.1 The Role Definition

The role is an abstract representation of a functionality, a service or an identification which allots an agent of higher level to an agent of lower level. We said that the agent of lower level plays the role with respect to the agent of higher level. The sight of the role (to be distinguished from attribution) can be done between all the levels.

$$Role = \langle Goal, Properties, Resources, States \rangle \tag{8}$$

Notice: An agent having necessary resources can ask, to an agent of higher level, for the attribution of a role.

Example: Within the framework of a modeling of goods' flow between companies, the conveying role can be allotted to an agent by a company. The agent playing this role is visible as a conveyor not only by the company but also by other agents of the same level as him, other conveyors for example. Those can meet to form a trade union, economic agent as well as the company.

Our concept of role is defined by four notions: goal, properties, resources and states.

Goal The goal corresponds to a satisfaction function of the agent for its role. The agent defines a global goal by fixing a priority on its roles and consequently a priority on its goals.

Example: The goal for a conveyor could be the maximization of quantity of transported matter.

Properties

$$Properties = \langle Specifications, Dependent Behaviors, Persistent Behaviors \rangle \tag{9}$$

A property can be:

Preexistent: Specifications of Behavior/Attribute/Role which an agent must satisfy to be able to play this role.

Dependent: Behavior received by the agent when it plays this role. It is unusable apart from the role.

Persistent: Behavior received by the agent when it plays this role. It is reusable apart from the role.

We distinguish dependent and persistent properties in optics to use individual mechanisms of learning.

Example: The conveying role can define the following properties:

Preexistent: to be able to play the role of conductor, and to have the behavior "toEstablishRoute(Departure, Destination)".

Dependent: "deliver(Matter, Departure, Destination)", the conveyor can deliver a matter to a company only when it plays the aforementioned role.

Persistent: "invoice()" the conveyor will be able to use this behavior when it plays other roles.

Resources

$$Resource = \langle Id, ObjectSpecification \rangle \tag{10}$$

They are descriptions of the elements (distinct from the agent) used by the behaviors defined in the role. A resource can be:

Preexistent: resource which an agent must have, to be able to play this role.

Dependent: resource received by the agent when it plays this role unusable apart from the role.

Persistent: resource received by the agent when it plays this role reusable apart from the role.

Example: For the conveying role:

Dependent: The truck.
Persistent: The map.

The concept of resource makes it possible to distinguish the concepts of agent and situated object. A situated object seems to be a resource easy to handle by the agent in an environment.

States

$$State = \langle PreConditions, PostConditions, ListOfElements \rangle \qquad (11)$$

States are dependent on the role. A state can be:

Internal: synthesizing values of attributes, behaviors (active - inactive) or states of the agent, observable only by the agent itself when it plays this role

External: synthesize value of attribute, behavior, or state of the agent, observable by other agents when it play this role.

A state is determined by:

Pre-conditions: attributes in a zone to specify, behaviors active/inactive, states in a zone to specify.

Possibly a threshold: set of critical values. This makes it possible to carry out a local detection being able to activate mechanisms of recombining in a group.

Post-conditions: attributes in a zone to specify, behaviors active/inactive, states in a zone to be specified.

Example: For the conveying role:

– External: workload
   • Pre-conditions: deliver(Matter, Departure, Destination) active.
   • Threshold: $monthlyHoursWorking > 160$.
   • Post-conditions: deliver(Matter, Departure, Destination) inactive

When the workload becomes too significant, local detection allows the company or the trade union to reorganize.

It is possible to specialize a role in this case, Properties and States of the father role are inherited by the son role. An agent can be informed of the available roles by requiring it of one of its supervisors. It can obtain a role only from one of its supervisors, and can always make the request of it if it has a part or even the totality of necessary resources. An agent of higher level can also propose a role to an agent of lower level. The agent of higher level must provide necessary resources to the agent if it agrees to allot the role.

An agent loses a role in one of the following cases:

– If it loses associated resources with the role.
– If it does not want to play the role any more.
– When the agent of higher level (or one of its supervisors), which has given the role, decides to dispossess it.

To summarize, we use the traditional concept of role and define a precise architecture, adapted to the domain of simulation. Thus we distinguish three types of properties (preexistent, dependent and persistent) allowing an opening to the use of individual learning mechanisms (re-use of the behaviors defined in a role for another role). We define also resources used in the behaviors of roles. And finally, states providing facilities of observation on the agents.

3.2   Role and Collective Organizations

We note that the role's definition allow to allot to agents, behaviors defined according to resources. The following remarks are direct results. We regard the group as being a role played by an agent of a level higher than the one of its members.

The agent playing this role has some specific properties and resources:

- Structure containing its elements and relations between these elements (forming part of the resources associated with the role).
- Techniques of messages diffusion to the members of the group.
- Mechanisms of recombining.

Considering a group as a role may seem surprising. Actually it also depends on the point of view or level on observation. Indeed, on the one hand, we can regard a cell on the level of a sponge as an agent; what interests the observer is then existing interactions between cells of sponge. On the other hand, the cell itself is regarded as a group of all the micro-organisms constituting it; on the level of the cell what the observer sees are the interactions between the various micro-organisms which are under the influence of cell's proper behaviors.

The Society is a specialization of the Group role, this role is held by the onliest agent supervising all the others. This agent plays a role, therefore it is supervised by an agent of higher level. In order to avoid an infinite regression it is considered that it is his own supervisor.

3.3   Advantages

Like many multi-agents models existing, this representation allows:

- An interesting modeling of some systems where agent's behavior is better translated by the collective behavior of its components (agents) . For example, the behavior of a cell eucaryote can be modeled like the collective behavior of its components.
- The groups' dynamic creation through mechanisms of emergence.

Moreover, it allows:

- A uniform sending of message. There are only agents which can exchange messages. Agents communicating with groups can thus do it easily. For example a large fish perceiving the signal emitted by a bank of small fish.
- The addition of finer level of granularity is easier. Indeed, one initially could have modeled a cell like an agent with simple behaviors. Then, to want finer observations of which occurs on the cell's level and for this reason to decompose it into micro-organisms. It is then simple to make the cell play the role of group thus enabling it to diffuse some signals towards its micro-organisms.
- The simulation of agents passing by various stages on the structural level. For example, a volcanic eruption is at the beginning a whole of magma lenses which becomes later a lava flow.

4 Case Study: The Biomas Project

We applied this meta-model in order to develop the framework of the Biomas project. The article [GCC+98] has been written within the framework of this large life size application and is based on this model. This work aims at modeling the practices of management of breeding's wastes in a rural locality in order to simulate the exchanges of organic matter, costs of transfer, and negotiations between farmers. The objective is to be able to characterize abnormal operations and to test organization's alternatives of actors making it possible to decrease the environment's pollution risks.

4.1 The Multi-Agents System

First, we consider the Mas, Biomas as a locality made up of:

Agents: At level 0 of the organization (Cf. § 2.) we define basic physical entities which act in environment by the intermediary of situated objects. These entities are Farms (Breeding's units (E), Cultivations (C)) and Transformers (transformation of rough organic matter: composting platforms, purification stations...). At level 1, we define Farmers and then the Farmer's groups at the level 2.

Situated Objects: LiveStockBuilding, Cultivated land, Transformation units, Vehicle (Tanker, Tractor, 4*4).

Messages sending: "Offer" of organic matter (MO) and "Demand" for fertilizing matter are caused by, respectively, breeding's units and cultivations. A "Demand" likely to be satisfied by an "Offer" subject to adequacy (quality, quantity, availability and cost). When a contract is established between two farmers, a delivery must be accomplished from livestock building towards cultivated lands. The producer sends a "delivery" request to a conveyor whose characteristics (availability, capacity, cost) are compatible with the terms of the negotiation.

Roles: We define the principal roles entering the process of negotiation, MO Producer (PMO), MO consumer (CMO) and MO conveyor (CMO).

4.2 Role and Agent, Association

A farmer is an agent which can handle at least one of the following roles: PMO, CMO, or TMO.

Theses roles allow the farmer to use protocols of negotiation to obtain satisfaction. When playing these roles a farmer can exert control on basic physical agents (cultivation, breeding, unit of transformation). For example a breeder-farmer can have direct informations for his cultivations.

Roles	[Agent, Resources]			
	level one			level zero
	[Breeder, breeders]	[Farmer, cultivation]	[Conveyor, vehicle]	[Transformer, transformation unit]
PMO	+	-	-	+
CMO	-	+	-	+
PMO	-	-	+	-

Table 1. Correspondence between agents and roles in Biomas

4.3 Role Centered Methodology

We worked with experts of the domain and noted that a methodology centered on the role brought directly more usable information.

The representation has similarities with OMT [RBP+91]. Various scenarios of potential interactions between agents are defined through roles which they can play and not by the only fact that an agent is of a given type.

4.4 Roles Definitions

The table 2 describes the main roles' features of the application.

Roles	Preexistent properties		Dependent properties	Resources
	attributes	behaviors	behaviors	
PMO	- labourForce		- moOfferSending(Mo,Vo) - analyzesMoRequest(Mo,Vo) - decision() - commandOfDelivery() - updateStock(Mo,Vt)	- breedings - liveStockBuilding
CMO	- labourForce		- analyzesMoOffer(Mo,Vo) - moCommand(Mo,Vo) - noteDecision() - updateStock(Mo,Vt)	- cultivations - cultivated lands
TMO	- labourForce	-toEstablishRoute (Departure, Destination)	- commandReception(Mo,Vt) - takeMo(Mo,Vt,Departure) - deliverMo(Mo,Vt,Recipient)	- vehicles

Table 2. Roles descriptions

4.5 Computational Framework

The application can be on the one hand represented by a diagram of agent and potential roles for each agent's type (biomas.agent). And on the other hand, by a unit resources handled by the agents (biomas.environment).

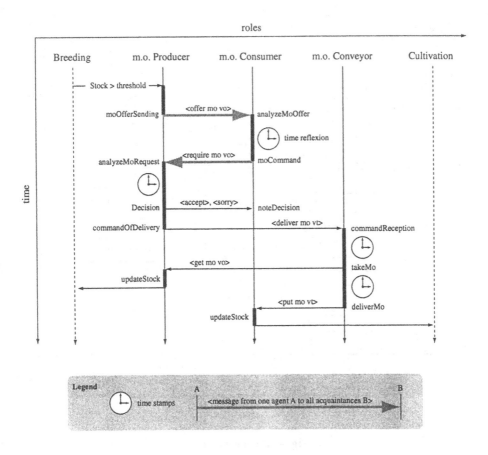

Fig. 3. Model of negotiation

4.6 Advantages and Weaknesses

Now we consider the advantages and weaknesses of our approach for this application.

- Our role centered methodology allows us to distinguish several aspects of an agent. These aspects are matched with roles and enable us to organize agents's interactions within more simple communication protocols. (A farmer playing the roles of CMO, PMO uses corresponding protocols).
- A good abstraction level for defining role compouned with preexistent properties enables us to define more easily some aspects of different agents. Thus we reduce the size of specific code for this agent (Zut is an agent defined by conjunction of PMO and CMO roles).
- When an agent has the necessary resources it is able to learn new capacities, this can introduce a powerful agent's evolution (a CMO having some livestock buildings is able to play the PMO role).

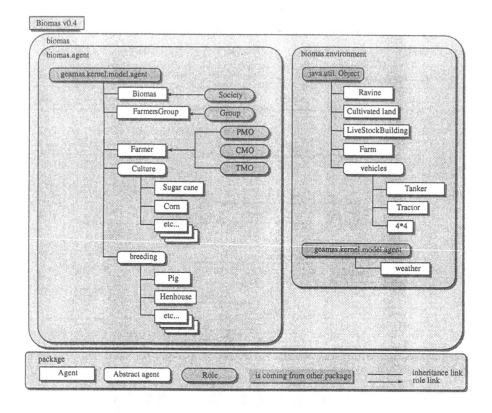

Fig. 4. Biomas model

The main weakness of our proposal is a bigger effort during the conception phase. We must identify not only the agents but also the roles. Thus, we have to define role's properties in an more or less complex organization.

5 Acknowledgments

We would like to thank F. Guerrin and the Cirad laboratory for their contributions in working on the "Biomas" application.

6 Conclusions

In this paper, we have introduced a conceptual role-centered design model for design of simulation MASs. The proposal allows an agent to be mainly defined as an aggregation of flexible roles that can dynamically be handled by agents depending on several well defined factors of the simulation process.

An Agent can handle at the same time a list of roles, and an agent can play a role if it includes preexistent associated entities: mainly if it includes the list of required attributes, resources and a list of pre-defined behaviors. When an agent changes its role, he can keep some knowledge entities such as resources, or behaviors which are defined as persistent one. The Agent has then a kind of memory of what he has done in the system and can handle new role at specific step of its life-cycle. This flexible notion of role is used in a very natural way to define a generic powerful representation of collective organizations.

We show in section 3 that we obtain with this approach a simple issue to represent groups of agents with several knowledge representation benefits. We then present a life-size application case study which is based on this model. The described application is used by the CIRAD research center to simulate the management of breeding's wastes in the Reunion Island in order to minimize the risks of environment pollution. As we show in the section 4, this application is design around the concept of role and gives promising results. It was presented in the JFIAD symposium to illustrate the contributions MASs in simulation systems.

References

[BG96]   T.R.J Bossomaier and D.G Green. *Complex systems*. Cambridge University Press, Amsterdam, 1996.

[CM98]   R. Courdier and P. Marcenac. Un processus de développement en spirale pour la simulation multi-agents. *L'Objet*, 4(1):73–86, March 1998.

[FBC98]   A. Dury F., Le Ber, and V. Chevrier. A reactive approach for solving constraint satisfaction. In Jörg P. Müller and al, editors, *Proceedings of the international workshop on Agent Theories, Architectures, and Languages – ATAL'98*, pages 289–303, July 1998.

[FG98]   Jacques Ferber and Olivier Gutknecht. A meta-model for the analysis and design of organizations in multi-agents systems. In *Proceedings of the International Conference on Multi-Agents Systems – ICMAS'98*, pages 128–135, Paris, France, July 1998. IEEE Computer Society Press.

[Fis98]   M. Fisher. Building representing abstract agent architecture. In Jörg P. Müller and al, editors, *Proceedings of the international workshop on Agent Theories, Architectures, and Languages – ATAL'98*, pages 33–47, July 1998.

[GCC+98] François Guerrin, Rémy Courdier, Stéphane Calderoni, Jean-Marie Paillat, Jean-Christophe Soulié, and Jean-Dany Vally. Conception d'un modèle multi-agents pour la gestion des effluents d'elevage à l'echelle d'une localité rurale. In *Actes des 6ᵉ Jounées Francophones en Intelligence Artificielle et Systèmes Multi-Agents*, Nancy, France, November 1998. Hermes.

[JBM97]   W. Joosen, S. Bijnens, and F. Matthijs. Building multi-agent systems with correlate. In Van De Velde, editor, *Proceedings of the 8ᵗʰ European Workshop on Modelling Autonomous Agents in a Multi-Agent World – MAA-MAW'97*, volume 1237 of *Lecture Notes in Artificial Intelligence*, pages 197–209, May 1997.

[KC86]   S. N. Khoshafian and G. P. Copeland. Object identity. In Norman Meyrowitz, editor, *Proceedings of the Conference on Object-Oriented Programming Systems, Languages, and Applications (OOPSLA)*, volume 21, pages 406–416, New York, NY, November 1986. ACM Press.

[LGMG96] F. Lahaie, J.R Grasso, P. Marcenac, and S. Giroux. Self-organized critical-
ity as a model for eruptions dynamics: validation on piton de la fournaise
volcano. Technical report, Académie des Sciences de Paris, 1996.

[MG98] Pierre Marcenac and Sylvain Giroux. *GEAMAS: A Generic Architecture
for Agent-Oriented Simulations of Complex Processes*, chapter not yet available. International Journal of Applied Intelligence, Kluwer Academic Publishers, 1998.

[MGG96] Pierre Marcenac, Sylvain Giroux, and J.R. Grasso. *Designing and Implementing Complex Systems with Agents*, chapter not yet available. Software
Engineering for Parallel and Distributed Systems. Chapman & Hall, March
1996.

[RBP+91] J. Rumbaugh, M. Blaha, W. Premerlani, F. Eddy, and W. Lorensen. *Object-
Oriented Modeling and Design*. Prentice Hall, Englewood Cliffs, NJ, 1991.

[SV98] P. Stone and M. Veloso. Task decomposition and dynamic role assignment
for real-time strategic teamwork. In Jörg P. Müller and al, editors, *Proceedings of the international workshop on Agent Theories, Architectures, and
Languages – ATAL'98*, pages 369–381, July 1998.

[Tam96] M. Tambe. Teamwork in real world. In *Proceedings of the International
Conference on Multi-Agents Systems – ICMAS'96*. IEEE Computer Society
Press, 1996.

Desiderata in Agent Architectures for Coordinating Multi-Agent Systems

Jaeho Lee

Department of Electrical Engineering
The University of Seoul
90 Cheonnong-dong, Tongdaemun-gu, Seoul 130-743, Korea
jaeho@ee.uos.ac.kr

Abstract. Agents for real applications often operate in complex, dynamic, and nondeterministic environments and thus need to function in worlds with exogenous events, other agents, and uncertain effects. In this paper, we present our reactive agent view to describe agents for real-world applications and introduce our two agent architectures: UM-PRS and Jam. UM-PRS has been applied to both physical robots and software agents and demonstrated its sufficiently powerful representation and control scheme as a general reactive agent architecture. The Jam agent architecture has evolved from UM-PRS and implemented in Java for maximum portability and mobility. We first identify agent tasks and environments and then highlight the relevant features in our agent architectures.

1 Introduction

Current trends toward ubiquitous, portable and mobile information systems in the open, distributed and heterogenous environments has brought the proliferation of agent-based systems (Huhns and Singh 1997). In this paper, we present general agent architectures for agent-based systems that have been evolved from the Procedural Reasoning System (PRS) (Georgeff and Ingrand 1989) via the University of Michigan Procedural Reasoning System (UM-PRS) (Lee, Huber, Durfee, and Kenny 1994) to the Jam agent architecture.

Agents for real applications often operate in complex, dynamic, and nondeterministic environments. Complex environments make it hard for an agent to build or maintain a faithful model of the environment. The dynamic nature of environments does not allow an agent to fully control the changes in the environment since changes can occur as a result of the actions of other agents and of exogenous influences which in turn affect the behavior of the agents. The nondeterministic nature of environments makes it impossible to predict with certainty the results of actions and the future situations. Agent systems for real applications thus need to have the capability to function in worlds with exogenous events, other agents, and uncertain effects.

Our approach to the problem of describing actions of the agents working in such complex, unpredictable, and nondeterministic environments is to regard agents as *reactive systems*. The key point concerning reactive systems is that they maintain an ongoing interaction with the environment, where intermediate outputs of the agent can influence subsequent intermediate inputs to the agent. Over the years, this reactive view of agents has often been used to describe the behavior of agents in dynamic environments (Georgeff and Ingrand 1989; McDermott 1991).

In this paper, First, we identify popular agent tasks and the characteristics of the environments in which agents need to operate. Second, we present the general concepts and basic features of PRS that motivated us to adopt it as a conceptual framework for the development of UM-PRS. We then describe our UM-PRS implementation and extensions in terms of our plan representations and plan execution semantics. We also describe how UM-PRS has been used to accomplish tasks in dynamically changing environments. Finally, we discuss how the Jam agent architecture has evolved from the UM-PRS architecture.

2 Tasks and Environments

In this section, we lay out some popular agent tasks and the characteristics of the environments in which agent need to operate. From these tasks and environments, we can draw out the common features and provide a basis to identify the desired features of agent architectures and rationales for our design of agent architectures. Tasks and environments relevant to reactive agent systems include:

Information Services: Dynamic teaming and interactions among information services in a digital library.

Coordinated Unmanned Vehicles: Coordinated, reactive mission achievement by unmanned vehicles that are decentrally controlled.

Operator-in-loop Coordination: Responsive display of situated intelligence that is coordinated with the needs and expectations of an operator.

Automated Monitoring and Controlling Systems: Dynamic movement of time-critical tasks among software and human agents in an automated monitoring and controlling system.

Flexible Manufacturing Systems: Coordinated activity without deadlocks or resource conflicts in a flexible manufacturing system.

For these tasks and environments, each application exhibits specific characteristics and requires certain capabilities. Some common features are as follows:

Real-time execution: The agent needs to be responsive to its environment and predictably *fast enough* to act on the changes in the environment.

Interruptible execution: A dynamically changing environment demands that the agent be able to stop its current activity and gracefully switch to other more urgent or higher priority activities.

Real-time execution and interruptible execution are necessary because most tasks of interest require that an agent responds fast enough to react to changes in the environment and response to changes requires that an agent be able to stop one activity and switch to another.

Multiple foci of attention: The agent needs to maintain multiple foci of attention to interact with multiple agents and the environment simultaneously. This ability requires that an agent's activity be not only *interruptible*, but also *resumable*. Agents with this capability are typically implemented with multiple threads of execution. The agent saves resumable activities by saving the context of the activities. However, there exists a tradeoff between *saving* the context of previous activity and *reestablishing* the context. The balance between these two overheads depends on how dynamically the environment is changing.

Hierarchical plan refinement and revision(mix and match strategies): The agent can progressively decompose high-level tasks into smaller subtasks. High-level tasks are considered independent of lower level tasks and the low-level tasks are chosen based on the current high-level goals and the current situation. The agent can *mix and match* among the relative strengths of the plans being combined.

Purposeful behavior (minimizing high-level plan revision): The agent works methodically toward its goals in a coherent manner. Purposeful behavior is easy to understand by others, including humans, and minimizes high-level plan revisions because even if details of how things are done change, the high-level methods stay consistent.

Purposeful behavior and adherence to predefined strategies are desired features in domains where others need to recognize the plans of the performing agent or where others are relying on the agent's expected behavior such as Coordinated Unmanned Vehicles, Operator-in-loop Coordination, Flexible Manufacturing Systems, and Information Services.

Adherence to predefined strategies: The agent behaves in a way that is consistent with what others expect (like following doctrine or executing interaction plans exactly as the operator told it to). Operator-in-loop Coordination and Automated Monitoring and Controlling Systems rely heavily on this feature.

Task migration: An agent architecture capable of task migration needs the ability to shed or accept tasks from other agents. Cooperating agents often need to reallocate workload among agents. When a workload imbalance among agents occurs, then the appropriate agents may shed or accept workload. This capability is critical in Automated Monitoring and Controlling Systems and Information Services.

Goal-driven and data-driven behavior: Agents may be goal-driven, where the agent is motivated by high-level statements about a state of the world to achieve or activities to perform. Agents may also be data-driven, where their behavior is motivated by low-level, perhaps transient data states, such as proximity to danger. Coordinated Unmanned Vehicles and Information Services especially demand both goal-driven and data-driven behavior.

Checkpointing and Mobility: The agent have the functionality for capturing the runtime state of the agent in the middle of execution and functionality for subsequently restoring that captured state to its execution state possibly on a different machine. This feature can be beneficial especially to the task such as Information Services and Automated Monitoring and Controlling Systems.

Explicit strategy articulation: The agent can explicitly articulate, transfer, and modify strategies. The internal representation of strategies needs to be explicitly expressible and convertible into a transferable textual representation. The transferred strategies also need to be dynamically interpreted and incorporated. This capability is required for the agents in Automated Monitoring and Controlling Systems, Flexible Manufacturing Systems, and Information Services to coordinate effectively.

Situation summary and report: The agent can summarize local situations and report them to other agents. The reports should provide the receiving agents with a global view of the situation and allow them to coordinate with other agents effectively. All the tasks we listed above seem to need this capability to coordinate with other agents or operators.

Restrainable reactivity: Coordinating with other agents involves commitment to a constrained choice of behaviors. Coordinated Unmanned Vehicles and Flexible Manufacturing Systems especially need this ability to constrain reactivity to enable coordination.

In the rest of this paper, we describe how our agent architectures satisfy the required capabilities and provide rationales for our design of agent architectures.

3 UM-PRS

UM-PRS is an implementation of the conceptual framework provided by the Procedural Reasoning System (PRS) (Georgeff and Ingrand 1989). UM-PRS maintains a library of alternative procedures for accomplishing goals and selectively invokes and elaborates procedures based on the evolving context. In contrast to the traditional deliberative planning systems, UM-PRS continuously tests its decisions against its changing knowledge about the world, and can redirect the choices of actions dynamically while remaining purposeful to the extent allowed by the unexpected changes to the environment.

The system interacts with its environment, including other systems, through its database (which acquires new beliefs in response to changes in the environment) and through the actions that it performs as it carries out its selected plans.

UM-PRS is completely written in C++, particularly to meet the need for real-time requirements of real-world applications, and thoroughly tested over years of applications. In this section, we describe basic UM-PRS components and our design decisions in developing UM-PRS.

3.1 World Model

In our implementation, the *world model* is a database of facts which are represented as relations. A relation has a name and a variable number of fields. Initial facts are asserted at the beginning of a UM-PRS program by the user. Facts can be either asserted, retracted, or updated by Knowledge Areas (see Section 3.3). The relations in the world model can be tested or retrieved using unification between constants, variables, and expressions.

A simple representation using relations allows us to use *unification* to perform sophisticated pattern matching between facts. Goals in UM-PRS (see the following section) also are represented as relations, thus uniform treatments between facts and goals are possible.

3.2 Goals

Goals in UM-PRS are the world states that the system is trying to bring about (or maintain, etc.). Goals are represented as relations with arguments, and thus pattern matching operations are allowed between goals. A goal can be either a top-level goal, which controls the system's highest order behavior, or a subgoal activated by the execution of a KA body (see Section 3.3).

Top-level Goals are the highest-level goals that the agent has. Top-level goal specifications are usually given to the agent and can be communicated to one agent from another agent. The agent also can use the POST action within plans to add top-level goals.

Top level goals are *persistent*. That is, they are pursued until they are satisfied (by successful plan execution or opportunistically by some other means, such as another agent) or are removed explicitly using an UNPOST action within a plan.

Subgoals are goals that the agent creates from within plans during plan execution. Plan actions are used to invoke subgoaling and the invocation is pattern-directed and context-based, thus the invocation mechanism is different from function calls in general programming languages.

Subgoaling can be performed to arbitrary depth levels and can be recursive, where a plan for a particular goal can subgoal to the same goal. Subgoals are *not persistent* by default. If a plan fails for a subgoal, the subgoaling action is considered to have failed as if it were any other type of valid plan action.

With this operationalization of top-level goals and subgoals, agent have a low level of commitment to all top-level goals, and a strong level of commitment to goals that have intentions associated with them.

3.3 Knowledge Areas

A *Knowledge Area* (KA) is a declarative procedure specification of how to satisfy a system goal or query. It consists of name, documentation, purpose, context, body, priority, effect section, and failure section as described below:

Name is the label for the KA.
Documentation is a description of the KA for human readers.

Purpose specifies the goal that successful execution of the KA body will satisfy. During execution of UM-PRS, this purpose is matched against system goals when the system looks for applicable KAs.

Context specifies the situations in which the KA may be applied. The context consists of a mixed sequence of patterns to be matched against the world model and expressions to be satisfied using the variable bindings established during the matching.

The context is checked throughout the execution of a KA, to make sure that the KA is still applicable to the intended situation. The context specification is described in terms of a list of expressions. Each expression is evaluated in turn, and its return value checked. The context may contain world model actions to check for particular world states.

A SOAK (Set Of Applicable KAs) is a collection of KAs which have been instantiated to achieve a goal (purpose) that has just been activated. Each KA in the SOAK is applicable to the specific situation, as one role of the context is to filter out KAs that are not relevant to a particular situation.

Body specifies the execution steps required to satisfy the KA purpose in terms of primitive functions, subgoals, conditional branches, and so on. The body can be viewed as a plan schema. The schema is instantiated with the bindings which are generated when the purpose and the context of the KA are checked during SOAK generation.

PRS uses a graphical network to specify the KA body, but UM-PRS uses a structured procedure representation inspired by Structured Circuit Semantics for explicit, transferable meaning.

Priority is an optional UM-PRS extension and specifies the priority of the KA when multiple KAs are applicable for the same situation. The priority can be any expression including variables and function calls.

Effect section of a KA is an optional UM-PRS extension, and is used to represent a simplified and abstract procedural representation of the real procedure. This section of a KA is executed when UM-PRS is run in simulation mode.

Failure section of a KA is an optional UM-PRS extension, and specifies a procedure to be executed when a KA fails.

3.4 Actions

Each action in the KA body can specify a goal or condition to ACHIEVE. In addition, a KA action can be a low-level function to EXECUTE directly, an ASSERTion of a fact to the world model, a RETRACTion of a fact from the world model, an UPDATE of a fact in the world model, a FACT or a RETRIEVE statement that retrieves relation values from the world model, or an ASSIGN statement that assigns the results of run-time computations to variables. Furthermore, iteration and branching are accomplished through WHILE, DO, OR, and AND actions. For convenience when testing KA failure (or for other reasons) there is also a FAIL action which is an action that always fails.

3.5 Intention Structure

The intention structure maintains information related to the runtime state of progress made toward the system's top-level goals. The agent will typically have more than one of these top-level goals, and each of these goals may, during execution, invoke subgoals to achieve lower-level goals. With the current implementation, a goal that is being pursued may be interrupted by a higher priority goal and then later resumed (if possible). To manage this, the intention structure keeps track of which top-level goals are being pursued, and which action in each KA is currently being executed.

When a goal gets suspended, due to a higher level goal becoming applicable, the current state of execution of the current goal is stored. When the suspended goal becomes the highest priority goal again, it is *reactivated*. The reactivation process is identical to normal execution. However, due to the possibility that the world model has been changed during the pursuit of other goals, the contexts of the resumed top-level goal and its subgoals may no longer be valid. If they are all still valid, execution resumes at the exact place where it was suspended. However, if one of the KA's context expressions fails, that KA and any of its subgoals are considered to have failed. This is the normal behavior for KAs whose context fails.

3.6 The Interpreter

The UM-PRS interpreter controls the execution of the entire system. Whenever there is new or changed information in the world model or goals, the interpreter determines a new SOAK. From this SOAK is selected the most appropriate KA, which is placed in the intention structure. When there are no SOAKs being generated, the interpreter checks the intention structure for the currently active KAs and executes the next primitive action. If this action changes the goals (by creating a subgoal or by satisfying a goal) or world model, a new SOAK is created and the cycle starts over. If a new SOAK is not created, then the next step in a leaf-level KA is executed.

With this implementation, the interpreter facilitates switching to more important goals according to the situation. The UM-PRS interpreter can exhibit the following behaviors:

- Incremental elaboration to identify appropriate actions.
- Recovery from a failed context.
- Suspension of one goal and pursuit of another.
- Interruption by new goals.
- Refocus due to a change of context.

3.7 Applications

UM-PRS has been applied to both physical robots and software agents, and has demonstrated its sufficiently powerful representation and control scheme as a general reactive agent architecture. Applications for physical robots include robotic control of two indoor mobile robots, and also of an outdoor robotic vehicle (Kenny, Bidlack, Kluge, Lee, Huber, Durfee, and Weymouth 1994).

Software agents implemented using UM-PRS include mediator agents in the University of Michigan Digital Library (UMDL) project (Birmingham, Durfee, Mullen, and Wellman 1995) and UM-PRS agents in the Ship Systems Automation (SSA) project (Durfee, Huber, Kurnow, and Lee 1997). In the SSA project, UM-PRS successfully handled the tasks of controlling the sequencing and execution of interaction plans, as well as executing plans for operator load management and alert prioritization.

In these projects, UM-PRS has demonstrated how it provides the critically needed level of representation for agent plans in dynamic, unpredictable domains, because it allows agents to pursue long-term goals by adopting pieces of relevant procedures depending on the changing context, rather than having to blindly follow a prearranged plan.

4   Jam Agent Architecture

Jam is an intelligent agent architecture that combines the best aspects of several leading-edge intelligent agent frameworks, including PRS, UM-PRS and the Structured Circuit Semantics (SCS) representation of Lee (1995).

Each Jam agent is composed of five primary components: a *world model*, a *plan library*, an *interpreter*, an *intention structure*, as in the UM-PRS architecture, and a Jam-specific *observer* component (see Section 4.3). In this section, we highlight the new features and execution semantics of Jam and describes the theory and purpose of the features.

4.1   Agent Goals

A Jam agent's top-down behavior is invoked by specifying goals that the agent is to achieve, perform, or maintain. A Jam agent may have a number of alternative plans for accomplishing a single goal. It is Jam's built in capability to reason about the alternatives, to select the best alternative given the particular situation, and to switch between alternative goals as utilities for doing each goal change, that are some of it's strongest advantages over standard programming paradigms.

The agent checks all the plans that can be applied to the goal are checked to see if any of them are relevant to the current situation by filtering out plans based upon their precondition and context fields. Those plans that are applicable are collected into what is called the Applicable Plan List (APL – SOAK in PRS terminology). A utility value is determined for each plan in the APL and the highest utility plan is selected and intended to the goal. If the intended goal has the highest utility among all goals with intentions, then its plan is executed. Otherwise, a previous intention still has a higher utility and that plan is executed.

As the utilities of the various goals change as the situation changes, the agent will switch between goals in order to continually pursue the highest-priority goal.

An agent's goals are divided into two categories, top-level goals and subgoals, as in UM-PRS (see Section 3.2). Jam, however, provides refined subgoaling actions as follows:

ACHIEVE: An achieve action causes the agent to establish a goal achievement subgoal for the currently executing plan. This then triggers the agent to search for plans in the plan library that can satisfy the goal given the current context.

If the invoked plan fails and the goal was specified as a subgoal of a plan, then the achieve action fails with ramifications identical to the failure semantics as for any other plan body action that fails.

PERFORM: Perform subgoals differ from achieve subgoals in several important aspects. The agent checks to see whether the subgoal has already been accomplished. Only if the goal has not been accomplished, the plan does subgoal.

The agent continually monitors for goal achievement. Typically, the plan selected for the subgoal will be the means by which the subgoal is accomplished. However, if the agent detects (opportunistic) accomplishment of the goal (perhaps by another agent), it will consider the subgoal action successful and discontinue execution of the plan established to achieve the subgoal.

MAINTAIN: A maintain goal indicates that the specified goal must be reattained if it ever becomes unsatisfied. A maintain goal is very similar to an achieve goal except that a maintain goal is never removed from the agent's goal list automatically. The only way that a maintain goal is removed from the agent's intention structure is to perform an explicit unpost action within a plan or Observer definition. A maintain goal only make sense as a top-level goal of an agent.

QUERY: A query action is functionally identical to an achieve action. It is provided to allow the programmer to be more explicit about the semantics of the action's goal.

WAIT: The wait action causes plan execution to pause until the specified goal is achieved or the specified action returns successfully. Execution of the plan continues *in place*, with the agent checking the goal or action every cycle through the interpreter. This action never fails.

4.2 Plans

A plan in Jam corresponds to a KA in the UM-PRS. A plan defines a procedural specification for accomplishing a goal. Its applicability is limited to a particular goal or data-driven conclusion, and may be further constrained to a certain precondition and maintained context.

Plan Precondition: The optional precondition field specifies the initial conditions that must be met before the plan should be considered for execution.

The contents of the precondition are identical to the context field. Note that the precondition of a plan is checked only when a plan is being considered for inclusion in an APL; unlike a plan's context, the precondition expression is not checked during runtime.

Plan Context: The agent developer can specify the situations that plans are valid in by including the optional context field of a plan. A plan's context specifies one or more expressions that describe the conditions under which the plan will be useful throughout the duration of plan execution.

The context field of a plan is first checked when a plan is being considered for inclusion in an Applicable Plan List (the APL), a list of plans that could be used to solve a goal. The context field's conditions are also checked during execution of a plan to make sure that the plan is still applicable even in the face of a changing environment. In contrast, the precondition field, described later, only specifies the initial conditions that must be met before the plan should be considered.

If the context check is not satisfied during APL generation, the plan is not considered applicable to the situation and is dropped from consideration for execution. Also, if the context of a currently executing plan fails, the entire plan and any of its subgoals are deemed invalid and removed from the agent's intention structure.

Jam agents can exhibit both *goal-driven* and *data-driven* behavior. Agents may be goal-driven, where the agent is motivated by high-level statements about a state of the world to achieve or activities to perform. Agents may also be data-driven, where their behavior is motivated by low-level, perhaps transient data states, such as proximity to danger.

Plan Goal: Goal-driven behavior is specified by including a GOAL field in a plan. This field's contents specify the goal or activity that successful execution of the plan's procedural body will accomplish. During execution, the interpreter matches this goal expression against the agent's top-level goals. If the plan's goal specification matches and if the plan's precondition and context expressions pass, the plan may then be instantiated and intended.

Plan Conclude: Data-driven behavior is indicated by using a CONCLUDE field in a plan. This specifies a World Model relation that should be monitored for change. If the given World Model relation changes in some way (i.e., it is asserted or updated), the agent's interpreter considers the plan for execution. If the plan's precondition and context expressions pass, the plan may then be instantiated (i.e., have values from the current situation assigned to plan variables) and intended (i.e., added to the agent's intention structure).

The body of a plan describes the sequence of actions, a procedure, to be taken in order to accomplish a goal. The body may contain Jam-provided actions, Jam-provided primitive functions, and user-defined primitive functions, and can be organized into any of a number of different constructs. A plan executes until it reaches the end of its encoded procedure. The plan is also considered to have completed successfully if the plan is an achieve or maintain goal and the goal expression becomes true during the middle of execution of the body.

A plan body will fail if an action within the body fails and there are no alternative paths to procedure completion. For example, a plan body with a simple sequence of actions will fail if any action in the sequence fails (this applies to subgoal actions such as achieve and perform as well). Branch constructs such as OR and DO_ANY can be used to provide alternate execution paths to protect against action failure.

The *effect* section and the *failure* section have refined semantics in Jam. The effects section is executed when the plan completes successfully. On the other hand, the failure section is executed when the plan fails as described below:

Plan Effects: Each plan may have an optional effects field that provides a place to specify a procedure that will be executed when the plan completes successfully. The syntax of the effects field's contents is identical to a plan's body but is typically used to modify the agent's world model.[1] The only limitation the effects field has with respect to a plan's body field is that there can be no subgoaling within an effects section. Other than this, everything that can be done within a plan's body can be done within the plan's effects. The procedure of the effects section is executed atomically. That is, it cannot be interrupted by the agent interpreter, for example, in order to switch execution to another, perhaps higher utility, plan.

Plan Failure: The optional failure field of a plan allows the agent designer to specify a procedure to be executed when the plan fails. If the plan fails, for example because the context fails, the agent interpreter will execute the actions found in the failure section before switching to other plans or goals. Execution of this section is performed as if the entire procedure were an atomic action. That is, the procedure is executed without the possibility of interruption by other plans or even from the normal interleaving of execution of actions with normal interpreter activity.

When a plan fails, the agent considers the failed plan and all of the failed plan's subgoals to have failed. In this case, the failure sections of each of the failed plan's subgoal's plans are executed from the plan for the goal at the bottom of the subgoal stack back up to the failed plan.

Another unique field in Jam is an *attributes* field, which provides a place for a programmer to put information concerning plan characteristics that can be reasoned about during plan execution and/or metalevel reasoning.

4.3 Observer

The observer is a lightweight plan that the agent executes between plan steps in order to perform functionality outside of the scope of its normal goal/plan-based reasoning. The Jam agent architecture supports arbitrary processing to

---

[1] like an add/delete list in STRIPS (Fikes and Nilsson 1971).

occur every cycle through the interpreter. This functionality, typically used to update the world model independently from the normal plan execution cycle, is provided in procedural body called the Observer. The Observer's behavior is specified in a syntax identical to that of a plan body in one of the files parsed during initialization. This procedure may contain any plan action or construct that a normal plan body can contain except for subgoaling. Subgoaling is not supported because execution of the Observer procedure is outside of the normal execution of the interpreter (see sec:jam-interpreter).

4.4   The Jam Interpreter

The Jam agent interpreter is responsible for selecting and executing plans based upon the goals and context of the current situation. Associated with the interpreter is the intention structure, a run-time stack (stacked based upon subgoaling) of goals with and without instantiated plans.

The basic flow of the agent's interpreter is to first execute the Observer procedure (if it exists) and then reason about what to execute within the agent's intention structure. If generation of an Applicable Plan List (APL) results in one or more entries, then the agent goes into *metalevel* reasoning; that is, it reasons about how to decide which of the APL elements to intend to its intention structure. The agent may have multiple ways of performing this decision-making, so that metalevel reasoning about its metalevel reasoning may ensue. Metalevel reasoning ends when the interpreter no longer generates a non-null APL, indicating that the agent has no means for deciding between alternatives.

If the agent performs metalevel reasoning, then it eventually executes a metalevel plan that reasons about lower-level alternatives and selects and intends the plan it deems best. Note that intending a metalevel plan does not ensure that the plan will be executed immediately. Utility values still determine which plan gets executed and there is no inherent preference for metalevel plans over *concrete level* plans. This ensures that the Jam agent maintains its ability to *do the best thing*, even while performing metalevel reasoning.

If the agent does not perform metalevel reasoning, then the agent selects randomly between the APL elements that share the highest utility and then intends that plan.

When APL element selection is not performed by metalevel reasoning, it is performed based upon APL element utilities. In the current implementation of the Jam agent architecture, the interpreter selects the highest utility plan instance from the APL. The interpreter selects randomly between plan instances if there is more than one plan instance that has the highest utility.

4.5   Jam Agent Checkpointing and Mobility

Jam agents are capable of checkpointing themselves. That is, we have implemented functionality for capturing the runtime state of a Jam agent in the middle of execution and functionality for subsequently restoring that captured state to its execution state.

One use of this functionality is for periodically saving the agent's state so that it can be restored in case the agent fails unexpectedly. Another use of this functionality is to implement agent mobility, where the agent migrates from one computer platform to another. A third possible use of this functionality is to clone an agent by creating a checkpoint and restoring it execution state without terminating the original agent.

5 Conclusions

In this paper, we identified the tasks and environments in which agents need to operate (Section 2) and then showed how our two agent architectures, UM-PRS and Jam, satisfy the required features for the tasks.

As a reactive agent architecture, UM-PRS satisfies most of the features requiring real-time interruptible execution, multiple foci of attention. It also naturally supports hierarchical plan refinement and revision, purposeful behavior, adherence to predefined strategies. Especially, in the SSA project (Durfee, Huber, Kurnow, and Lee 1997), UM-PRS demonstrated effective task migration capability. Jam inherits all of the above capabilities and supports additional explicit data-driven behavior, checkpointing and mobility.

The explicit strategy articulation capability is strengthened by incorporating the SCS execution semantics Lee (1995) into Jam and is also supported partly by Jam's refined goal actions and plan conditions.

Other capabilities, situation summary/report and restrained reactivity are especially required for coordinated agent plan execution and are being studied in the context of explicit specification of execution semantics in the agent plan (Lee 1997).

6 Acknowledgement

Jam is implemented by Marc Huber in Intelligent Reasoning Systems (IRS) and the author of this paper. The most description of Jam is also quoted from the Jam manual written by Marc Huber (marcush@home.com).

References

Birmingham, W. P., E. H. Durfee, T. Mullen, and M. P. Wellman (1995, March). The distributed agent architecture of the university of michigan digital library (extended abstract). In *AAAI Spring Symposium Series on Information Gathering from Distributed, Heterogeneous Environments*.

Durfee, E. H., M. Huber, M. Kurnow, and J. Lee (1997, February). TAIPE: Tactical assistants for interaction planning and execution. In *Proceedings of the First International Conference on Autonomous Agents (Agents '97)*, Marina del Rey, California, pp. 443–450.

Fikes, R. E. and N. J. Nilsson (1971). STRIPS: A new approach to the application of theorem proving to problem solving. *Artificial Intelligence 2*, 189–208.

Georgeff, M. P. and F. F. Ingrand (1989). Decision-making in an embedded reasoning system. In *Proceedings of the Eleventh International Joint Conference on Artificial Intelligence*, Detroit, Michigan, pp. 972–978.

Huhns, M. N. and M. P. Singh (Eds.) (1997). *Readings in Agents*, Chapter 1, pp. 1–23. Morgan Kaufmann.

Kenny, P. G., C. R. Bidlack, K. C. Kluge, J. Lee, M. J. Huber, E. H. Durfee, and T. Weymouth (1994, May). Implementation of a reactive autonomous navigation system on an outdoor mobile robot. In *Association for Unmanned Vehicle Systems Annual National Symposium (AUVS-94)*, Detroit, MI, pp. 233–239. Association for Unmanned Vehicle Systems.

Lee, J. (1995, March). On the design of structured circuit semantics. In *AAAI Spring Symposium on Lessons Learned from Implemented Software Architectures for Physical Agents*, pp. 127–134.

Lee, J. (1997, January). *An Explicit Semantics for Coordinated Multiagent Plan Execution*. Ph. D. thesis, University of Michigan, Ann Arbor, Michigan.

Lee, J., M. J. Huber, E. H. Durfee, and P. G. Kenny (1994, March). UM-PRS: an implementation of the procedural reasoning system for multirobot applications. In *Conference on Intelligent Robotics in Field, Factory, Service, and Space (CIRFFSS '94)*, Houston, Texas, pp. 842–849.

McDermott, D. (1991, June). A reactive plan language. Technical Note YALEU/CSD/RR #864, Department of Computer Science, Yale University.

Time-Bounded Negotiation Framework for Multi-Agent Coordination

Kyoung Jun Lee[1] and Yong Sik Chang[2]

[1] School of Business, Korea University
Anam-Dong, Sungbuk-Ku, Seoul 136-701, Korea
leekj@kuba.korea.ac.kr
[2] Graduate School of Management, Korea Advanced Institute of Science and Technology
207-43 Cheongryangri-Dong, Dongdaemoon-Ku, Seoul 130-012, Korea
yschang@msd.kaist.ac.kr

Abstract. For the efficient and informative coordination of multiple agents, a time-bounded agent negotiation framework is proposed utilizing time-based commitment scheme. By attaching the commitment duration to agent messages, the traditional Contract Net Protocol is extended to a time-bounded environment, thereby giving rise to a *Time-Bounded Negotiation Framework* (TBNF). The proposed negotiation framework has a new message type to agree upon the extension of a commitment duration, and a novel commitment concept in the form of Negative Commitment. We interpret the semantics of the messages with the commitment duration, and then formally define and compare the three typical negotiation protocols - nothing-guaranteed protocol, acceptance-guaranteed protocol, and finite-time guarantee protocol - which can be incorporated into TBNF. The Time-Bounded Negotiation Framework should provide a background for efficient and effective agent coordination while accommodating each agent's adaptive negotiation strategy.

1. Introduction

Efficient coordination of multi-agents is very important for the performance of each agent and the whole system. The Contract Net Protocol [7, 14] has been the most commonly used method for coordinating agents in negotiation. The Contract Net Protocol specifies communication and control in a distributed problem solver [3], that is, how contract managers announce tasks to other agents, how potential contractors return bids to the manager, and how the manager then awards the contract (A manager is responsible for monitoring the execution of a task and processing the results of its execution, and a contractor is responsible for the actual execution of the task). The basic steps of the protocol is as follows.

- A manager issues a task announcement describing the task to be done and the criteria for bids.
- Contractors send bids to announce their willingness and ability to perform a task.

- The manager sends the award message to a successful contractor
- The contractor sends an acknowledgement of the award, either accepting or rejecting it.

Since the Contract Net Protocol can be somewhat simple for a specific purpose and needs to be modified to satisfy various system requirements and improve performance, there have been a couple of researches on the extension of the protocol by:

- Introducing new speech acts such as temporal grant, temporal reject, definitive grant, definitive reject for the case when tasks exceed the capacity of a single agent. The context involves an extended Contract Net Protocol [5].
- Fuzzy theoretic method for determining next task announcement and the best fitting bid [17].
- Using directed contract and forgetting by case-based reasoning to reduce communication load [15].
- Enabling agents to choose level of commitment dynamically for iterative task allocation negotiations [10].

In this paper, we propose a negotiation framework emphasizing the commitment duration attached to every message (Commitment is an agreement or pledge to do something in the future [7,12]). The time-bounded framework provides a good background for choosing a proper negotiation protocol especially for dynamic situation where desired tasks and available resources may be changing as the system is executing tasks. The following is the scenario from the delivery problem in a virtual shopping mall, which inspired this research. When a virtual shopping mall receives product orders from customers, it needs to make delivery orders automatically without human intervention, generate a request for proposal (RFP) and announce it to multiple delivery companies. Then, the mall and delivery companies will negotiate over the price and quality (e.g. delivery date) of a specific delivery service. In this case, each agent is self-interested, contractor agent (i.e. delivery company) is resource-constrained, and the status of agents is fast changing.

Example scenario from delivery problem in virtual shopping mall context

1. A shopping mall agent (SMA1) asks a delivery company agent (DCA) whether it can deliver a product (PA) to its buyer from a warehouse in three days.
2. DCA schedules its own facility (e.g. trucks) for the delivery of the product PA and replies 'Yes' to SMA1.
3. However, SMA1 has not yet awarded the bid to DCA.
4. During the meantime, another shopping mall agent SMA2 asks the delivery company agent (DCA) whether DCA can deliver a product PB to its buyer from a warehouse in three days.
5. DCA tries to schedules its own facility for the delivery of PB and comes to know that it cannot deliver PB to the buyer for SMA2 on time without canceling the capacity reservation for SMA1.

In this case, what should DCA do? We can consider using three alternative protocols to cope with this problem: 1) *Nothing-Guaranteed Protocol*, 2) *Acceptance-*

Guaranteed Protocol, and 3) *Finite-time Guarantee Protocol*. The next section briefly explains each of them.

2. Three Candidate Protocols for the Scenario

2.1. Nothing-Guaranteed Protocol (NGP)

Most of protocols based on traditional Contract Net Protocol assume this [8,9,13,16]. In this protocol, no one has to take any responsibility before reaching mutual agreement on the task. In our scenario, DCA feels free to reply 'Yes' to SMA2, and waits for the confirming messages from either SMA1 or SMA2. Under this protocol, the messages need not have any time concept because there is no commitment or responsibility before the final agreement. Therefore, each agent feels free to send a message to another agent. However, since nothing is guaranteed until a mutual agreement is made, some agents can feel nervous and the global coordination performance can be degraded. For example, when SMA1 receives the bid from DCA and decides to award the bid to DCA, but in the meantime, DCA can contract with SMA2, then DCA cannot accept the bid awarded from SMA1. In this case, SMA1 should start negotiation from the beginning. Traditional Contract Net Protocol is a protocol which does not guarantee anything before the final agreement. Even though the manager awards the bid immediately after receiving it, the contractor's rejection is inherently possible, which can result in an inefficient negotiation process. In addition, each agent can be unsettled because it has no further information until the final agreement.

2.2. Acceptance-Guaranteed Protocol (AGP)

In this protocol, an agent guarantees the positive response to the other agent's message. For example, a manager agent can guarantee the acceptance of a bid submission to a contractor agent when the manager agent announces a task, which means that the task announcer automatically will award the bid to the bidder on the condition that the submitted bid satisfies the constraints of the initial announcement. In addition, a contractor agent can guarantee the unconditional acceptance of the bid awarded from a manager agent. This protocol can be useful when a task announcer agent contacts only one bidder agent or a bidder agent contacts only one manager. This situation can be interpreted as the extreme case of audience restriction, which was discussed in [16]. For example, there might be only one bidder, or the announcer could have preferences among the bidders. One of the merits of the acceptance-guaranteed protocol is reducing the communication effort between agents. This protocol can be used for hierarchical (vertical) coordination between high-level agents and lower-level agents, where the high-level agents have only one partner in negotiation. If we apply this protocol to the above scenario, which assumes that DCA guarantees the acceptance of the bid awarded from the SMA1, then DCA should reply 'No' to SMA2 because DCA already submitted the bid to SMA1.

2.3. Finite-time Guarantee Protocol (FGP)

When a message has a kind of guarantee, that is, commitment, then the message needs to have a lifetime because an agent cannot wait a long time to establish a contract with the other agent. In addition, if an agent wants to hold a task but needs more time to confirm its resource availability, it should send a message requesting the extension of the message life. The finite-time guarantee protocol addresses such needs by making every message have its own timed token over a valid duration. The message with the token is valid during the duration specified in the token and the timing token can be attached to request messages as well as reply messages. We may rewrite the above scenario using the protocol below.

1. SMA1 asks DCA whether it can deliver a product PA to its buyer in three days.
2. DCA schedules its own facility for the delivery of the product PA and replies 'Yes' to SMA1 with a timed token valid for 30 minutes.
3. SMA1 has not awarded the bid to DCA yet.
4. During the meantime, another shopping mall agent SMA2 asks DCA whether it can deliver a product PB to its buyer in three days.
5. DCA checks the current time.
- (a) If 30 minutes have passed: DCA schedules its own facility for the delivery of PB without reserving its resources for SMA1 and replies 'Yes' to SMA2 with the timed token valid for 30 minutes. DCA need not feel any responsibility toward SMA1. (See (a) in Fig. 1)
- (b) If it is before the deadline (for example, it has taken 20 minutes after replying to SMA1): DCA should try to schedule its own facility for the delivery of PB with capacity reservation for SMA1. As the result, DCA knows that it cannot deliver PA for SMA2 on time without canceling the capacity reservation for SMA1. DCA replies 'No' to SMA2 but it asks SMA2 to try to request the order again after 10 minutes or wait 10 minutes to confirm message. (See (b) in Fig. 1)

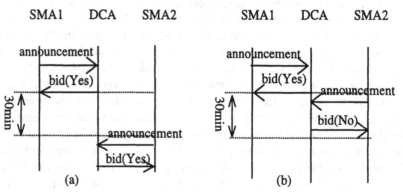

Fig. 1. Two situations when using finite-time guarantee protocol

3. Time-Bounded Negotiation Framework

To synthesize the above three protocols into a framework, we propose the Time-Bounded Negotiation Framework (TBNF) which is a meta-model of the Contract Net Protocol emphasizing the commitment duration attached to each negotiation message.

3.1. Definition of Time-Bounded Negotiation Framework (TBNF)

Time-Bounded Negotiation Framework (TBNF) is a negotiation framework where agents negotiate with messages with *commitment duration* (denoted by T in this paper). When a message has a zero-length commitment duration (T = 0), it has no commitment in it (*Zero-time commitment*). On the other hand, when a message has an infinite-length commitment duration (T = ∞), the message is interpreted to be valid eternally by the agent's commitment (*Infinite-time Commitment*). When a message has a finite-length commitment duration (T = α, $0 < \alpha < \infty$), the message is valid for the specified duration (*Finite-time commitment*).

3.2. New Message Type for Efficient Negotiation

The explicit use of the commitment duration leads to a new type of message for efficient negotiation. If an agent is computing its resource for decision making on an ongoing negotiation but the commitment duration given by its partner is almost expiring, it needs to send a message asking the extension of the commitment duration to its partner. Without this message type, the negotiation can be terminated despite both agents want to continue their negotiation process. We call this message as Request for Extending Commitment Duration (ReqECD) and its response is named as Response to Extending Commitment Duration (ResECD).

3.3. Motivations of Using and Demanding Commitment Duration

To justify the real world applicability of the Time-Bounded Negotiation Framework, we need to check each agent's motivation of using commitment duration for itself or demanding commitment duration to its partner. For example, in a cooperative and mediated environment, a central agent can ensure the global performance by enforcing the use of commitment duration. On the other hand, in a self-interested environment, each agent can generate a message with commitment duration for self-interest as follows.

- *Committed task announcement*: Manager agent can use a committed announcement of a task to contact the contractor agents sequentially and select one of them.
- *Committed bid submission*: Manager agent can demand a committed submission to contractor agents for a safe choice among committed alternatives. On the other hand, contractor agents can use the committed bid submission for

1. increasing the probability of getting the award from manager agent by providing a safe choice or
2. maintaining internal consistency for itself and escaping the responsibility of the future possible rejection of the award from the manager agent.

- *Committed bid awarding*: Bid awarding is inherently a committed action. Manager can use finite-time commitment to contract sequentially with contractors or expedite the acknowledgement of the contractors.

4. Semantics of Each Message with Commitment Duration

By analyzing the meaning of the commitment duration, the semantics of any negotiation message can be precisely interpreted. Before the introduction of the commitment duration concept, strictly speaking, each message can only be an announcement without guarantee or commitment. Under TBNF, every message can have the option regarding whether it commits or not to a specific task, and a new commitment concept, *negative commitment*, is suggested. The following is the interpretation of each message.

4.1. Task Announcement with the Commitment Duration

- *Common interpretation*: "Submit the bid about this task to me (Manager) within duration T, if you submit the bid within T then I will award the grant to you".
- *Infinite-time commitment ($T = \infty$)*: It says that contractor agent has only to submit the bid at any time. Awarding is guaranteed (Automatic Awarding). This scheme can be used between cooperating agents such as in internal hierarchical scheduling.
- *Finite-time commitment ($T = \alpha, 0 < \alpha < \infty$)*: It means that if a contractor agent submits the bid before α, the grant should be awarded to the contractor agent.
- *Zero-time commitment ($T = 0$)*: It is implicitly interpreted that even if a contractor submits the bid to manager, there is no guarantee it would be awarded. Interestingly, even using the expiration time of the task announcement message [14] corresponds to the case where the commitment duration is zero because the expiration time has nothing to do with the manager's commitment. The commitment duration is not the same as the deadline for receiving bids. As pointed out in [10], it should be noted that when the commitment duration is longer than zero, the number of recipients of the announcement message should be one since the same task set cannot be awarded exclusively to multiple agents.

4.2. Bid Submission with the Commitment Duration

- *Common interpretation*: "I (Contractor) am submitting this bid to you and I'll reserve my resource for the task for the duration T".

- *Infinite-time commitment (T = ∞)*: The manager agent does not have to send the bid awarding message to a contractor agent because the contractor agent already committed its resource for the bid.
- *Finite-time commitment (T = α, 0 < α < ∞)*: If the manager agent awards the bid within α, the contractor agent can afford to use its resource for the bid.
- *Zero-time commitment (T = 0)*: It is implicitly interpreted that even though the manager agent awards the bid as soon as it receives the submission, there is actually no guarantee that the contractor will commit its resources for the bid.

4.3. Bid Rejection with the Commitment Duration

It is interesting to see that even the message of the rejection of a bid has a concept of commitment. We may call this *Negative Commitment*.
- *Infinite-time commitment (T = ∞)*: Due to the limited capacity of the contractor agent, it will not be able to submit the bid for the task forever.
- *Finite-time commitment (T = α, 0 < α < ∞)*: Though the contractor agent cannot submit the bid right now, but after the duration α the contractor agent may be able to submit the bid.
- *Zero-time commitment (T = 0)*: It is implicitly interpreted that the contractor agent cannot submit the bid right now, but it may be able to submit the bid soon.

4.4. Bid Awarding with the Commitment Duration

For the resource-bounded contractors, the final step for the agreement should not be the bid awarding by the manager, but should be the acknowledgement of the bid awarding by the contractor because the bid submission cannot guarantee the acceptance of a bid award without any pre-commitment. In the traditional Contract Net Protocol, it is assumed that if manager awards the bid to a contractor, then the contractor can accept or reject it, and the manager accepts the response unconditionally. So, the bid awarding in traditional Contract Net Protocol can be viewed as an eternally committed message. Therefore, we can interpret that the traditional Contract Net Protocol is a special case protocol where the committed awarding message have infinite commitment duration and both the task announcement message and the bid submission message have zero-commitment duration. Under TBNF we can give the finite-time commitment duration to the bid awarding message in order to demand rejection or acceptance from the contractor in the specified time.
- *Infinite-time commitment (T = ∞)*: The contract is completed and the contractor agent do not have to reply to this.
- *Finite-time commitment (T = α, 0 < α < ∞)*: For the final agreement, the contractor should send acknowledgement within α. If not, the award can be canceled.
- *Zero-time commitment (T = 0)*: Irrelevant to the semantics of bid awarding.

4. 5. Acknowledgement (Award acceptance/rejection)

The final confirmation message inherently has the infinite commitment duration (T = ∞)

5. Comparison of the Three Protocols in Time-Bounded Negotiation Framework (TBNF)

By employing the length of the commitment duration in TBNF, we can formally define the above three typical negotiation protocols as follows.

1. Nothing-Guaranteed Protocol (NGP) is defined as the protocol where every negotiation message has zero-length commitment duration (T = 0).
2. Acceptance-Guaranteed Protocol (AGP) is defined as the protocol where the task announcement message or the bid submission message has infinite-length commitment duration (T = ∞).
3. Finite Time-Guarantee Protocol (FGP) is defined as the protocol where one or more message types have finite-length commitment duration (T = ∞).

The protocols have the comparative characteristics along the several criteria, which are summarized in Table 1.

Table 1. Protocol comparison summary

Protocols	NGP	AGP	FGP
contract process	simple	simple	complex
negotiation efficiency	inefficient when highly resource-constrained	efficient	efficient when highly resource-constrained
predictability & informativeness	low	high	high
alternative availability	high	low	high
communication overhead	high when highly resource-constrained	low	high when not optimized
implementation complexity	simple	simple	complex
strategic variety	low	low	high

- *Contract process complexity*: In terms of the contract process complexity, Finite-time Guarantee Protocol is the most complex because it has to deal with the new message types such as ReqECD and ResECD and the concept of the negative commitment.
- *Negotiation efficiency*: Since agents in Nothing-Guaranteed Protocol do not guarantee anything until the final agreement, the negotiation process can be inefficient

when resources are highly constrained or the decision making time (deliberation time) of agents is relatively long. On the other hand, Finite-time Guarantee Protocol can be effective in highly constrained situation as we see in the example scenario. Acceptance-Guaranteed Protocol has a simple contract process and is efficient in negotiation, but it can be used only for a special situation such as the hierarchical or cooperative coordination of agents.

- *Predictability and informativeness*: In Finite-Guarantee Protocol, agents can enjoy more predictability (e.g. Managers can select the pre-committed bid). Finite-time Guarantee Protocol is the most informative protocol among the three protocols since each agent can infer the resource status or the intention of the other agent from the commitment duration. The informativeness can expedite the agreement between participating agents. Agents in Nothing-Guaranteed Protocol cannot have sufficient information on the status of other agents, which can lead to inefficiency in negotiation.

- *Alternative availability*: In Acceptance-Guaranteed Protocol, alternatives for the contract partner of an agent are much reduced because it should communicate with the agents to which it can guarantee the acceptance of the offer from its partner. On the other hand, in Finite-time Guarantee Protocol , agents can enjoy more availability. Manager agents can use a finite-time commitment in task announcement message to choose a good candidate by sending the task announcement sequentially. In addition, manager agents can contact sequentially the contractor agents who submitted the bid by using the finite-time commitment in bid awarding message.

- *Communication overhead*: In highly constrained and dynamic situation, the communication overhead can be high from the negotiation failure especially under Nothing-Guaranteed Protocol. Under a Finite-time Guarantee Protocol, too short a commitment duration can lead to unnecessary communication for confirmation and computation for feasibility checking. On the other hand, in a Finite-time Guarantee Protocol with too long a commitment duration, agents may respond negatively to requests from their partners. Therefore, it is necessary to find an optimal lengrh of the commitment duration. The optimal lifetime of messages can be determined for each agent's performance or for global performance. In addition, if the computation time of an agent is unpredictable, it should send many ReqECD (Request for Extending Commitment Duration), which increases the amount of communication.

- *Implementation complexity*: In Finite-time Guarantee Protocol, each agent should have a sophisticated action scheduling mechanism and a message management procedure such as the local scheduler [4] for managing message transmission and its own resources. To react in such a time-constrained situation, each agent may need a kind of anytime algorithm capability [1]. In addition, Finite-time Guarantee Protocol, a time dependent scheme, requires that the sending or receiving time of a message be verified by both parties [10]. That is, there should be a mechanism for all agents to agree on the message arrival time. To solve such a problem, a method has been proposed [11], which can carry out electronic commerce transactions that does not require any third-party enforcement.

- *Strategic variety*: Finite-time Guarantee Protocol has more strategic varieties over the other two protocols. For example, contractor agents can use the finite-time guarantee to promote bid award from manager agents.

6. Experiment in Electronic Commerce Context

One of the benefits from using TBNF is that it provides a background for finding an appropriate architecture and protocol for a specific domain and situation. In this section, we show the usefulness of TBNF by the experiment which finds an optimal commitment duration in bidding message when the contractor's resource is highly constrained.

6.1. Design of Experiment

For the experiment, we assume that we have three manager agents (i.e. shopping mall agents) and two contractor agents (i.e. delivery company agents). Each delivery company is assumed to have one unit resource (i.e. a truck), which is used up when a contract is set-up and becomes available when a certain time (i.e. delivery time is randomly distributed from 6 seconds and 10 seconds in this experiment) is passed after the contract. To simplify the experiment and see the pure effect of the commitment duration in bidding message, we set each commitment duration in task announcement and awarding to zero. The acknowledgement message inherently has the infinite commitment duration. All these message flows in the contract process is depicted in Fig. 2.

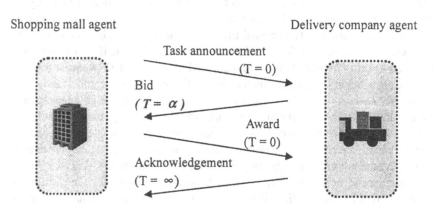

Fig. 2. Commitment duration in bidding message

When the contract process begins between the two agents, as described in Table 2, there can be four kinds of results such as bid rejection by contractor (**B**), award rejection by manager (**Q**), acknowledgement rejection by contractor (**X**), and successful contract (**Y**). In the experiment, we will see the frequency of each result by changing the commitment duration in bid submission. The optimal commitment duration will be the duration which maximizes the number of successful contracts.

Table 2. Contract success and rejection types

Negotiation types	B		Q		X		Y	
Agent	S	D	S	D	S	D	S	D
Task announcement	O.K.		O.K.		O.K.		O.K.	
Bid		No		O.K.		O.K.		O.K.
Award			No		O.K.		O.K.	
Acknowledgement						No		O.K.

B : Bid rejection by contractor (delivery company)
Q : Award rejection by manager (shopping mall) after bid
X : Acknowledgement rejection by contractor (delivery company) after award
Y : Successful contract
S : Shopping mall agent
D : Delivery company agent

We implemented the test bed of agents for the experiment using Oracle Database and C language in UNIX environment and the user interface on the WWW. The current architecture (Fig. 3) is simplified for the experiment but has a scalable structure.

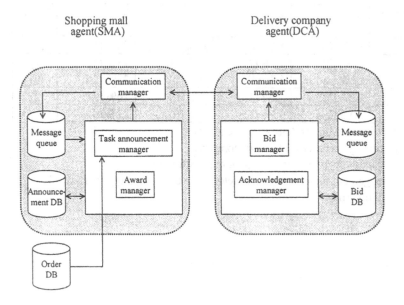

Fig. 3. Architecture of agents for experiment

The multiagent system is composed of shopping mall agent and delivery company agent. Each has a communication manager sending and receiving messages and a message queue storing the incoming messages. The shopping mall agent has a task announcement manager building and announcing task, a task announcement history database, and an award manager which awards the bid to a selected delivery company agent. The delivery company agent has a bid manager which analyzes an announcement and submits a bid to the shopping mall agent, a bidding history database, and an acknowledgement manager which receives an award and finally sends a confirmation message to the shopping mall agent. In order to implement such an agent system operating successfully under real electronic commerce environment, each agent needs a kind of action scheduling module which can optimally allocate the time and resources for his decision making [1]. To improve the performance of TBNF, it is important to implement the optimal decision making on message prioritizing and reallocating the decision resources for new arriving messages. However, for this experiment, we implemented a simple system where each agent processes messages in message queue by FIFO (First-In First-Out) method.

6.2. Result of the Experiment

We observed the trend of frequencies of each result in the contract process while increasing the commitment duration of the bidding message by 5 seconds per experiment from zero to 20 seconds. Table 3 summarizes the result and Fig. 4 shows the trend of the contract result.

Table 3. Result of the experiment

Commitment duration	B	Q	X	Y	Total
T = 0	0 % (0)	5% (1)	69% (13)	26% (5)	(19)
T = 5	17% (3)	12% (2)	47% (8)	23% (4)	(17)
T = 10	62% (49)	5% (4)	0% (0)	33% (26)	(79)
T = 15	62% (50)	12% (10)	0% (0)	26% (22)	(82)
T = 20	60% (24)	18% (7)	0% (0)	22% (9)	(40)

(The numbers in parentheses denote the frequencies.)
B : Bid rejection by contractor (delivery company)
Q : Award rejection by manager (shopping mall) after bid
X : Acknowledgement rejection by contractor (delivery company) after award
Y : Successful contract

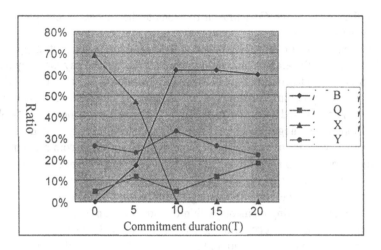

Fig. 4. Trend of contract result

As we see in Fig. 4, negotiation success ratio depends on the length of bid commitment duration; it is not good when the bid commitment duration is too short or too long. That is, there exists the optimal length of the commitment duration in bidding message, which maximizes the contract success rate. It means that a proper use of a commitment duration in messages can result in better result than the nothing-guaranteed protocol which has been frequently used so far, and for the best performance it is necessary to find the optimal commitment duration for a specific situation. The trend of the bid rejection confirms the plausible fact that the longer the commitment duration of bidding message the more conservative in bid submission. On the contrary, we can see that the acknowledgement rejection decreases as the commitment duration of bidding increases.

7. Related Research

A field similar to the commitment duration, Time Valid Through, was suggested in the extension of the Contract Net Protocol [10]. This field describes how long an offer on an alternative is valid and suggested as one of various commitment methods with the penalties of decommiting. If the negotiation partner has not answered by that time, the sender of the message gets decommitted from that alternative. While the research deals with a rational decommiting scheme based on marginal cost calculation, we do not include the issues of decommitting in this paper. Instead, we try to formalize the CNP (contract net protocol) based negotiation framework by emphasizing the concept of the commitment duration, introducing new message types such as ReqECD (Request for Extending Commitment Duration) and creating new commitment concept in bid rejection, that is, *Negative Commitment* to promote the successful completion of the negotiation between agents.

In [12], the commitment concept is studied at the negotiation agent's strategy level while TBNF treats it at the architecture and protocol levels. We can say that they used the 'oscillation-type' of adaptive strategy between two extremes (T=0 and T=∞), while TBNF provides the opportunity to employ an adaptive strategy between moderate alternatives (such as T=0 and T=α, T=α and T=β, T=β and T=∞, when $\alpha < \beta$). We expect that a moderate strategy can outperform the oscillatory strategy in many situations. Furthermore, we can give each heterogeneous agent different commitment duration depending on its various characteristics and each agent can change the length of the commitment duration at its own and employ flexible strategies.

Collins et al. [2] study the temporal strategies in Contract Net Protocol and show how the selection of the timing elements within the protocol can affect the behaviors of the agents involved in the negotiation. However, a temporal strategy of an agent without commitment is only a declaration, so it does not have any enforcing mechanism for the contract between two agents. Therefore, in their scheme a mendacious agent can have an advantage over the other honest agents.

8. Conclusion

We expect TBNF will be suited well to choose a good protocol for the situation where self-interested and resource-constrained agents negotiate in a dynamic situation.

In summary, the merits of TBNF we can consider are as follows:
1. TBNF provides a more informative framework with richer semantics.
2. TBNF provides the framework for promoting and expediting the negotiation process by allowing agents more strategy alternatives.
3. TBNF provides the background for finding an appropriate architecture and protocol for a specific domain and situation.
4. TBNF provides the background for efficient and effective multi-agent coordination while accommodating agent's adaptive negotiation strategy.

The future research topics related to TBNF include the research on the desirable architecture of agents under the framework and the optimal commitment scheme for competition and cooperation between agents. In addition, the research on a time stamping mechanism is necessary for all agents to verify and agree on the sending or receiving time of a message, which is regarded as one of the functions of certificate authorities for electronic commerce.

References

1. Boddy, M., Dean, T.: Solving Time-Dependent Planning Problems, Proceedings of the Eleventh International Joint Conference on Artificial Intelligence (1989) 979-984

2. Collins, J., Jamison, S., Gini, M., and Mobasher, B.: Temporal Strategies in a Multi-Agent Contracting Protocol, Proceedings of AAAI-97 Workshop on Using AI in Electronic Commerce, Virtual Organizations, Enterprise Knowledge Management to Reengineer the Corporation (1997) 50-56

3. Davis, R., Smith, R.: Negotiation as a metaphor for distributed problem solving, Artificial Intelligence 20(1) (1983) 63-109

4. Decker, K.: Environment Centered Analysis & Design of Coordination Mechanisms, Ph.D. Dissertation. University of Massachusetts at Amherst, Department of Computer Science (1995)

5. Fisher, K., Muller, J., Pischel, M., Schier, D.: A Model for Cooperative Transportation Scheduling, Proceedings of the First International Conference on Multi-Agent Systems (1995) 109-116

6. Gu, C., Ishida, T.: Analyzing the Social Behavior of Contract Net Protocol, Agents Breaking Away; MAAMAW'96, Lecture Notes in Artificial Intelligence, Vol. 1038. Springer-Verlag, Berlin Heidelberg New York (1996) 116-127

7. Jennings, N.: Commitments and Conventions: The Foundation of Coordination in Multi-Agent Systems, Knowledge Engineering Review 8(3) (1993) 223-250

8. Lin, G., Solberg, J.: Integrated Shop Floor Control Using Autonomous Agents, IIE Transactions 24(3) (1992) 57-71

9. Malone, T., Fikes, R., Grant, K., Howard, M.: Enterprise: A Market-like Task Scheduler for Distributed Computing Environments, The Ecology of Computation, North-Holland (1988) 177-205

10. Sandholm, T., Lesser, V.: Issues in Automated Negotiation and Electronic Commerce: Extending the Contract Net Framework, Proceedings of the First International Conference on Multi-Agent Systems (1995) 328-335

11. Sandholm, T.: Unenforced E-Commerce Transactions, IEEE Internet Computing, (1997 Nov/Dec) 47-54

12. Sen, S., Durfee, E.: The Role of Commitment in Cooperative Negotiation, International Journal of Intelligent and Cooperative Information Systems 3(1) (1994) 67-81

13. Shaw, M., Whinston, A.: Task Bidding and Distributed Planning in Flexible Manufacturing, Proceedings of the Second IEEE Conference on Artificial Intelligence Applications, Miami (1985) 184-189

14. Smith, R.: The contract net protocol: High-level communication and control in a distributed problem solver, IEEE Transactions on Computer 29 (1980) 1104-1113

15. Takuya, O., Kazuo, H., Yuichiro, A.: Reducing Communication Load on Contract Net by Case-Based Reasoning -- Extension with Directed Contract and Forgetting --, Proceedings of the Second International Conference on Multi-Agent Systems (1996) 244-251

16. Van Dyke Parunak, H.: Manufacturing experience with the contract net. In Proceedings of the Distributed Artificial Intelligence Workshop (1985) 67-91

17. Vojdani, N.: Distributed Manufacturing Control Using Fuzzy Contract Net. In: Jamshidi, M., Zadeh, L. (eds.): Applications of Fuzzy Logic, Prentice Hall Canada (1997)

A Fuzzy Game Theoretic Approach to Multi-Agent Coordination

Shih-Hung Wu and Von-Wun Soo

Department of Computer Science
National Tsing Hua University
Hsin-Chu City, 30043 Taiwan, R.O.C.
E-mail: shwu@cs.nthu.edu.tw, soo@cs.nthu.edu.tw

Abstract. Game theoretic decision making is a practical approach to multi-agent coordination. Rational agents may make decisions based on different principles of rationality assumptions that usually involve knowledge of how other agents might move. After formulating a game matrix of utility entries of possible combination of moves from both agents, agents can reason which combination is the equilibrium. Most previous game theoretic works treat the utility values qualitatively (i.e., consider only the order of the utility values). This is not practical since the utility values are usually approximate and the differences between utility values are somewhat vague. In this paper, we present a fuzzy game theoretic decision making mechanism that can deal with uncertain utilities. We thus construct a fuzzy-theoretic game framework under both the fuzzy theory and the game theory. The notions of fuzzy dominant relations, fuzzy Nash equilibrium, and fuzzy strategies are defined and fuzzy reasoning are carried out in agent decision making. We show that a fuzzy strategy can perform better than a mixed strategy in traditional game theory in dealing with more than one Nash equilibrium games.

1 Introduction

Previous work shows that rational agents are able to coordinate and cooperate under a game theoretical deal-making mechanism [15], [18]. However, the payoff values in the game matrix maybe uncertain values, that will affect the result of the decision making. In order to deal with the uncertainty of payoffs, the agents are required to introduce the ability of fuzzy reasoning into the conventional game theory.

The payoff value may be uncertain is a problem in the process of constructing a game matrix in a real world situation. When the payoff is given in the form of fuzzy rather than crisp numbers, fuzzy reasoning may help in game theoretic decision making. For example, the payoffs of the game matrix in **Fig. 1** are not crisp numbers but in terms of such fuzzy words as best, good, fine, bad, and worst. These words can be mapped into numbers. However, if we map the fuzzy concepts into crisp numbers and then make decision, the result could be very different on even a very little difference in the word-to-number mapping. In **Fig. 2**, where best worst, good and fine are mapped to 90, 10, 49 and 51 respectively. The mapping gives two similar matrices, but they give a different result on the computation of Nash equilibrium. In

Fig. 2 (a), each agent has a dominant strategy and the game has a unique Nash equilibrium at the strategy combination (b, d). However, in **Fig. 2** (b), there is no dominant strategy for any agent and no Nash equilibrium exists in the game. The only difference between **Fig. 2**(a) and **Fig. 2**(b) is the different value assignment of good and fine. In (a), good is 49 and fine is 51, while in (b), good is 51 and fine is 49. Small change of the payoff value gives drastically different result. Thus

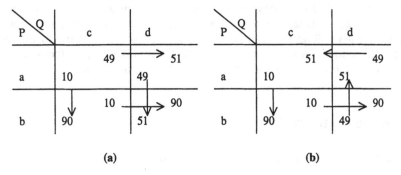

Fig. 1. Game Matrix of a game with fuzzy payoff.

Fig. 2. Mapping the game matrix in Fig. 1 into crisp numbers. The game may have (a) unique equilibrium or (b) no equilibrium at all.

Rational agents make decisions based on the different principles of rationality, which involve the knowledge of how others move. The most common definition of rationality is assuming both agents in the game are expected utility maximizers [8], [15]. Most works treated the utility values qualitatively (i.e., considered only the ordinal relation among the utility values instead the exact values) [4], [3], [18]. This is unpractical when the utility values are approximated value or the utility values are fuzzy. In a game theory, all decisions are made through the comparison of the utility values (payoffs) associated with the outcome of the different combination of strategies. When the utility values are not exact, the exact comparison is not realistic. In this situation, we introduce the notion of fuzzy comparison by changing the "greater than" relation in defining the dominant strategy into a fuzzy relation. This approach gives an interesting concept of a fuzzy strategy, which is related to but different from the traditional mixed-strategy in game theory. In game theory, a mixed strategy equilibrium is a concept, where agents can take separate pure strategies with different probabilities. A mixed strategy can deal with games with no pure equilibrium or multiple equilibria. In the previous work, we have listed all the possible cases, which are a unique equilibrium, multiple equilibria, and no equilibrium [19]. In one equilibrium case, agents will agree on the equilibrium, unless there are better solutions than the equilibrium for both agents (the prisoner's dilemma). In the multiple equilibrium case, it needs a communication protocol to choose among these focal points. In no equilibrium case, there is no easy mechanism to reach an agreement, therefore, a negotiation protocol is needed.

Traditional game theory mostly dealt with uncertainty in a probabilistic way, i.e., Bayesian games. A nature agent is assumed to move before or after each agent's move. The payoff cannot be certain because the moves of nature agent cannot be deterministically predicted. In fuzzy theory, a lot of pioneers had investigated the fuzzy decision making for single agent under uncertain situation [2], [6], [20], [21], [17]. A traditional game can involve a set of agents. Each agent can have a set of strategies to play and have a utility function that maps every outcome (a combination of strategies) to a payoff value. There can be many ways of extending a traditional game into a fuzzy game. Orlovsky [11] [12] fuzzified the notions of strategies so that agents could choose among a fuzzy set of strategies, namely, the choice of strategies for agents is fuzzy but the payoff values are crisp. Aubin [1], Butnariu [5], Sakawa & Nishizaki [16] studied the fuzzy coalition where the memberships for an agent to participate a team is fuzzy, namely an agent may not be one hundred percent of participating a team. Ragade [13] studied the notion of fuzzy preference that is much closer to our notions of fuzzy dominance concepts. In this work, we focused on the definition of fuzzy dominance relations and fuzzy Nash equilibrium.

2 The Basic Framework of a Game

In this section we review important definitions in game theory [14].

Game
A game involves a set of agents; each agent has a set of strategies to play. And each agent has a utility function that maps every combination of strategies into payoff value. Here we discuss only 2-person game, which can be represented in a 2 by 2 matrix.

Payoff value
The payoff value for each agent in a combination of strategies is denoted as $\pi_i(s_i, s_{-i})$, where i is the index of agent, $-i$ denoted the other agent and player i plays strategy s_i while agent $-i$ plays strategy s_{-i}.

Dominant strategy
The strategy $S_i{}^*$ is a dominant strategy if it is player's strictly best response regardless the other player's strategies S_{-i}. Mathematically, the dominant strategy gives the highest payoff as following:

$$\pi_i(s_i^*, s_{-i}) > \pi_i(s_i', s_{-i}) \forall s_{-i}, \forall s_i' \neq s_i^* \tag{1}$$

Based on the traditional assumption of rationality, if an agent has a dominant strategy, the agent will play the dominant strategy definitely.

Nash equilibrium
An equilibrium state is a combination of strategies, in which when agents reach such a state, it is irrational to leave the state alone. [9]

Mixed strategies
A mixed strategy is a set of strategies, where each strategy is associated with a probability.

Mixed strategy equilibrium
In game theory, a mixed strategy equilibrium is a useful concept, where each agent can take a separate pure strategy with a different probability. Mixed strategies can deal with games with no pure equilibrium or multiple equilibrium. Here is an example taken from [14]. Consider a game matrix in fig 3. Assume that agent P will take a mixed strategy with a probability p_a to take strategy a, and probability p_b to take strategy b, and agent Q will take a mixed strategy with probabilities p_c and p_d to take strategies c, and d respectively. Note that $p_a + p_b = p_c + p_d = 1$. The expected payoff of P is:

$$E[\text{ Payoff}_p] = 2p_a p_d + 2p_b p_c + p_b p_d = p_a + p_c - 3p_a p_c + 1 \qquad (2)$$

Differentiating the formula with respect to p_a, and assign the value to be zero (for the maximization condition), then, we can obtain that $p_a = 1/3$, $p_b = 2/3$, $p_c = 1/3$, $p_d = 2/3$, and the expect payoffs of P and Q are both 4/3.

Games with no equilibrium can also use this approach to find a mixed-strategy equilibrium to obtain the maximum expected payoff. But to asymptotically get the expected payoff, agents must play a large number of the same games repeatedly. And each agent must play undeterministically each time.

P \ Q	c		d	
		0		2
a	0		2	
		2		1
b	2		1	

Fig. 3. Game matrix of a game with 2 pure-strategy equilibria.

3 A Fuzzy Game

A fuzzy game theoretic decision making is a new approach to multi-agent coordination. We try to deal with the uncertainty in a game using fuzzy theory. This approach gives interesting notions, a fuzzy strategy, which is related to but is different from the mixed-strategy in traditional game theory. Since the payoff values cannot be certain, the domination among strategies cannot be certain either. We have to introduce the fuzzy notion of domination. Consequently, the concept of equilibrium can be fuzzy too due to it is based on the domination. We therefore have to redefine the whole notion of a fuzzy game.

Fuzzy payoff

Suppose a payoff value for a combination of strategies for a given agent can be a fuzzy number instead of a crisp number, say v1/f1; v2/f2; v3/f3. Namely, values v1, v2, v3 with different possibilities (fuzzy memberships) f1, f2 and f3 respectively. It is then possible to defuzzify the fuzzy payoff number into a crisp number by either
1) taking the value which has the maximum fuzzy membership; or
2) taking the value of the center of gravity of the fuzzy number.
   Or we might also treat the fuzzy payoff as a fuzzy number and define the fuzzy distance operation to obtain the concept of a fuzzy dominant relation. In this paper, we assume that the fuzzy payoff can be defuzzified into a crisp number. We will leave the fuzzy distance operation in future work.

Fuzzy relation [21]

Fuzzy relations are fuzzy subsets of $X \times Y$, that is, a mapping from X to Y; $X \to Y$. Here only binary relations are considered; n-ary relations can be generalized easily. Let X, $Y \subseteq \Re$ be universal sets, then the set

$$\tilde{R} = \{((x, y), \mu_{\tilde{R}}(x, y)) \mid (x, y) \subseteq X \times Y\} \tag{3}$$

is called a fuzzy relation on $X \times Y$. In order to define a fuzzy dominant relation, we need a fuzzy greater-than relation.

Fuzzy greater-than relation

The fuzziness of a value x is greater than a value y is defined in terms of their difference. The greater the difference between them the more likely the greater than relation is established. Therefore, we could define a fuzzy membership function over any pair of (x, y) values. As we could see, there could be many different ways to define the fuzzy greater-than relation.

Fuzzy dominant relation

Assume the membership function of the fuzzy greater than relation $\mu_{\tilde{R}}$ is defined.

Then the membership value of a strategy s_i^* belonging to a dominant strategy set can be defined as:

$$\mu_{\underset{D}{\sim}}(s_i^*) = \underset{\forall s_{-i}}{min}\underset{\forall s_i' \neq s_i^*}{min}\mu_{\underset{R}{\sim}}(\pi_i(s_i^*, s_{-i}), \pi_i(s_i', s_{-i})) \tag{4}$$

Each strategy has an associated membership value, which indicates the degree of possibility of being dominant.

Fuzzy Nash equilibrium
Also, the membership value of a strategy combination (s_i^*, s_{-i}^*) belonging to the Nash equilibrium set can be computed as:

$$\mu_{\underset{NE}{\sim}}(s_i^*, s_{-i}^*) = \bigvee_i \underset{\forall s_i' \neq s_i^*}{min}(\mu_{\underset{R}{\sim}}(\pi_i(s_i^*, s_{-i}^*), \pi_i(s_i', s_{-i}^*))) \tag{5}$$

Each strategy combination has an associated membership value to indicate the degree of membership of being a Nash equilibrium.

Example 1
Given a game matrix as the one in Fig. 2 (a). Where player P has two strategies a and b, and player Q also has two strategies c and d. We can get the fuzzy membership value of a strategy being a dominant strategy by defining a suitable fuzzy greater-than relation.

Suppose a "fuzzy greater-than" relation is defined as following:

$$\mu_R(x, y) = 0 \qquad \text{for } y\text{-}5 <= x; \tag{6}$$

$$= 1 \qquad \text{for } x>=y+5;$$

$$=(x\text{-}y+5)/10 \quad \text{for } y\text{-}5<x<y+5$$

This fuzzy relation can be illustrated in Fig. 4. Note that if x is equal to y, then the membership value is 0.5. We can later use 0.5 as a threshold to defuzzify the result.

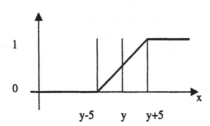

Fig. 4. A possible membership function of the fuzzy relation x >= y.

Then, for agent Q, the membership value of strategy c being a dominant strategy is:

$$\mu_{\underset{D}{\sim}}(c) = min(\mu_{\underset{R}{\sim}}(\pi_Q(a, c), \pi_Q(a, d)), \mu_{\underset{R}{\sim}}(\pi_Q(b, c), \pi_Q(b, d))) \tag{7}$$

$$= min(\mu_{\underset{R}{-}} (49, 51), \mu_{\underset{R}{-}} (10,90))=min(0.3 , 0) = 0$$

and the membership value of d being a dominant strategy is:

$$\mu_{\underset{D}{-}} (d) = min(\mu_{\underset{R}{-}} (\pi_Q (a, d), \pi_Q (a, c)), \mu_{\underset{R}{-}} (\pi_Q (b, d), \pi_Q (b, c))) \qquad (8)$$

$$= min(\mu_{\underset{R}{-}} (51, 49), \mu_{\underset{R}{-}} (90,10))=min(0.7 , 1) = 0.7$$

Similarly, for agent P, the membership value of strategy a being a dominant strategy is:

$$\mu_{\underset{D}{-}} (a) = min(\mu_{\underset{R}{-}} (\pi_P (a, c), \pi_P (b, c)), \mu_{\underset{R}{-}} (\pi_P (a, d), \pi_P (b, d))) \qquad (9)$$

$$= min(\mu_{\underset{R}{-}} (10, 90), \mu_{\underset{R}{-}} (49,51))=min(0 , 0.3) = 0$$

And the membership value of the strategy b being a dominant strategy is:

$$\mu_{\underset{D}{-}} (b) = min(\mu_{\underset{R}{-}} (\pi_P (b, c), \pi_P (a, c)), \mu_{\underset{R}{-}} (\pi_P (b, d), \pi_P (a, d))) \qquad (10)$$

$$= min(\mu_{\underset{R}{-}} (90, 10), \mu_{\underset{R}{-}} (51, 49))=min(1 , 0.7) = 0.7$$

Then we can see there are strategy for each of the agent, which has a membership value 0.7 greater than the threshold 0.5. We can say, since the membership is above 0.5, we have the confidence that take such a strategy is rational to the degree of 0.7.

Example 2
Consider the game matrix in Fig. 2 (b). As we mentioned before, the game matrix in Fig. 2(b) is very similar to the one in Fig. 2(a) but they have a totally different result. The game in Fig. 2(a) has a Nash equivalent (b, d) while the game in Fig. 2(b) has no dominant strategies and no Nash equilibrium. But, still we can find the fuzzy membership of dominant strategies and Nash equilibria, which can tell us how far is the game from having a Nash equilibrium. Follow the same calculation in Example 1. We can get:

$$\mu_{\underset{D}{-}} (c) = 0, \ \mu_{\underset{D}{-}} (d) = 0.3, \ \mu_{\underset{D}{-}} (a) = 0, \ \mu_{\underset{D}{-}} (b) = 0.3 \qquad (11)$$

Since no memberships are greater than the threshold 0.5, we can conclude that there is no dominant strategy for each agent, though d and b are possible ones to a degree 0.3. We can then calculate the membership of each strategy combination of being a Nash equilibrium as:

$$\mu_{\underset{NE}{-}} (a, c) = min (\mu_{\underset{R}{-}} (\pi_P (a, c), \pi_P (b, c)), \mu_{\underset{R}{-}} (\pi_Q (a, c), \pi_Q (a, d))) \qquad (12)$$

$$=min (\mu_{\underset{R}{-}} (10, 90), \mu_{\underset{R}{-}} (51, 49)) = min(0, 0.3)=0,$$

$$\mu_{\underset{NE}{\sim}}(b, c)=0,$$

$$\mu_{\underset{NE}{\sim}}(a, d)=0.3$$

$$\mu_{\underset{NE}{\sim}}(b, d)=0.3$$

Since no membership values are greater than the threshold value 0.5, we can conclude that there is no Nash Equilibrium in the game. However, strategy combination (a, d) and (b, d) have a tendency to a degree 0.3. If to reach a equilibrium is necessary, but cannot find one, there is a need to employ some negotiation protocol find one as in the work [19].

Example 3
Consider the game matrix in Fig. 5 with the same 2 Nash equilibria as the game in Fig. 3 but with less symmetry. The game in Fig. 5 also has no dominant strategy but has 2 Nash equilibria. Follow the same calculation in section 2, we can get the mixed strategy and the expected payoff: $P_a =1/3$, $P_b = 2/3$, $P_c= 1/3$, $P_d = 2/3$, E[Payoff $_p$] = 1.5, E[Payoff $_Q$] = 2. Now we compare the result of traditional game to the fuzzy game.

The fuzzy membership values also show that there is no dominant strategy since none of the strategies yield a dominant relation degree up to 0.5.

$$\mu_{\underset{D}{\sim}}(c) = 0.3, \ \mu_{\underset{D}{\sim}}(d) = 0.4, \ \mu_{\underset{D}{\sim}}(a) = 0.3, \ \mu_{\underset{D}{\sim}}(b) = 0.3 \qquad (13)$$

But the membership value of being Nash equilibrium shows a different result:

$$\mu_{\underset{NE}{\sim}}(a, c) =0.3, \qquad (14)$$

$$\mu_{\underset{NE}{\sim}}(b, c)=0.6,$$

$$\mu_{\underset{NE}{\sim}}(a, d)=0.7$$

$$\mu_{\underset{NE}{\sim}}(b, d)=0.3$$

As we expect, there are two Nash equilibria. But the membership values of the two Nash equilibria are different. This means the strategy combination *(a, d)* is more likely to be a Nash equilibrium.

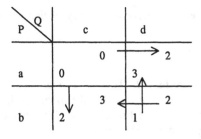

Fig. 5. Game Matrix of a game with 2 Nash equilibria.

The reason why (a, d) is picked instead of (b, c) is quite obvious that the tendency of moving from d to c for Q is weaker than the tendency of moving from b to a for player P due to the asymmetry. If agents play the game repeatedly by picking up the most likely Nash equilibrium state (a, d), the expected payoff of the player P is 3 and Q is 2. This is a better result than the mixed strategy.

4 Discussion

In the cases where there are no equilibrium or multiple equilibrium, both a fuzzy strategy and a mixed strategy can help the decision-making. A fuzzy strategy is similar to a mixed strategy, but more interesting in the sense that is can provide a measure of quality of decision making. Based on the measurement, a deterministic strategy can be then selected. Agent that takes mixed strategies can be quite useful to force other agents not to guess its move, then they must also play the mixed strategies that lead to an equilibrium. However, at each game, taking a certain strategy can become meaningless if another player plays with a mixed strategy.

4.1 Reduce the Fuzzy Game to the Traditional Game

If the "large or equal than" relation is defined as a step function as in Fig. 6:

$$\mu_R(x, y) = 0 \quad for\ y < x; \tag{15}$$

$$= 1 \quad for\ x >= y$$

Then the fuzzy dominant strategy is exactly equivalent to the crisp dominant strategy with a membership value 1. And the fuzzy Nash equilibrium is reduced to the traditional Nash equilibrium with a membership value 1.

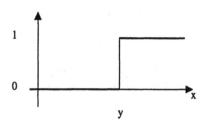

Fig. 6. Another possible membership function of the fuzzy relation x >= y.

Example 4
Consider the game matrix in Fig. 7. This is also a game with a unique Nash equilibrium as the game matrix in Fig. 1(a) but the membership of Nash equilibrium at (b, d) is worse than that of non-equilibrium (a, c). The membership value of each strategy combination being Nash equilibrium is:

$$\mu_{\underset{NE}{\sim}}(a, c) = 0.3, \tag{16}$$

$$\mu_{\underset{NE}{\sim}}(b, c) = 0.4,$$

$$\mu_{\underset{NE}{\sim}}(a, d) = 0.4,$$

$$\mu_{\underset{NE}{\sim}}(b, d) = 0.6$$

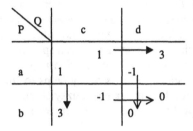

Fig. 7. Game Matrix of the prison's dilemma.

In this case, the fuzzy strategy will indicate state (b, d) is a better Nash equilibrium state to be picked. However, the better state is actually (a, c). This is a kind of prisoner's dilemma games. Fuzzy strategy cannot escape from the prisoner's dilemma if the Nash equilibrium is the only source of information to be based on.

4.2 Multi-agent Coordination Based on the Fuzzy Game Theory

Multi-agent coordination can be modeled as an N-person game [18]. Fuzzy games can also be extended into N-person fuzzy games. Although in the examples of this paper, only 2 agents and 2 by 2 game matrices are illustrated, the fuzzy game definition can be in fact applied to N by N game matrices and can also be extended to N-person fuzzy games. In an N-person game, each agent models others as rational agents and tries to find a unique Nash equilibrium. In fuzzy N-person game, each agent models others as fuzzy rational agents and tries to find a fuzzy Nash equilibrium that will achieve the highest fuzzy payoff. The method to solve 2-person games can also be extended to solve N-person games. However, since the number of strategy combinations will grow exponentially, solving an N-person game is computational costly, most relative works dealt only with 2-person games.

In a non-benevolent and loosely coupled agent society, each agent may pursue the highest expected utility while also modeling others as expected utility maximizers. One agent may perform some action that benefits others only if that action also benefits itself. Agents may wish to help each other and thus create a joint plan to achieve a common goal. Agents may wish to share load or compromise over goal satisfaction [22]. There are also situations that agents may encounter conflicts or dilemma situations that are hard to resolve due to selfishness or rationality of agents. Therefore multi-agent coordination is a must. Multi-agent coordination can be achieved through many mechanisms: organizational structuring, contracting, multi-agent planning and multi-agent negotiation [10]. Among them, the game theoretical negotiation seems to be more practical to deal with [22], [18]. In order to implement multi-agent coordination based on the fuzzy game theory, we need to also incorporate the negotiation mechanisms that have been investigated in other work [19].

5 Conclusion

In this paper, we defined the notions of fuzzy dominant relation, fuzzy Nash equilibrium and fuzzy strategies by adopting a suitable fuzzy relation. If the fuzzy relation is simplified to the 0/1 logic, the fuzzy game reduces to the traditional games. Therefore, traditional game theory can be viewed as a special case of the fuzzy game. Fuzzy game theory can be a useful tool for decision making. As we have seen, in Multi-agent coordination situations, fuzzy strategy helps to find a more stable Nash equilibrium in the multiple equilibrium games. Fuzzy strategy can select a state that obtains a better expected payoff than the traditional mixed strategy.

As a preliminary result of establishing a fuzzy game framework, there are still many different ways to improve. Firstly, since each payoff value can be a fuzzy set, we need to define fuzzy greater-than operation directly instead of de-fuzzifying over the payoff values into crisp numbers and then defining their fuzzy greater-than relations. Secondly, the fuzzy greater-than relation can be defined in a number of ways. In particular, different agents may have different greater-than concept depending on their scale over utility value. We could have different greater-than relations for two players. In this case, we might observe different results in the same game. Thirdly, continuous strategies can be used to the problems where there is no restriction on the choice of strategies. Fuzzy strategy can be used on both of the cases.

Acknowledgment

This work was financially supported by National Science Council of Taiwan, Republic of China, under grant No. NSC88-2213-E-007-05.

Reference

1. Aubin, J. P.: Fuzzy core and equilibrium of games defined in strategic form. In: Ho, Y.C., Mitter, S.K.(eds.): Directions in Large-Scale Systems, Plenum, New York(1976)371-388
2. Bellman, R.E., Zadeh, L.A.: Decision Making in a Fuzzy Environment. Management Sci. Vol.17(1970)141-164
3. Brafman, R., Tennenholtz, M.: On the Foundations of Qualitative Decision Theory, In: Proceedings of the National Conference on Artificial Intelligence, Portland, OR(1996)
4. Brams, S.J.: Theory of Moves, American Scientist Vol.81(1993)562-570
5. Butnariu, D.: Fuzzy Games: A Description of the Concept. Fuzzy Sets and Systems Vol.1(3), (1978)181-192
6. Dubois, D., Prade, H.: Fuzzy Sets and Systems: Theory and Applications, Academic Press, New York(1980)

7. Genesereth, M.R., Ginsberg, M.L., Rosenschein, J. S.: Cooperation without Communication. In: Proceedings of the National Conference on Artificial Intelligence. Philadelphia, Pennsylvania (1986)51-57

8. Mor, Y., Rosenschein, J.S.: Time and the Prisoner's Dilemma, In: Proceedings of the First International Conference on Multi-Agent Systems (1995)276-282

9. Nash, J.F.: Non-cooperative Games, Ann. of Math. 54(1951)286-295

10. Nwana, H.S., Lee, L.C., Jennings, N.R.: Coordination in Software Agent systems, BT Technology Journal,Vol.14,No.4(1996)79-88

11. Orlovski, S.A.: On Programming with Fuzzy Constraint Sets, Kybernetics 6, (1977)197-201 (Reference from [6])

12. Orlovski, S.A.: Fuzzy Goals and Sets of Choices in Two-person Games. In: Kacprzyk, J., Fedrizzi, M.(eds.): Multiperson Decision Making Models Using Fuzzy Sets and Possibility Theory. Kluwer Academic Publishers, Dordrecht(1990)288-297

13. Ragade, R.K.: Fuzzy Games in the Analysis of Options. J. Cybern. 6, (1976)213-221. (Reference from [6])

14. Rasmusen, E.: Games and Information: An Introduction to Game Theory. Basil Blackwell, Oxford(1989)

15. Rosenschein, J.S., Genesereth, M.R.: Deals among Rational Agents. In: Proceedings of the Ninth International Conference on Artificial Intelligence (1985)91-99

16. Sakawa, M., Nishizaki, I.: A Lexicographical Solution Concept in an n-Person Cooperative Fuzzy Game. Fuzzy Sets and Systems, Vol.61(3), (1994)265-275

17. Sakawa, M., Kato, K.: Interactive Decision-making for Multi-objective Linear Fractional Programming Problems with Block Angular Structure Involving Fuzzy Numbers. Fuzzy Sets and Systems. Vol.97 (1998)19-31

18. Tennenholtz, M.: On Stable Social Laws and Qualitative Equilibria. Artificial Intelligence Vol.102(1998)1-20

19. Wu, S. H., Soo, V. W.: Escape from a Prisoners' Dilemma by Communication with a Trusted Third Party. In: Proceedings of the Tenth International Conference on Tools with Artificial Intelligence. IEEE, Taipei(1998)58-65

20. Zimmermann, H.J.: Fuzzy Sets, Decision Making, and Expert Systems. Kluwer Academic, Boston(1986)

21. Zimmermann, H.J.: Fuzzy Set Theory and its Applications. 2ed. Kluwer Academic, Boston(1991)

22. Zlotkin, G., Rosenschein, J. S., Compromise in Negotiation: Exploiting Worth Functions over States, Artificial Intelligence Vol.84(1996)151-176

Partial Plan Recognition Using Predictive Agents

Jung-Jin Lee and Robert McCartney

Department of Computer Science and Engineering
University of Connecticut
Storrs, CT 06269-3155 U.S.A.
[jjl|robert]@engr.uconn.edu

Abstract. This work explores the benefits of using user models for plan recognition problems in a real-world application. Interface agents are designed for the prediction of resource usage in the UNIX domain using a stochastic approach to automatically acquire regularities of user behavior. Both sequential information from the command sequence and relational information such as system's responses and arguments to the commands are considered to typify a user's behavior and intentions. Issues of ambiguity, distraction and interleaved execution of user behavior are examined and taken into account to improve the probability estimation in hidden Markov models. This paper mainly represents both ideal and simplified models to represent and solve the prediction problem on a theory basis.

1   Introduction

When humans predict the future for what's coming next, ones try to discover existing facts at present time and employ past findings and experiences which have been learned from the past and utilize them to envision the future. These are the core concepts we want to transform from humans to our predictive agents. Our agent is designed for the prediction of resource usage. The agent observes the actions taken by a user, learns patterns of user behavior in using resources from the user's previous actions, predicts the user using the resources by referring previously learned behavior.

Either cooperative or self-interested agents try to improve their ability to recognize the likely actions of other agents in multiagent systems. The recognition of other agents' intentions is an important task [1][2][3]. It is particularly so when an agent is expected to produce some useful information in an interactive computing environment, where acquiring knowledge of the current world serves as a basis for immediate or future actions of the system. Examples of such systems include intelligent help systems, decision support systems, immunity-based systems that protect the system from potential problems, and forecasting and risk assessment systems.

As part of acquiring knowledge of the current world, we focus on acquiring knowledge of a user such as its behavior or preferences. The behavioral patterns from the user information demonstrate the user's preferences in a particular situation, a tendency towards certain stereotypical command sequences and/or the level of his/her expertise [4]. Finding regularities in data is a basis of knowledge acquisition hence the user preference is hard to model in a pre-defined plan structure. However, the model can be acquired through long-term observations of user behavior.

Systems that reason about real-world problems can represent only a portion of reality [5]. The incompleteness and uncertainty about the state of the world and about the consequences of actions are unavoidable. In practice, uncertainty is particularly acute when dealing with multiple users, complex preferences, and long-term consequences. Moreover, the observation of a user itself is not easy [6]. The source of uncertainty could come from imperfect observation and inferencing of the sequence of actions. The observation could be harder (or more ambiguous) if an observer agent doesn't have a particular goal or interest to watch for. The agent's discernibility of what to observe will contribute to patternize user behavior of using resources by dealing with both uncertainty of the state of the world and the complexity of user behavior. Our agent is a predictive interface agent whose interest is focused on managing its own resources such as printer or file system in the UNIX domain;it is for, specifically, assessing the likelihood of upcoming demands by users on limited resources and detecting potential problems by observing human-computer interactions. The agent scheme in our work utilizes plan recognition as its primary means of acquiring the information necessary to manage its resources and uses the information to predict the resource usages.

The general area of inferring the goals and intentions of people through observations is commonly known as *plan recognition*. Inducing the plan of observed actions can be useful for predicting the agent's future behavior, interpreting its past behavior, or taking actions to influence the plan.

The plan recognizer in this work is a *reactive* agent: it assesses the various hypotheses, selects the best, and takes some actions based on what is *currently* recognized. The complete plan recognition problem in this role is extremely difficult; however, for some problems, *partial* recognition may be sufficient to predict the next behavior of a user, the usage of resources, or a short-term goal conflict [7]. Employing agent technologies, we challenge the problem of recognizing partial/particular plans from the perspectives of the agent by dealing with uncertainty and incompleteness of information. Instead of having pre-defined generally guessed plan structure, we build individual user models and have emerging plan structures from user behavior.

In plan recognition community, the integration of probabilistic reasoning into plan recognition is done mostly based on the traditional assumptions of plan recognition, such as complete plan structure [8], and/or the observed actions are all purposeful and explainable [3]. Machine learning techniques have been employed to acquire plan libraries in an effort to overcome the traditional problems [4], [9], [10]. Bauer[4] applies decision trees to obtain regularities of user behavior within a plan hierarchy and uses the Dempster-Shafer theory to reason about a user's actions for assessing plan hypotheses. The work by Lesh and Etzioni [9] uses version spaces [11] to represent the relations between actions and possible goals and pursues recognizing a goal by pruning inconsistent actions and goals. Another work by Albrecht et al. [10] uses a dynamic belief network in order to guess a player's current quest and predict his/her next action and location in the "Shattered Worlds" Multi-User Dungeon (MUD) domain. Once a particular structure of their Bayesian network, without the notion of a plan it uses a brute-force approach to collect statistical data about the coincidental occurrence of a player's action, a location, and a quest.

2 Recognition/Prediction Problem

Our domain of interest is human-computer interaction in a large, ongoing, and dynamic environment such as UNIX and WWW. Some difficult features in these domains include the nonstrict temporal orderings of actions, the interleaving of multiple tasks, the large space of possible plans, some sequence of actions are shared, suspended, and resumed to lead to multiple goals, and conditional plans where the condition is neither explicit nor directly observable. The UNIX domain is used as a testbed for this work.

Suppose that the recognizing agent has three resources to manage: printer, router, and memory resources. The recognizing agent will exploit the likelihood of resource usages by observing the sequence of actions from users (random variables). It has an underlying Markovian finite-state structure for abstract plans of using resources and the underlying stochastic process of the states has another set of stochastic processes that produce the sequence of observations. Only the user actions and system responses are observed. The action sequence depends very much on the individual bias(preferences), the transition probabilities between various states(plans), as well as on which state is chosen as the starting point for the observations.

As to the benefits of such predictions, the agent can use the prediction to take control actions both to help users and to better manage resources. For users, the agent can suggest, upon the predictions of their behaviors, users to send a file to printer2, since printer1 is jammed and printer3 has many jobs in the queue. This is a kind of *information push*, that is, the agents are constantly trying to push information and services toward the user [12] rather than users always take initiative to pull some information. For overall system performance, based on the measure of predicted use of printers, the agent can take the action of changing cartridges or warming up the printers or pull some information from other agents. We look at three prediction problems: predicting next behavior, predicting the possibility of using resources with the partial sequence of actions observed, and predicting which resource is more likely to be used among competing ones. Issues of ambiguity, distraction and interleaved execution of user behavior are examined using general action knowledge and taken into account to improve the probability estimation in hidden Markov models. In this paper, we focus on the formal theory of the models in particular.

3 The Hybrid Approach of Agent Systems

The user preference varies in detailed levels of actions and a stochastic approach is taken to learn user models. While a sequence of actions is observed, which actions are optional or shared by multiple plans are hidden from the observation. We use hidden Markov models (HMMs) to represent the ambiguity of actions towards plans within underlying structure. Due to the simplicity and efficiency of its parameter estimation algorithm, the HMM has emerged for modeling discrete time series of stochastic processes and sequences and speech recognition [13]. In the double embedded structure of this model, the outcomes of user actions are observable random variables, called the *observation sequence*, that each depend only on an underlying state variable (*output probability*). The hidden state variables which represent plans in turn depend only on their immediate predecessors (*Markov chains*).

The agent system for the recognition/prediction problem has two major parts: building user models and using them to predict the resource usages from the users. The emphasized modeling methodology is building individual models based on his/her respective relative frequencies of actions through human-computer interactions. The assumption is taken and explored that regularities of user behavior are different enough to be modeled individually, in particular, when there are large spaces of possible plans and actions in a large and dynamic domain such as *UNIX* and *WWW*. The models are refined from coherent partial sequences that are extracted based on their correlations. The learned demonstrates user preferences and regularities, that is, how the user behaves in using particular resources.

The parameters generated from these models are inputs to the prediction system of each hidden Markov model, which construct a probabilistic plan structure of each user. Then the prediction of resource usage is made by comparing each user's currently observed behavior to the model. Predictions of overall resource usage at current times are based on the aggregated predictions from currently logging-in users. This work puts an emphasis on producing *better* parameters for the hidden Markov models, namely, state transition probability and output probability. They are produced through data analysis by filtering and extracting relevant information only and using them to disclose hidden states of behaviors from real data. instead of randomly guessing numbers of parameters for the HMMs.

3.1 Assumptions

There are some assumptions we are making in the approach.

1. **Coherent Partial Sequence under a Single Plan** Each extracted partial sequence is assumed to be coherent and involved in at least one same plan of using a resource.
2. **Final Actions as a Fixed Feature** In a command-driven system like *UNIX*, a plan of using a particular resource is completed by issuing the

final actions of the plan, for instance, 'lpr' for the printing plan. We use the final actions as a feature to uncover states of actions.

3. **Multiple States for an Action** The issues of user behavior: distraction, ambiguity, and interleaved plans are examined by locating shared actions as a basis of correlations. Finding a shared action implies that an action can be involved in multiple states, that is, an action leads to multiple plans.

3.2 Formal Theory

The formal model of user interaction is described in this section. The formal model is based on the probabilities associated with coherent sequences of user commands. The sample space, SS, is defined as all possible coherent sequences of UNIX commands with length less than or equal to n: the window size for an observation. If C is the (finite) set of all UNIX commands, then the sample space is a subset of all possible sequences of elements of C up to size n. That is

$$SS \subseteq \bigcup_{i=1}^{n} C^i$$

$$\begin{aligned}
= \{ & lpr,\ prtex,...,\ vi\text{-}lpr,\ cd\text{-}ls\text{-}prtex\text{-}ls,\ lpr\text{-}lpr\text{-}prtex, \\
& mail,\ ftp,...,\ compress\text{-}ftp,\ from\text{-}mail\text{-}from,\ mail\text{-}mail\text{-}mail, \\
& latex,\ uncompress,\ cc,...,\ emacs\text{-}latex\text{-}emacs,\ latex\text{-}latex, \\
& cd,\ who,\ ...,\ cd\text{-}ls\text{-}cd\text{-}ls,\ emacs\text{-}latex\text{-}ghostview\ \}
\end{aligned}$$

The events of interest here are those that correspond to the use of particular resources. An element of SS is defined to be in an event corresponding to the use of a particular resource if it includes an action that actually uses that resource. More specifically, we define event S_1 (the 'PrinterUse' plan) as the set of all elements of SS that have actions that use the printer (from the set $\{lpr, prtex\}$), S_2 (the 'RouterUse' plan) as the set of all elements of SS that have actions that use the router (from the set $\{ftp, mail, ping, telnet, netscape, gopher\}$), and S_3 (the 'MemoryUse' plan) as the set of all elements of SS that have actions that use lots of memory (from the set $\{uncompress, cc, gcc, latex, tar, dvips\}$). Define event S_t as the set of all elements of SS that do not fall into one of the other three events.

For example, the sequence $cd\text{-}ls\text{-}prtex\text{-}ls$ is a member of the event corresponding to using the printer resource, $from\text{-}mail\text{-}from$ to using the router resource, and $emacs\text{-}latex\text{-}ghostview$ to using the memory resource. cd, who, $cd\text{-}ls$, and $cd\text{-}ls\text{-}cd\text{-}ls$ are members of the event corresponding to not using any of the resources that we are interested in. An element of SS may fall into more than one event: $emacs\text{-}latex\text{-}prtex$ is in both S_1 and S_2.

Given that we have a probability function $f(x)$ for the elements of SS, for event E,

$$P(E) = \sum_{s \in E} f(s)$$

Since our events are not disjoint, we see that

$$\sum_{i=1,2,3,t} P(S_i) \geq 1$$

Additionally, we observe sequences one command at a time, that is, we are observing prefixes of the coherent sequences in the sample space. The P is extended to handle these subsequences in the following way: let q be any sequence of UNIX commands. Then

$$P(q) = \sum_{s \in SS \wedge q \text{ is a prefix of } s} f(s)$$

That is, the probability of a subsequence is the sum of the probabilities of its possible extensions.

Finally, the problem of interest here is calculating the probabilities of using the various resources given a subsequence of commands w, that is, $P(S_i|w)$. Using the definition of conditional probability and the Bayesian rule, we calculate

$$P(S_i|w) = P(S_i \& w)/P(w) = P(S_i * P(w|S_i)/P(w) \tag{1}$$

3.3 Action Reasoning for Data Analysis

The fundamental shortcoming of using statistical model only is that no analysis of data is involved to improve the quality of the data to be used. Reasoning about actions is conducted to find correlations of actions in terms of ambiguity, distraction, and interleaved plans of user behavior. The analysis of actions tackles the structure of learning user behavior in an incremental way. It is expected to produce better input parameters for the prediction system.

Correlations among actions are determined by coherence rules and general action knowledge such as command and argument coherence, data dependency, anytime action, redundant action, and conditional sequence actions. Correlations are used to extract coherent partial sequences and the presence of final actions determines the states of the partial sequence.

Action Knowledge The knowledge of general actions and coherence rules are represented in predicate forms. Some of action rules are represented in Figure 1.

The *Path* for an action represents the current working directory of the action issued and the *Paths* are compared to make sure the actions compared for correlations are in the same directory. The *Arg* represents any argument each action might have. The *Effect* is a result of an action from the UNIX system and the *Time* describes the sequence of two actions. For instance, if the current action takes an argument from the result of its previous action then the *data dependency* rule is attached as a link and the link represents the two actions are correlated with the data dependency relation.

```
Data Dependency Rule (DDR)

IF    Path(Ai) and Path(Aj) are equal      AND
      Arg(Aj) is from Effect(Ai)           AND
      Time(Ai) < Time(Aj)
Then  Link(Ai --> Aj)  as DDR


Action Coherence Rule (ACR)

IF    Path(Ai) and Path(Aj) are equal                  AND
      Arg(Ai) and Arg(Aj) are equal or compatible      AND
      Time(Ai) < Time(Aj)
THEN  Link(Ai --> Aj)  as ACR


Redundant Action Rule (RAR)

IF    Path(Ai) and Path(Aj) are equal      AND
      Arg(Ai) and Arg(Aj) are equal        AND
      Effect(Ai) and Effect(Aj) are equal  AND
      Time(Ai) < Time(Aj)
THEN  Link(Ai --> Aj) as RAR
```

Fig. 1. General Action Knowledge

3.4 Ambiguity and Interpretation of Partial Sequences

Consider our domain of probability theory related to coherent partial sequences of actions, namely, pattern-of-actions identification. Extracting coherent partial sequences is done for both excluding possible extraneous and irrelevant actions and branching out possible interleaved user behavior based on actions' correlations from a real observation. In interpreting the coherent partial sequence extracted, the ambiguity of each action is examined. At an action level of the interpretation, shared actions likely involve in multiple plans and final actions of one plan can also involve in other plans as an action of subsequence of the partial sequence. At a sequence level of the interpretation, with assumption 1, the partial sequence is coherent based on correlations and with assumption 2, partial sequences are represented with states the sequences involve in according to the retrieval of final actions in each plan. Therefore, the prediction problem here is that determining the most likely resource to be used given a sequence of ambiguous actions.

Suppose a coherent partial sequence of an observation in a training phase is *'latex-compress-prtex-ftp'* as in Figure 2. By the definition of a partial sequence, the observed partial sequence in the example can be viewed as using three multiple resources : 'latex' itself completes a 'MemoryUse' plan, 'latex-compress-prtex' as a pattern of using printer resource, and 'latex-compress-prtex-ftp' as a pat-

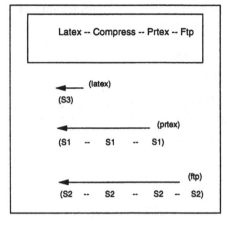
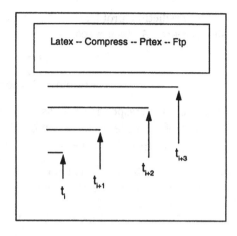

(a) Ambiguity of a Partial Sequence

(b) Prediction at Different Times

Fig. 2. A Partial Sequence

tern of using router resource. Therefore, the sequence is represented as a state of $(S_1 S_2 S_3)$.

Once a model is built from this analysis and when we observe the same coherent partial sequence or a prefix of the sequence in a testing phase, the prediction questions we can have at different times are : at time t_i the probabilities of $P(S_1|'latex')$, $P(S_2|'latex')$, $P(S_3|'latex')$, and $P(S_t|'latex')$ and at time t_{i+1} $P(S_1|'latex - compress')$, $P(S_2|'latex - compress')$, $P(S_3|'latex - compress')$, and $P(S_t|'latex - compress')$ and so on as in Figure 2.

Using the formula of conditional probability, we compute the likelihood of the coherent partial sequence to be a pattern or a part of a pattern of using each resource. In order to make such a prediction, the appropriate model needs to be built. The pure statistical model is hard to get enough observation to obtain the true probabilities of occurrences of partial sequences. And it has been known that the general method to improve reliability of the statistical model is to use the information of some of local context in data [14]. Action reasoning in our work is conducted to obtain the local context of the sequence of user interaction.

3.5 Theory on Models

Uncovering hidden states for each partial sequence in this work is resolving the ambiguity of the partial sequence and it is represented each combination of multiple resource use into a state. The formal model is to handle all subsequences of observed coherent partial sequences by representing a state of multiple resource use for every observed partial sequence.

The prediction problem in our work can be restated as the probability of using resource A given a sequence w at a time T_i, that is,

$$\sum_{i:\ \text{resource } A \text{ used in } s_i} P(S_i|w)$$

If resource A corresponds to S_1 as resource B to S_2 and resource C to S_3, then the states of multiple resource combinations that the resource A is used are S_1, S_{12}, S_{13}, and S_{123}. Then the computation we need are,

$P(S_i)$ the probability of each state
$P(s)$ the probability of every sequence s in all states, which is

$$P(s) = \sum_{i:S_i \leftarrow all states} P(S_i)P(s|S_i)$$

$P(w|S_i)$ if w: a prefix of s, is observed, get the probability $P(w|S_i)$ for all i, that is,

$$P(w|S_i) = \sum_{w \text{ is a prefix of } s} P(s|S_i)$$

The issue of choosing a model is a problem of either representing multiple states for every partial sequence or representing multiple states for every action by chopping the sequence into an action level.

The ideal model for the problem is having all possible partial sequences as observation symbols and finite states for using multiple resources. A set Σ of observation symbols for each state in the model is then equal to the possible number of partial sequences which are up to

$$\Sigma = \sum_{k=1}^{n} |C|^k$$

where n is a window size of an observation and the size of UNIX command C is $|C| < \infty$. Each state of a combination of multiple resources can be represented as all possible subsets of the number m of resources. For instance, if resource $r1$ and $r2$ are in interest then the possible states are represented as S_{r1}, S_{r2}, S_{r1r2}, S_t. That is, the number of possible states $TOTstates$ for each subsequence is

$$TOTstates = ((m+2) + \sum_{k=2}^{m-1} C_k^m)$$

where m states for representing a single resource, one state for representing all resources in use, and one state for representing no use of resource and k-multiple states for representing states of using more than one resource but less than all resources. The number of states in the model increases exponentially as the number of resources in interest grows. Although the model could be manageable with a small number of resources in concern the size of observable symbols will grow exponentially as the window size n of an observation increases. Furthermore, it is unrealistic in a practical point of view to obtain reliable probabilities for each possible partial sequence from real observations.

As an alternative model, we've looked at representing multiple states with a single command as an observation symbol, that is, if a current state is in state S_i the user will use resource i between an initial state S_I and a final state S_F. The model represents states for multiple resource use and each action is separated from a partial sequence and represented as an observation symbol. In this model, the size of observation symbol set Σ is kept to the size $|C|$ of UNIX command C and the problem of obtaining probabilities for observation symbols are mitigated by chopping a sequence of actions into a single action and representing states of multiple resource use for each action involved in to include action information. Also considering a prediction problem makes an observation one command at a time and the observed coherent sequence is increased by an action at a time, this way of representing each action and computing probabilities seems more practical to produce prediction at any time by letting the computation for one action at a time. However, the lost of prediction accuracy at some degree is expected due to the simplification comparing to having an ideal model. Specifically, since the probability of each action is computed separately and combined together with this model, the ordering information of actions is not kept strictly. A practical problem with this model remains to keep the number of states at a manageable level as in the previous model, since the number of states is close to 2^R when the number of resources is R.

For a general problem in a HMM, the *conditional probability* $P(x|M)$ of a sequence of actions x: $(x_1x_2..x_T)$, given a HMM M, is the sum of all the joint probabilities of random walks through the model generating x:

$$P(x|M) = \{ \sum_{q_1...q_l \in Q^l} \pi_{q_1} b_{q_1}(x_1) a_{q_1 q_2} b_{q_2}(x_2)...a_{q_{T-1} q_T} b_{q_T}(x_T) \} \qquad (2)$$

Since the coherent partial sequence is assumed to be at least in a same plan with the possibility of being in multiple plans, the each probability $P(S_i|w)$ in the HMM M can be obtained from the sum of all the joint probabilities of each output probability and state transition probability from a state where S_i state is in to a state where S_i is also in through the model generating w:

The computations of getting information $P(S_i)$, $P(S_i|S_I)$ and $P(w)$ for the prediction question are similar in both ideal and simplified models except the computation of output probability $P(w|S_i)$ which is getting a probability of a whole partial sequence or a prefix of a sequence given a state S_i in the ideal model versus a joint probability of each action in a sequence to be in the same state given a state S_i.

When w is a prefix of sequences s and $w = C_1C_2...C_n$ The probability of a prefix w of sequences given a state S_i is computed differently in each model. In the ideal model, $P(w|S_i)$ can be obtained directly from the output probability by checking w to be a prefix of sequences s in a state S_i. In the simplified model, the probability of $P(w|S_i)$ can be computed from both state transition probability and output probabilities of each action in a state S_i. Let the initial state transition $P(S_i|S_I)$ from S_I to S_i be α_i and a state transition $P(S_i|S_i)$ from S_i to S_i be β_i then when $w = C_1 C_2 ... C_n$,

$$P(w|S_i) = P(S_i|S_I)P(S_i|S_i)..P(S_i|S_i)P(C_1|S_i)P(C_2|S_i)..P(C_n|S_i)$$
$$= \alpha_i \beta_i^{n-1} \Pi_{j=1,n} P(C_j|S_i)$$

and the probability of a prefix w: $P(w)$ can be computed in the simplified model as

$$P(w) = P(C_1 C_2 ... Cn) = \sum_{i:S_i \leftarrow allstates} P(S_i)P(w|S_i)$$

$$= \sum_{i:S_i \leftarrow allstates} \alpha_i \beta_i^{n-1} \Pi_{j=1,n} P(C_j|S_i)$$

If we could generalize the simplified model in terms of α and β, high probabilities of α_i denote high use of the resources corresponding to the states and $\alpha_i = 0$ implies no use of the particular resource corresponding to the state. β is another indicator for representing a tendency of a user's grouping behavior. If the $\beta_i = 0$ when its $\alpha_i <> 0$, then the resource corresponding to the state is used but rather accessed directly with a single action.

4   Experimental Results

Data collection for training models is done from four different users and the number of actions in each reference file varies with various periods of data collection as in the table below.

User	Data Size	Duration of Collection
User 1	1,948	4/15/98–5/15/98
User 2	427	3/22/98–5/04/98
User 3	1,430	9/22/97–3/30/98
User 4	734	3/27/98–4/21/98

The class/type of each user regarding the particular resource use is represented in the Figure 3 through the user models. User 1 never uses a printer resource within the training data, user 2 uses the resources memory, printer and router resource in order, user 3 uses router resource most, and user 4 uses any resource least among the users. For all of the users, the percentage of using the particular resources is rather low. Taking a user–2 model as an example, the Figure 4 represents the predictions of resource use given the observation of partial sequence PS made at a certain time. Some observations are selectively tested in the Figure to represent differences of observed and unobserved behaviors in each training model. For instance, an action dvips, which is a distinguished action of a "MemoryUse" plan, is observed in 60 percentage of training data but never

Resource / User	Ideal (%)				Simplified (%)			
	Printer	Router	Memory	Others	Printer	Router	Memory	Others
User 1	0	1.9	3.08	95.02	0	1.51	6.76	91.73
User 2	3.07	0.68	4.1	92.49	6.54	0.38	13.27	80.58
User 3	0.24	26.48	0.32	72.96	0.58	37.2	0.7	61.52
User 4	0.36	1.08	0	98.56	0.43	0.86	0	98.71

Fig. 3. Class/Type of Users

observed as a first action of the observed sequence in the user model. The simplified model predicts the memory usage 100 percentage as dvips is observed at the prediction time, while the ideal model predicts wrong. After the dvips is observed as a first action of extracted partial sequence in both (dvips lpr lpr lpr) and (dvips) sequences from 40 percentage of testing data, when 90 percentage of same data is taken as training data which includes the sequences above, both models predict the memory usage as dvips is observed at the prediction time.

In addition to the comparison of predictions between ideal and simplified models, we've examined labeling method on the sequence in learning predictive patterns excluding the segmentation of using contextual temporal information, that is, extracting partial sequences through correlations of actions, in order to evaluate the methods.

The prediction accuracy is again tested with both observed and unobserved behaviors in different ratio of training data sets. It needs to be noted that the criteria of prediction accuracy for this comparison is rather generous. Prediction hit ratio is measured as in Figure 5 by looking ahead of predicted results of testing data only knowing what likelihood of resource use has to be predicted but not knowing accurate predictions on the resources. For observed behavior, labeling method in an ideal model demonstrates lowest performance while labeling method in a simplified model demonstrates fairly good predictions for this particular user. However, for unobserved behavior, labeling method in both models predicts everything wrong while detecting irrelevant actions and grouping them differently bear out the segmentation and labeling method in both models.

Prediction (Training: 60% Testing: 40%)

PS	Ideal Model (%)				Simplified Model(%)			
	P	R	M	O	P	R	M	O
(ls vi)	0	0	11.11	83.92	0	0	0.12	99.87
(vi)	0	0	0	94.41	0	0	2.73	97.26
(dvips)	0	0	0	0	0	0	100	0
(xdvi vi)	0	0	0	0	0	0	100	0

Extracted PS using resources(40%)

Printer	(ls vi ghostview vi gs gs ghostview lpr), (dvips lpr lpr lpr), (ls vi gs gs ghostview lpr), (ls gs ghostview lpr), (lpq lpr (3)), (lpr lpr lpr)
Router	None
Memory	(dvips), (latex xdvi vi latex xdvi vi latex xdvi vi latex xdvi vi latex xdvi), (dvips lpr lpr lpr)

Prediction (Training: 91% Testing: 9%)

PS	Ideal Model (%)				Simplified Model (%)			
	P	R	M	O	P	R	M	O
(ls vi)	5.88	0	11.76	75.59	0.009	0	0.13	99.86
(vi)	0	0	0	91.79	0.23	0	2.46	97.31
(dvips)	50	0	100	0	2.01	0	100	0
(xdvi vi)	0	0	0	0	0	0	100	0

Fig. 4. Predictions of Resource Use given Observation PS from User 2

5   Discussion

The objective of this work is to develop a reactive and intelligent interface agent in a real-world application, solving plan recognition problems using user models. This paper is more focused on representing and comparing both ideal and simplified models in order to represent and solve the prediction problem on a theory basis. A data filtering tool is developed for automatic on-line data collection, encoding information from observation, capturing both sequential and relational information [15] from four individuals. These data are used for off-line analysis and evaluation of the predictions. In experimental results, simplified models outperform ideal models since it is easier to obtain reliable probabilities in the simplified model from the observations and also as there are many variations of a same plan in this domain, keeping the strict order of actions in a sequence of observation lowers the prediction accuracy. There are also many irrelevant actions in using resources within a whole sequence of observation, segmenting the sequences excluding those extraneous actions helped to learn the patterns. The results also demonstrate how the reality of having real data affects the view of both theory and practice as a real factor for an interface agent to decide how to meet the real world. When individual differences are more evident in some domains, using individual user models can also be beneficial to a user recognition/identification problem. We are examining pure statistical approache such as n–grams [16] to have a base line of measuring the predictability of our approach. In summary, our approach achieved that automatic acquisition of particular plans from users, that the supportive results of building individual models

User 2 (training : testing = 60 : 40 vs 90 : 10)

	Ideal				Simplified			
	Labeling		Segmentation &Labeling		Labeling		Segmentation &Labeling	
Data Ratio of Training	60%	90%	60%	90%	60%	90%	60%	90%
Number of Prediction Made (Observed Behavior of using resources in Training)	140	28	147	28	140	28	147	28
Number of predictions that were correct	9	4	84	26	120	28	147	28
Prediction Accuracy	6.43%	14.29%	57.14%	92.86%	85.71%	100%	100%	100%
Number of predictions that were error	131	24	63	2	20	0	0	0
Prediction Rate	93.57%	85.71%	42.86%	7.14%	14.29%	0%	0%	0%
Number of Prediction Made (Unobserved Behavior of using resources in Training)	45	0	52	0	45	0	52	0
Number of correct predictions	0	0	18	0	0	0	29	0
Prediction Accuracy	0%		34.62%		0%		55.77%	
Number of error predictions	45	0	34	0	45	0	23	0
Prediction Rate	100%		65.38%		100%		44.23%	

Fig. 5. Prediction Hit Ratio in Different Methods with Different Models

based on individual differences and that the development and verification of the models based on the real observation.

The presented work focuses on how to build and to use interface agents for prediction problem by modeling human agents. The learned models can be utilized not only through interface agents but also both through task and information agents by providing both correlation information from learned patterns and human factors in multi-agent systems. The work is expected to be extended using graphical user interfaces to better model inter-agent (both software and human) communications and cooperation in multi-agent systems.

References

[1] J. Allen. Recognizing intentions from natural language utterances, In *Computational Models of Discourse* M. Brady and R. Berwick eds, The MIT Press. 1983.

[2] D. Litman. Plan recognition and discourse analysis: an integrated approach for understanding dialogues. Ph.D. Thesis, University of Rochester. 1986.

[3] S. Carberry. Plan recognition in natural language, *Plan Recognition in Natural Language*. The MIT Press, Cambridge, MA. 1990.

[4] M. Bauer. Acquisition of user preferences for plan recognition, In *Proceedings of the Fifth International Conference on User Modeling* pp. 105–112. Kailua-Kona, Hawaii 1996.

[5] E. Horvitz, J. Breese and M. Henrion. Decision Theory in Expert Systems and Artificial Intelligence, *Int. J. of Approximate Reasoning* pp 2:247-301, 1988.

[6] D. Diaper. Task observation for Human-Computer Interaction, *Task Analysis for Human-Computer Interaction*, pp. 210–237, 1989.

[7] J.J. Lee. Case-based plan recognition in computing domains, (Doctoral Consortium), In *Proceedings of the Fifth International Conference on User Modeling* pp. 234–236. Kailua-Kona, Hawaii 1996.

[8] E. Charniak and R. Goldman. A Bayesian model of plan recognition. *Artificial Intelligence*, 64(1) pp. 53–79, Elsevier Science Publishers. 1993.

[9] N. Lesh and O.Etzioni. A sound and fast goal recognizer. In *Proceedings of the Fourteenth International Joint Conference on Artificial Intelligence*, pp. 1704–1710. 1995.

[10] D. Albrecht, I. Zukerman, A. Nicholson, and A. Bud. Towards a Bayesian model for keyhole plan recognition in large domains, In *Proceedings of the Sixth International Conference on User Modeling* pp. 365–376. Sardinia, Italy 1997.

[11] T. Mitchell. Generalization as search, *Artificial Intelligence*, 18 pp. 2-3–226. 1982.

[12] W. Van de Velde et al. Competition for Attention. in *Preproceedings of the 4th Int., Workshop on Agent Theories, Architectures, and Languages*, pp 282–296, Providence, RI. 1997.

[13] L. Rabiner. A tutorial on hidden Markov models and selected applications in speech recognition. In *Proceedings of the IEEE*, vol. 77, No. 2, pp. 257–286, 1989.

[14] J. Allen. Natural Language Understanding. The Benjamin/Cummings Publishing Company, 1995.

[15] K. Yoshida and H. Motoda. Automated User Modeling for Intelligent Interface. in *Int. J. of Human Computer Interaction*, 8(3):237–258, 1996.

[16] E. Charniak. Statistical Language Learning. The MIT Press, 1996.

Multi-Agent Coordination with OASIS *

David Ramamonjisoa

Faculty of Software and Information Science,
Iwate Prefectural University (IPU),
152-52 Sugo, Takizawa, Iwate 020-0193, JAPAN
david@soft.iwate-pu.ac.jp

Abstract. In this paper, we present Organic Agents for Software and Intelligent Systems (*OASIS*) as a original agents coordination framework. *OASIS* is based on expertises for building multi-agent system in defined environments.
We introduce the agent/environment interaction modeling and implementation. We describe several coordination techniques such as the negotiation with heuristics in multi-agent planning, and the organization structure in multi-agent actions and mobile agents. Then, these models and techniques are integrated into simulated multi-agent cars on crossroads. Agents are coordinated through common knowledge or negotiation according to the difficulty of the situation. Simulation results shows the coordination techniques comparison with OASIS.

1 Introduction

Coordinating the behavior of autonomous agents is a key issue in multi-agent systems today. It has been a concern of computing for decades but it continues to be an open research area. In the past, Gelernter and Carriero have noted that *computation* and *coordination* are separate and orthogonal dimensions of all useful computing, and have proposed *coordination languages* as a class of tools for managing interaction [1]. In the distributed artificial intelligence research, coordination is treated as a *problem of distributed control decision making under uncertainty, as collections of settled and unsettled questions about knowledge and action* [2]. Recently, researchers have evolved a range of mechanisms for coordination representation in different fields of agents systems (mobile agents, intelligent agents, interface agents) [3] [4] [5]. It is much more difficult, especially in the case of agents group, because conflicts are a permanent situation that must be solved through some coordination systems. Moreover, the environment changes and multi-agent must evolve to adapt to the changes. The multi-agent/environment interaction must be modeled. The environment glues the agents together and grounds their existence.

* This work was performed under the management of Information-technology Promotion Agency, Japan (IPA) as a part of the Industrial Science and Technology Frontier Program "New Models for Software Architectures" sponsored by NEDO (New Energy and Industrial technology Development Organization).

The architecture of our framework describes the clear separation of agents computation and coordination structure as we called OASIS. OASIS framework is able to resolve conflicts among agents designed by the agents primitive languages in using coordination expertises. Expertises concern the choice of the coordination mechanisms for each type of conflict or interaction. Using negotiation for a particular problem may be inappropriate rather using other mechanisms. For example, in case of application for decisions making with time constraint, long conversation during the negotiation may be a wrong one. Indeed, in the crossroad, negotiation is the last solution. Agents may be driven by some common knowledge to resolve conflicts and for the decisions control. In the crossroad, the common knowledge are the traffic light or priority according to the crossroad type. We discuss here some examples describing the different mechanisms and the result of a simulation. Agent is a knowledge based system that monitors and controls its own behavior. Environment is represented as objects, states and active common knowledge. OASIS model for agent-environment interaction describes this part. We are using agents primitive languages, Flage[6] [7] and GAEA[8] to implement agents. *Flage agents* are mobile and asynchronous concurrent objects which work in local or distributed computation systems. Each agent has a meta-base structure for autonomy. This language provides also another kind of objects, *fields*, for mobility and cooperability. *GAEA agents* are threads and execute concurrently. They may suspend waiting for an event, fork any number of child threads, or use to create a high-level interthread message communication. Agents can have sophisticated reasoning capabilities and fast reaction. Multiagent coordination concerns the threads control, communication, and synchronization.

The organization of the paper is as follows. In section 2, we present OASIS system and a formal multi-agent-environment interaction model. Section 3 provides an overview of the coordination techniques and implementation. In section 4 and 5 we illustrate uses of coordination in simulation and examples by presenting some statistic results.

2 OASIS

We describe basic definitions of world model on which to develop our framework. We use concepts and definitions given in (Katagiri [9]). The formalization emphasizes the role of environments in mediating between actions and knowledge states of agents. Then we detail our implementation languages.

2.1 Model for Multi-agent/Environment Interaction

A multi-agent model assumes one or more agents executing their programs in an environment. Execution of programs can bring about changes both in environment and in agents. One agent's program step may interfere with other agents' program step, and environment may intervene program execution and change the outcome.

Basics. We define a multi-agent system to be a set of n agents $\{a_1, ..., a_n\}$ executing their programs in an environment e.

States : A *system state* s can be described by a tuple of an environmental state and local states of each agents, $\{s_e, s_1, ..., s_n\}$. A *local state* s_i of each agent a_i at a given instant is taken from a corresponding set of local states S^i. An environmental state s_e is similarly taken from a set S^e. The behavior of the system can be specified as transitions in the set of system states S.

A *basic proposition* corresponds to a set of system states. We denote a set of system states in which a basic proposition p holds by S_p. A basic proposition is a *local state condition* σ_i of an agent a_i, if it is solely determined by a set of a_i's local state.

Protocols and transition functions : A *protocol* Π is a tuple of local protocol Π_i's. Π_i specifies which action to execute based on local states of a_i; $\Pi i : S^i \rightarrow 2^{ACT_i}$, where ACT_i is a set of actions for each agent a_i. Agents are deterministic, hence the value of Π_i is a singleton set for $i \geq 1$. A *transition function* τ specifies the transition of the entire system state given all the actions executed by agents and the environment: $s_{t+1} = \tau(act_e, act_1, ..., act_n)(s_t)$. τ represents the outcome of actions of all agents. This includes each agent's internal state change upon receiving information about actions performed.

Runs, points and systems : A *run* r is a function $r : N \rightarrow S$ which gives a system state $r(t)$ for each time point t. $\langle r, t \rangle$ is a *point* in a run r. For an agent a_i, points $\langle r, t \rangle$ and $\langle r', t' \rangle$ are a_i-*equivalent* if $r_i(t) = r'_i(t')$, and write $\langle r, t \rangle \sim_i \langle r', t' \rangle$. A *system (s)* is identified with a set of runs that corresponds to all executions of the protocol Π under the transition function τ.

Knowledge and time : Knowledge is a relational condition between agents' local states and entire system states. $K_{a_i}\varphi$ represents that agent a_i knows φ. Common knowledge in a group of agents is defined as $C_G\varphi \overset{def}{=} \wedge_{a_i \in G} K_{a_i}\varphi$. Agents in the group G knows φ if and only if for every agent a_i in G there is a time point t_i such that a_i knows φ at t_i.

Consistency in distributed knowledge base : Given a knowledge base protocol, let take two different systems. One system serves to give interpretations for knowledge conditions in the protocol, and the other system gives the result of the protocol execution. Knowledge consistency proposes to check the difference between the two systems. A *knowledge consistency* can be modeled as follows. Every run in the actual system is almost indiscernible for all the agents to some run in the dual system.

A run r is *knowledge consistent* with another run r', $r\|_{\preceq}r'$, iff there is a monotone increasing mapping $\rho_i : N \rightarrow N$ for each agent a_i such that $\langle r, t \rangle \sim_i \langle r', \rho_i(t) \rangle$ for all i.

Coordination : The *coordination* procedure is evaluated before each transition of the system state. This procedure uses the conflict detection and resolution functions as respectively a negative interaction *NegInt* and conflict resolution *ResolveConflict*. The *NegInt* function depends on the resource conflicts *ResConf* and incompatibilities *Incompa* in the environment.

$$ResConf(act_1, act_2) \Leftrightarrow \exists[t, t + \Delta t], \exists resource \in e, resource \in act_1 \wedge act_2$$

and

$$Incompa(act_1, act_2) \Leftrightarrow \exists[t, t + \Delta t], act_1 \wedge act_2 \neq \emptyset.$$

Thus,

$$NegInt(act_1, act_2) \Leftrightarrow ResConf(act_1, act_2) \vee Incompa(act_1, act_2)$$

and

$$NegInt(ACT_1, ACT_2) \Leftrightarrow \exists act_1 \in ACT_1, act_2 \in ACT_2, NegInt(act_1, act_2),$$

where ACT_i is a set of actions act_i for each agent a_i.
The coordination evaluation through the resolution is :

$$coordination(A, t) \Leftrightarrow ResolveConf(A, t)$$

and

$$ResolveConf(A, t) \Leftrightarrow \forall ACT_i, ACT_j \in A, i \neq j : \neg NegInt(ACT_i, ACT_j),$$

where A specifies all interacted agents $A \subseteq \{a_1, ..., a_n\}$.

These models are used to analyze the knowledge and actions in joint activities. They make also clear the coordination structure in generating forms of organization structures. With these models, we can make sure for the distributed knowledge consistency and the results of an implemented multi-agent system.

2.2 Implementation Languages

OASIS prototype is developed with two agent oriented languages Flage and Gaea [8]. Flage was designed for uses in software engineering and mobile agents applications [6]. We outline in this section the agent architecture and multi-agent platform. Agent is a knowledge based system composed of rules and objects in Flage and a process with a cell structure in Gaea. An agent can be a complex or simple structure in a given environment. We detail here multi-agent based on Flage and GAEA concept.

Flage. An *agent* is a concurrent object which has *attributes* to preserve data and *methods* to operate attributes and to communicate with others through messages. Methods and attributes are defined in two levels (*meta-level, base-level*). Messages are also classified into two levels.
A *field* is a virtual place where agents retrieve methods and other information or a place where agents work cooperatively with other agents. The machine running the language itself is also modeled as the special field, called also *node*.
Field is an important model of the agents environment. OASIS coordination place lies on it.

Gaea. Agent is structured according to the GAEA concept. The user does not have a predefined structure as in Flage, but he designs the agent through the bottom-up style. The user focuses his program on the processes assumed as the agents and their environments.

A cell is the level at which name to content mapping and background conditions are implemented. An environment of a given process is the collection of cells which are currently active for it. Agent performs some activities or gets some resources in the cells. The first picture in Fig.1 depicts agents as cars in the intersection represented with processes and cells. This describes the agent structure and its behavior. The second one represents a mechanism to synchronize cars in the intersection using cells as state transition that is common for all agents in the environment. We remind the model as $s_{t+1} = \tau(act_e, act_1, ..., act_n)(s_t)$.

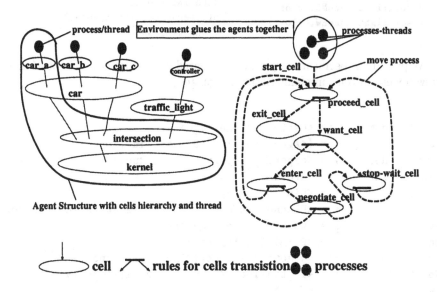

Fig. 1. GAEA concept

An example of the GAEA code is depicted below :

```
%%% Car structure as cells hierarchy     (check_cell_var(Name,lane);
car(Name,Pos,Plan,Loc,Lane):=                add_cell_var(Name,lane)),
begin_cell(Name),                         push(Name),
   (check_cell_var(Name,loc);             (name(Name);assert(name(Name))),
       add_cell_var(Name,loc)),           cv_write(Name,loc,Loc),
   (check_cell_var(Name,pos);             cv_write(Name,pos,Pos),
       add_cell_var(Name,pos)),           cv_write(Name,plan,Plan),
   (check_cell_var(Name,plan);            cv_write(Name,lane,Lane),
       add_cell_var(Name,plan)),          init_position(Name,Pos),
   (check_cell_var(Name,iloc);            push(proceed),
       add_cell_var(Name,iloc)),          output(initializing(Name,Loc)),
```

```
  repeat(e()),                                    ?-end_cell(light).
end_cell(Name).
?-begin_cell(light).                                  Somewhere in the program of the envi-
create_trafficlight():=                           ronment :
   (check_cell_var(light,laneNS);
   add_cell_var(light,laneNS)),                   ?-begin_cell(want).
   (check_cell_var(light,laneEW);                 %If the traffic light is red
   add_cell_var(light,laneEW)),                   %then change state to stop
   cv_set(light,laneNS,red),                      e():light(red):=name(Car),
   cv_set(light,laneEW,green).                        output(light_is_red_for(Car)),
                                                      swap_cell(want,stop).
change_state():=                                  ...
   cv_ref(light,laneNS,Color1),                   %else continue to enter
   cv_ref(light,laneEW,Color2),                   %the intersection
   cv_set(light,laneNS,Color2),                   e():=swap_cell(want,enter).
   cv_set(light,laneEW,Color1).                   ?-end_cell(want).
```

We provide a specification syntax represented in Extendted BNF notation as below for use in both implementation languages.

```
<CommandFormat>  ::= <Recipient><Message>
<Recipient>      ::= [<Agent_model>][<Dynamic_id>]
<Agent_model>    ::= <expert>|<supervisor>|<unknown>
<Dynamic_id>     ::= <Group><Role><Status>
<Group>          ::= <List_of_agents>
<Role>           ::= <Planner>|<Coordinator>|<Executor>|<Role_Free>
<Status>         ::= <waiting>|<moving>|<busy>
<Message>        ::= <Primitive>[<Fact>]
<Primitive       ::= <Negotiate>|<Act>|<Inquire>|<Report>
<Negotiate       ::= <Initialise>|<Submit-proposal>|<Reply>
<Fact>           ::= <Term>
```

3 Coordination Expertise

In this section, several coordination techniques to which agents are required to interact dynamically and coherently are represented. Some expertises of coordination are originally aquired from the book of Dr Von Martial [10]. However, the implementation is completely different. We describe how agents interact each other using a communication primitives and field/cell programming facilities of Flage/GAEA.

3.1 Mechanisms

In the microscopic model, we describe the coordination mechanism between agents as *how* to compose/decompose and allocate tasks between agents and achieve coherent interaction without conflicts. In the macroscopic model, we represent autonomous agents constrained by the environment in achieving a coherent interaction. We present *coordination* as the first one is based on the *negotiation* with planning, and replanning and the second on common knowledge as rules for agents to organize their behaviors.

During the planning, agents need to share and process substantial amount of information. The interaction between agents may be guided by protocols for communication. During the execution, the synchronization between the agents actions have to be monitored. This can be achieved by sending messages between the agents or by having a central instance monitoring the execution.

3.2 Coordination through Negotiation

We describe in this paragraph the implementation of the agents coordination with a centralized negotiation (as example the contract net protocol) and decentralized control.

The negotiation concerns about the actions planning coordination. Agents are communicating their plans to the others. They are negotiating and modifying their plans until achieving a consensus. The centralized negotiation has a coordinator to monitor the interaction. This coordinator decides to start, suspend or end the negotiation. In the planning, agents pass status and plans to others, the coordinator agent detects conflicts through negative interactions (resource conflicts or incompatibilities).

The interaction is focused to the communication as *message passing* in this type of coordination. This interaction views agents as *participating in* behavior, and does not distinguish between a sender and a recipient (eq. to *discussing* or *negotiating*). In general negotiation form, agents can have the roles as a Planner, an Executor or a Coordinator in a conversation during the interaction. The conversation model is composed of three parts as *states*, *message types*, and *conversation rules*. In figure Fig. 2, states are represented with circle, message types are the connections between states, rules are a set of pair states, and the negotiation is the set of rules in a dark shape.

Contract Net Protocol Implementation with Field. As example for implementation in Flage, we designed the negotiation place as a field. Agents need to meet in this field to negotiate. The user broadcasts all participants to enter the field. The field can be named "negotiation-place". It has several methods for negotiation primitives. When agents get into the field, they inherit the field methods and can have the same protocol. Once agents enter the field, they start to negotiate with the coordinator. This coordinator agent broadcasts the order (ORDER) to all agents in the field (bidders) and waits the reply from the participants. The participants submit a proposal (SUBMIT-PROPOSAL) to the coordinator. The coordinator decides which bid is the most suitable and awards actions (usually named *contract*) to the most appropriate bidder (contractor). According to the strategies in the coordinator, it sends for each participant a response as FAILURE or RESOLUTION and finally deal with the agent who

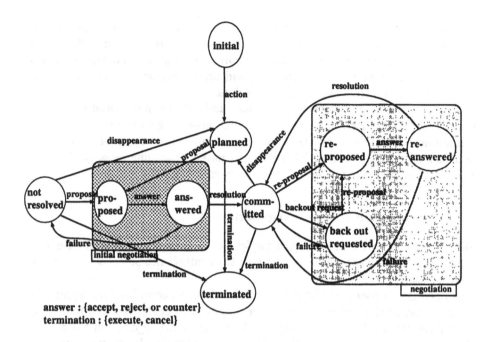

Fig. 2. Conversation Model

receives RESOLUTION response in privately. The negotiation is finished. The coordinator will continue to discuss with the selected agent and commit to terminate the conversation (see figure Fig.2).

```
broadcast(node, m(1,negotiation())).
% enter to the field negotiation-place
% choose the coordinator
broadcast(negotiation-place,
        m(0,negotiate(ORDER,Proposal)))
%From each participant:
send(agentCoordinator,
        m(0,negotiate(SUBMIT-PROPOSAL,Answer)))
%From the Coordinator: for each agent
%in the field negotiate-place.
send(agent-i,m(0,negotiate(SELECT,solution)))
broadcast(negotiation-place,negotiate(END)).
```

Negotiation with Decentralized Control Structure. According to the applications, it may be possible to use this technique to reach a consensus during the negotiation. This technique is used to dispatch elevators that we found very useful [11]. Agents are autonomous and using their limited planning capabilities to decide to what extent answering the request in achieving their goal. The agent then formulates a concise statement of its decision, which is generally a simple numerical bid. This numerical bid is calculated with a special heuristic function representing the agents's opinion with regard to the given request. As agents finish their self-evaluations, they communicate their bids to other agents, and the best situated agent is awarded the request by group consensus. This entire process of evaluating, bidding, and choosing a "contractor" is repeated for each new request. The group consensus is made by all agents. Every agent individually evaluates the situation and submits its recommendation to its fellows. By weighing these recommendations according to shared, predetermined rules, the group can reach consensus with a minimum of communication.

3.3 Coordination through Conflict Management

During the execution, the resource conflict must be solved. Agents are trying to access the same resource and can not perform the actions correctly. The strategies of conflict resolution are added to the agents during their lifecycle. Agents may use the negotiation strategy described in the paragraph 3.2 and coordination model defined in the section Sect.2.1, we resume here the resolution:
- detect the critical-region of conflict such as resource conflict,
- give priority to each action in eliminating the critical-region.
This mechanism may come from the study of the system to be implemented (i.e. applications) and organization of coordination structures. Composition and inheritance properties are the basic mechanisms to structure a collection of agents. Our platform uses the environment as *field/cell* to model the coordination structure.

3.4 Coordination through Organized Mobile Agents

We cite here the possibility to coordinate multi-agent in distributed systems through network with mobile agents. Mobile agents are self-contained entities that can navigate autonomously through the underlying network and perform a variety of tasks in the nodes they visit (see Fig.d in Fig.3). Scheduling, communicating and creating/destructing these mobile agents and their activities in the network are the main targets of the coordination. In OASIS, we propose the following facilities to achieve this coordination:

— Each host has an interpreter superimposed on the distributed system. Mobile agents program interpreter is running on each node of the network.
— Autonomous migration is implemented in the network with the meta-level. Mobile agents move autonomously according their state without commands from the users. Mobile agents carries out a schedule of activities to perform in other hosts through the meta-level. The meta-level methods can ensure the *round-trip* of the mobile agents.
— Negotiating multi-agent to work concurrently by assigning each subtasks from a controller agent is available. In using the negotiation coordination described in the previous paragraph, multi-agent are interacting coherently.

```
round-trip(Node1,Node2,Schedules)::    migrate(Field1,Field2,Result)::
( migrate(Node1,Node2,Result);         ( exit(Field1,ExitResult);
   if (Result=success) then              if ExitResult = success then
     execute(Schedules);                  (move_to(AnotherNode);
   // agent is in the other host          enter(Field2,EnterResult);
   // and performs activities.            Result=EnterResult)
   migrate(Node2,Node1,Result);)        else  Result = ExitResult )
```

Figure 3 depicts the possible coordination mechanisms with OASIS as mobile agents.

4 Traffic Intersection

We focus on the intersection problem for the regulation and interaction of vehicles.

An alternate approach to the problem uses autonomous agents and a distributed, decentralized control structure. Multi-agent system has properties such negotiation amongst agents and sharing a common goal.

The general model of vehicle agent and simulator can be found in the literature[12] [13] [14].

We designed the system that new agents can easily be plugged into the simulation to test different types of interagent communication and planning. Because of its distributed nature, the testbed is also dynamically scalable, agents can be added to or removed from a running simulation. The simulation displays a simple map of the crossroad and some blocks with animated icons representing the locations of all the agents. A special window accepts input allowing the user to control events such traffic light or run a prepared script or custom generate scenario. The simulation keeps track of a number of different run-time statistics (e.g. average time to go from one point to another), enabling objective comparisons of the performance of various scenarios.

We focus our problem to the decision making during the crossroad passing and the shortest way to reach the required locations.

Agents and environment are modeled with OASIS framework. The coordination of agents is managed with the knowledge level.

The common knowledge will give for each agent the priority level according to the environment. Agent uses first this priority before communicating to the other agents in case of conflict. As in common sense counterparts, when driver arrives at the intersection, his first reflex is to look at the intersection type as traffic light, stop line, etc. then his second reflex is to look at the other vehicles whether they exist or not. At each execution of the program, this priority is communicated to each agent in conflict from the environment. Agents in conflict cooperate according to this priority with messages sending and pass the crossroad correctly.

Agents in conflict cooperate according to this priority with messages sending and pass the crossroad correctly.

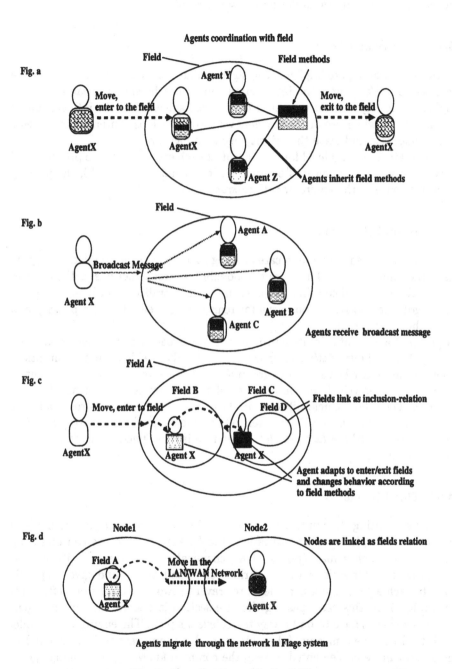

Fig. 3. Coordination with the fields

common knowledge : map of the intersection, priority according to the stop line or traffic light, or convoy of vehicles.

agent plan : list of its tasks during the simulation.

4.1   First Scenario

In this example, we are implementing agents simulating cars which pass over the intersection. We assume the intersection should not have more than one agent and the other agent must wait until the entered agent leaves the intersection. A conflict arises when two or more agents want to enter in the intersection. Agents must cooperate and leave the priority agent to pass first.

We generate a priority level for each agent at each execution of the program and this priority is communicated to each agent in conflict. In OASIS, the priority is an attribute of the *environment crossroad.*

4.2   Second Scenario

The agents will really communicate and negotiate during the conflict. All agents have the same priority. There are two possible control structures as the centralized or decentralized coordination one. In the decentralized coordination, agents are negotiating to reach consensus for rearranging themselves the priority and cross the intersection.

A group of agents are simulated to pass the crossroad. They are assumed to do it together without cutting their convoy with other vehicle. In this situation, coordination must be set for the group and the other vehicle. It is important to notice the other vehicle of the presence of the convoy as the first and the last vehicles. The other vehicle will wait until the last vehicle pass the crossroad. The other vehicle must have rule to interpret the meaning of the convoy *"If it is a convoy, wait until the last vehicle".* That rule is predefined for each vehicle as common rules.

4.3   Third Scenario

We are simulating the multi-agent system in boosting the agent knowledge and raising the complexity of the situation (Fig.4). For example, we can create an environment such a map (power plant, chemical depot, or set of city blocks) with several intersections within various crossroad types, and give a specific plan to each agent. Agent is modeled to travel to two dimensions (go left, right, or straight). In this case, passing the intersection is a small part of the agent tasks. The agent have to find a way to achieve his plan. The environment model with field became a meaningful architecture. Each intersection is considered as field and can be implemented to keep the common knowledge in helping agents coordination. Agent moves to reach his goal according to the information in each field. The hierarchy formed by the inclusion relation and linking of fields in the node are very useful in this case. The agent is not overloaded of information about the global map. It reduces the size of the agent knowledge during its planning and processing. Interaction among individual agents is reduced to each field. We propose a plan as a list of fields from the agent initial field to the final required one. This list can be built through a database field of the environment.

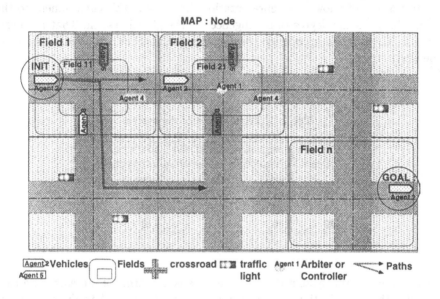

Fig. 4. Scenario

4.4 Results

The current simulator was tested as a prototype of multi-agent cars on a traffic "crossroad" where possible risk of collision and actions planning are the main problems. The proposed solution concerns to allow each agent to access the common knowledge as in the conflict zone to avoid collision. The other solution consists to give to agent some facility to negotiate with a controller. All agents in a conflict zone will be coordinated by this controller in arranging the "crossroad" flow regulation. The controller has a specific knowledge for the circulation and can be here considered as an intelligent traffic regulator like a police agent in the real world "crossroad".

According to our experience, the coordination with a controller is slower than the using common knowledge during the simulation. The coordination based on negotiation is a time consuming to the processing. However, it is more accurate and can solve traffic congestion in the "crossroad" if it happens. Indeed, the common knowledge such priority can not solve the flow regulation problem. Individual agents do not need to know how many agents are in the intersection or to communicate (to send a message) with the other. In an environment where the flow is not important, the controller is not necessary.

In terms of software modeling, agent based model is very easy to manipulate. Changes in the specification does not necessary implicate modification to the whole system. Flage allows us to implement the prototype rapidly. Modifications or changes are easily updated. Modeling the environment with a field is a natural way of knowledge representation. Interacting this environment to the agents brings some degree of intelligence for the global system. That is to say, we put the common knowledge (field attributes, methods, functions, rules) as the environment.

Table 1. Performance of the system

Number of cars	unsignalized intersection (sec)	signalized intersection (sec)	adaptive intersection (sec)
10	101	115	109
20	120	140	130
30	250	270	220

Performance of the system (Tab.1) is expressed in terms of crossing time that includes the computation time in the simulator. In term of traffic simulation, signalization is much safer for vehicle than using unsignalized crossroad.

5   Conclusions

In this paper, we presented coordination techniques of multi-agent independent to the programming language and agents models. With the multi-agent-environment interaction model, we could formalize the coordination knowledge base.

We represented forms of coordination as :

- rule based system for all agents in the environment that we call also *the influential and constraint behaviors from the environment*. Rules are set to the *field* as common knowledge for all agents in this environment. agents are assumed to be honest in respecting the rules.
- communication based coordination where a controller exists. Agents can negotiate according to the situation and their state in using conversation table we have implemented.
- mobility of agents to move from one *field* to another one.

We developed our coordination through negotiation with functional heuristics and group decisions strategies. This is used when conflict persists during the interaction. The effectiveness of the multi-agent interaction for each coordination is represented with statistic results in crossroad simulation.

The existence of the simulator greatly reduces the time required to develop and test new theories about interagent communication and interaction. It also provides a standard metric for comparing the performance of different agents.

Multi-agent coordination with OASIS does simplify the design process, providing a natural decomposition of large, difficult problems.

References

1. Gelernter,D. et al. : Coordination Languages and their Significance. *Communications of the ACM*, pp.97-107, 35:2, Feb. 1992.
2. Gasser,L. : DAI Approaches to Coordination. *DAI: Theory and Praxis*, Avouris and Gasser Eds., Kluwer Academic Press, pp. 31-51, 1992.
3. Baumann,J. and Radouniklis,N. : Agent Groups in Mobile Agent Systems,DAIS'97, In *Distributed Applications and Interoperable Systems*, H. Konig et al. Eds., Chapman & Hall, pp. 74-85, 1997.
4. Fukuda,M et al. : Distributed Coordination with MESSENGERS, *Sciences of Computer Programming Journal*, Special Issue on Coordination Models, Languages, and Applications, 31(2), July 1998.
5. Bijnens,S. et al. : Language construct for Coordination in an Agent Space, *MAA-MAW'94 Selected Presentation*, LNCS/LNAI 1069, Springer, pp.90-105, 1996.
6. Kumeno, F et al. : Evolutional Agents: Field Oriented Programming Language, Flage, In *Proceedings of Asian Pacific of Software Engineering Conference (APSEC95)*, Australia, pp.189-198, 1995.
7. Kumeno, F et al. : A Framework for Adaptive Software by Agents and Thesaurus, In *Proceedings of Software Engineering and Knowledge Engineering (SEKE'97)*, Spain, pp.430-439, June 1997.
8. Nakashima, H. et al. : *GAEA Version 2.2 Manual Revision 0*, Cooperative Architecture Project Team, Electro-Technical Laboratory Report, Tsukuba, 1998.
9. Katagiri,Y. : Belief Coordination by Default, In *Proceedings of the International Conference on Multi-Agent Systems (ICMAS)*, Japan,pp.142-149, Dec. 1996.
10. von Martial,F. : Coordinating Plans for Autonomous Agents, *LNCS/LNAI 610*, Springer, 1992.
11. Stanley Peters,J. et al. : Communication Strategies for Cooperative Behavior, In *Proceedings of the International Symposium in New Models for Software Architecture (IMSA)*, Kyoto, Japan, pp.27-36, Dec. 1996.
12. Ramamonjisoa,D. et al. : Real-time Knowledge-based System for Ploughing Support, In *Proceedings of the 11th IEEE Conference on Artificial Intelligence for Applications (IEEE-CAIA)*, Los Angeles, USA, pp.313-319, Feb. 1995.
13. Chaib-draa,B. and Levesque,P. : Hierarchical Model and Communication by signs, signals, and symbols in Multi-agent environments, *Distributed Software Agents and Applications, LNCS/LNAI 1069*, J.W. Perram and J.P. Muller Eds, Springer, 1996.
14. Resnick, M. : Changing the Centralized Mind, *Technology Review Magazine*, July 1994.

Personalized Web Retrieval: Three Agents for Retrieving Web Information

Jieh Hsiang

Department of Computer Science

National Chi-Nan University

Puli, Tantou, Taiwan

hsiang@csie.ntu.edu.tw

Hsieh-Chang Tu

Department of Computer Science

National Taiwan University

Taipei, Taiwan

tu@csie.ntu.edu.tw

Abstract

As information available over the Web grows, so does the need for more effective retrieval tools. In this paper we describe three information retrieval agents currently being developed at the National Taiwan University. While each agent serves a different purpose, they share the common feature of incorporating the need of the users. In other words, all three agents offer *personalized* services. The first agent is an IR agent that utilizes categorical information to assist a user find relevant Web pages. The second one is a *website browsing* agent which provides various services in an integrated interface to help a user navigate through a content-rich website. The third is designed to help users find on-line papers in computer science.

This research is partly supported by grant NSC 87-2213-E-002-012 of the National Science Council of the Republic of China.

1 Introduction

Web retrieval is the process of acquiring useful information from the World Wide Web. Having realized the power of Web technologies, more and more people are making resources available on the Web. Instead of finding more useful information, however, it has become increasingly difficult for an average user to weed out garbage from the interesting. There is a general feeling that the task of information retrieval should be more personalized. That is, information retrieval (IR) should be tailored to accommodate individual preferences and be more "intelligent".

In this paper we present an agent technology approach to Web information retrieval. We describe three IR agents, all developed at the National Taiwan University, for different retrieval purposes. Although somewhat different in their use, they all share the common feature of personalization. The first agent, presented in Section 2, is a meta search engine for retrieving ordinary webpages. We introduce a notion of *category*, which is used to classify documents. Categories are used in different ways; to identify a user's interests, to pre-process a query accordingly by including more keywords, and to post-process query results. Our notion of categories is different from the usual notion of clusters in that the name of a category has semantic meaning and that a user can defined her own personal categories.

In Section 3 we present an agent for *website browsing and navigation*. There are more and more websites devoted to a specific topic. Such websites are attractive because they are often better organized, and are the easiest places to gather information about a specific domain. The structureness makes possible to design dedicated website search engines and navigation tools to provide better performance. We call the process of traversing through a website and collecting information *website browsing and navigation*. *website* browsing is different from *Web* browsing in that the former is mainly designed for navigating and retrieving information *within* a particular website. Although the problems posed by website browsing are superficially similar to those of Web browsing, they are different in magnitude and solvability. For instance, a frequent user may want to know if the contents of the website has been modified since the last visit and if so, what the changes are. As we shall see, this type of service is possible for *website* browsing. It is obviously impossible, on the other hand, to provide such information for the entire Web.

Using the agent technology, we propose a methodology for designing user-friendly interfaces to provide personalized services for website browsing. We demonstrate how the idea works by presenting a website browsing agent for the Digital Library and Museum of the National Taiwan University.

The third agent, presented in Section 4, is for retrieving, over the Web, on-line papers in computer science. We use the categorical approach developed in the first agent to improve retrieval performance, and employ the technologies discussed in the second agent to provide navigation services.

2 Personal Web IR Agent

A *Web information retrieval agent* (or *Web IR agent* for short) is a program to help users retrieve webpages. General purpose search engines such as AL-TAVISTA[1] and EXCITE[2] can be considered as primitive versions of Web IR agents. A user formulates a request as a *query* q, and a search engine returns a list of abstracts of Web pages (denoted by R_q) it deems relevant to q.

Most search engines use text-based *term retrieval* techniques [2, 12, 19] to index and retrieve Web pages. In the term retrieval model, a user query is a sequence of *keywords*. Since keywords are the only means to differentiate among webpages, it is important for a user to enter a "good" query in order to obtain a satisfactory R_q, where "satisfactory" means that relevant webpages are returned and irrelevant one are not returned. Unfortunately, users usually do not know

---

[1]http://www.altavista.com (January 28, 1999).
[2]http://www.excite.com (January 28, 1999).

which terms are appropriate to compose a good query. Some Web search engines provide *query refinement* mechanisms to help a user modify her queries. Given a query q, the search engine suggests a set of keywords $k(q)$ (called *candidate keywords*) from which the user may select a subset to modify q. See [17] for more information about query refinement.

An issue arises here is that different users prefer different webpages. Thus there should be different sets of candidate keywords for different users to choose from according to their retrieval habit. In the following we introduce a notion of categories to achieve this goal. Specifically, we present the notion of *category profiles* in Section 2.1, and describe how it is used in a personal Web IR agent in Section 2.2.

2.1 Categorical User Profiles

Text-based term retrieval systems often regard a user profile as a set of keywords with weights (called a *simple profile*). One may use a simple profile as a *pre-filter* to modify a user query, or as a *post-filter* to filter out webpages returned by other IR systems. Experiments done by Sung and Korfhage suggest that information about the user may indeed improve retrieval performance [13].

Employing user profiles is a technique similar to the traditional *relevance feedback* [3, 5, 11], which is a process of automatically altering an existing query by the relevance information (supplied by the user) of previously retrieved documents. In relevance feedback, the retrieval system makes use of keywords K in the relevant documents to modify the previous query into a (hopefully) better one. The keyword information K is discarded after the user completes a search request. In practice, since a user usually have the same interests during a period of time, it is helpful to collect relevant documents found in this period. We may then regard keywords computed from these documents as a user profile.

A user may have several different interests. Since webpages about different topics usually have different keywords, a single user profile is not sufficient to represent all the preferences of a user. To solve this problem, we divide a user profile into several *category profiles*, where each profile represents a *category*. A *category* is defined as a collection of webpages relevant to a certain semantic concept. For instance, a collection of Web pages relevant to computer viruses is a category which may be named computer virus.

A category profile is a set of keywords, each associated with a weight. Formally, let V be the vocabulary of all possible keywords. (A *stop words* is not considered as a keyword.) Let C be a set of topics. Given $c \in C$, let n_c be a *name* to describe what the category is. (Category names allow a user to specify which categories are relevant to what she wants.) Given $c \in C$ and $v \in V$, let w_{cv} denote the weight of keyword v with respect to the category c. We define a *category profile of the topic c* to be a tuple $\mathcal{K}_c = \langle n_c, \mathbf{w}_c \rangle$, where $\mathbf{w}_c = (w_{cv})_{v \in V}$ is a vector indexed by the vocabulary V. A *(categorical) user profile* is then defined as the vector of category profiles $(\mathcal{K}_c)_{c \in C}$.

Two problems arise: How to produce the category set C, and how to construct the category profiles. There are two ways to acquire interesting categories.

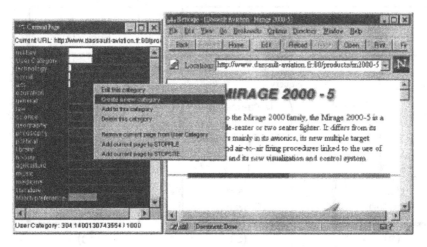

Figure 1: An example of creating a personal category. A user creates a new category which initially contains the page currently being browsed. The agent then asks the user to specify a category name. The left window displays the *category scores* of all existing categories with respect to the page being browsed. In this example military and User Category are the two categories with the highest category scores.

One approach is to define, a priori, all categories likely to be interesting and ask the user to choose a subset; and the other method requires the user to define the category herself. We adopt a hybrid approach. We provide several pre-defined categories for the user to choose from. But the user may also create her own category by giving it a name and specifying webpages belonging to the category. Figure 1 illustrates how a user may create a personal category.

The profiles of the pre-defined categories are provided by the system developer. The remaining problem is to compute the category profile $\mathcal{K}_c$ of a user-defined category c. Recall that when creating a personal profile, the user should provide a name, n_c, and a set of webpages, T, belonging to the category. T is then used by the system as the set of *positive* training webpages, from which a weight vector $\mathbf{w}_c$ is computed.

Informally, we want $\mathbf{w}_c$ to be computed in such a way that a keyword v which appears frequently in T has a larger weight. Traditional IR studies often use the measure $tf \cdot idf$ (*term frequency* times *inverse document frequency*) to compute the weight vector. However, since our Web IR agent is designed as a meta search engine and that most existing search engines have already taken idf into account, it is unnecessary for our agent to compute idf again. Let f_{dv} be the number of occurrences of a keyword v in a document d. Let $f_{cv} = \sum_{d \in T} f_{dv}$ be the number of occurrences of v in the training set T. The weight vector $\mathbf{w}_c = (w_{cv})_{v \in V}$ is computed by normalizing $(f_{cv})_{v \in V}$:

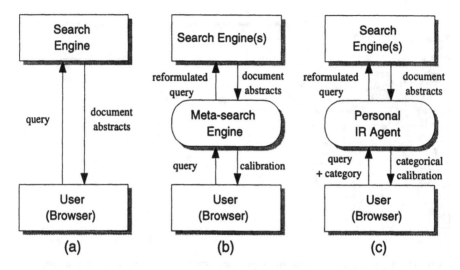

Figure 2: A comparison of search strategies. (a) search directly via a search engine, (b) search via a meta-search engine, (c) search via a personal IR agent.

$$w_{cv} = \frac{f_{cv}}{\sqrt{\sum_{v \in V} f_{cv}^2}}.\tag{1}$$

For instance, let the training set for category c contain only one document, whose content is a single sentence

A computer virus is not a biomedical virus.

After eliminating stop words **a, is,** and **not,** we have (vector components with zero weights are omitted for simplicity)

$$(f_{cv})_{v \in V} = (\text{computer: } 1, \text{ virus: } 2, \text{ biomedical: } 1),$$

and

$$\mathbf{w}_c = (\text{computer: } \tfrac{1}{\sqrt{6}}, \text{ virus: } \tfrac{2}{\sqrt{6}}, \text{ biomedical: } \tfrac{1}{\sqrt{6}}).$$

Using the normalized vector allows the agent to determine whether a re-trieved webpage belongs to a category (cf. Figure 1). More detailed discussions about how to compute the score of a retrieved page with respect to a category can be found in [6] and [15].

In next subsection, we show how category profiles can be used to suggest candidate keywords and to re-rank webpages returned by a search engine.

2.2 Categorical Web Search

There are already a number of powerful search engines with enormous data bases that are available on the Web. It is therefore unnecessary for us to build our

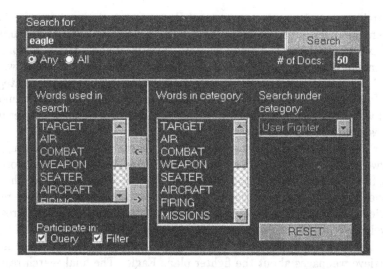

Figure 3: Search interface of the personal Web IR agent. The (personal) category User Fighter is created from the webpage shown in Figure 1. In this example, the user enters a word **eagle** as the original query, and chooses the (user-defined) category User Fighter. The top-10 ranked keywords in the category profile are automatically added into the "words used in search" box. The user may add or remove these auxiliary keywords.

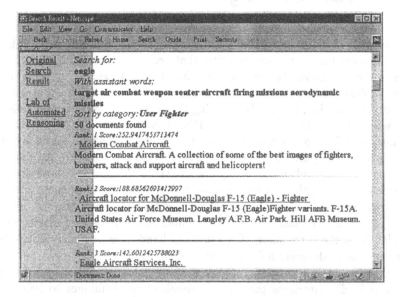

Figure 4: The search results of the user query **eagle** with the relevant category User Fighter. It can be seen that the top three ranked Web pages are relevant to the Eagle *fighter plane* as opposed to the bird.

own search engine. Instead, our personal IR agent takes advantage of existing search engines and improves upon their retrieved results. Figure 2 compares the differences among a search engine, a meta-search engine, and a personal IR agent. In short, a personal IR agent acts as an information broker between a user and the search engines. It accepts a user query and a relevant category, reformulates (and refines) the query into forms acceptable by the search engines, receives webpages returned from the search engines, and re-ranks the returned webpages as the actual search result.

After the user issues a query and a relevant category $c \in C$, the agent suggests ten keywords (i.e., those with largest weights) in $\mathbf{w}_c$ as auxiliary keywords to be sent to the search engines in conjunction with the original query. The user may choose none or several of them. After the (external) search engines return the retrieved results, $\mathbf{w}_c$ is used as a post-filter to re-rank the returned results. Intuitively, a returned page with more important keywords in $\mathbf{w}_c$ is ranked higher [6]. We demonstrate, in Figure 3, how the agent uses category profiles to help a user retrieve webpages about the fighter plane Eagle. The final search result is shown in Figure 4.

In our experiments, we have found that employing the simple formula (1) usually yields a satisfactory category profile. In particular, it is shown that a small training set (which contains three to ten webpages) is often sufficient to produce a good category profile [7].

3   Website Browsing Agent

A *website* is a repository of information accessible through a Web browser. The main purpose of building a website is for users to visit and find useful information. There are more and more websites that are devoted to a single topic. Such websites are attractive because they are often better organized, systematic, and are the easiest places to gather information that the user needs about a special domain. We call the process of traversing through such a website and collecting information *website browsing and navigating* to emphasize that, even though the user may visit Web pages not belonging to the site (through hyperlinks), she is focusing on finding useful information from within the website. Although the problems posed by website browsing are similar to those of web browsing, they are different in magnitude and solvability. For instance, a frequent user may want to know if the contents of the website has been modified since her last visit and, if so, what the changes are. As we shall see, this type of service can be provided for *website* browsing. On the other hand, it is obviously not possible to provide such information for the entire Web.

Using the agent technology, we have developed a methodology for designing user-friendly interfaces that use *personalization* techniques to help a user navigate through a website. The agent contains different features tailored for users who are familiar or unfamiliar with the website. The main mechanism we used in achieving personalization is through *user profile*, which we explain in Section 3.1. Based on our methodology, we have implemented a website browsing agent for navigating the *National Taiwan University Digital Library and Museum* (NTUDLM). This system is briefly described in Section 3.2.

3.1 Profiles for Suggesting New website Content

There are quite a few issues involved in website browsing and navigation. Due to the length constraint of this paper, we only briefly discuss the issue of notifying a user of new website content. Interested readers should read [16] for other problems and details of our proposed solutions.

The content in a website may change. Although the website may contain a large database from which most of its information is drawn, we can still regard the website content as website pages, since the website must present the content in a browser-readable form so that a user can read the content through a browser. Let D_n be the website pages which are *added* within the last n days, then a "what's new" subagent is responsible for returning D_n, for some predefined n, to a user.

Assuming that $n = 30$ and that a registered user had visited the subagent one week ago. Then obviously it is more reasonable to simply report what had been added within the last 7 days. To achieve this goal, the subagent needs to simply maintain a number t_u in the user's personal profile which indicates that the user u did not check for new content in the last t_u days. Then the subagent may return D_x, where $x = \min(30, t_u)$, as new website content.

This straightforward solution is not satisfactory if a massive amount of information had been added recently. We propose two possible approaches to this problem. If a new collection has been added, the subagent can simply provide the user with a link to the homepage of the new collection. Concurrently, the subagent can also utilize the user's preference. Assume that the website pages have been classified into several categories, and that the user's preference identifies one or several of the categories as being interesting, then only the new website pages that fall into those categories need be reported.

What was described above can be done as follows. Given a user u, let C_u be the set of categories preferred by u and let V_u be the set of website pages visited by u. We denote by $V_u(c) \subseteq V_u$ the set of visited pages that are in the category c. The set V_u can be obtained by keeping a record of which website pages have been visited. The set of interesting categories C_u can be obtained either by asking a user to subscribe to interesting categories, or by employing learning techniques to the set V_u [15]. For instance, we may regard a category c as interesting to user u if $|V_u(c)|$ exceeds a certain threshold. Once the personal profile $P_u = \langle t_u, C_u, V_u \rangle$ is obtained, new website pages in category c, where $c \in C_u$, can be highlighted as new content that may be interesting.

The category information C_u in a personal profile P_u is also useful for other subagents for different tasks. For instance, a user may want to find visited pages relevant to the one currently being browsed. A "user history" subagent is a program that offers such a service. Let p be the current page and c be its corresponding category. The subagent may suggest $V_u(c)$ as formerly visited pages relevant to p.

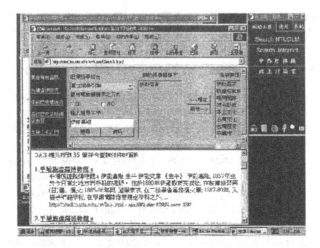

Figure 5: An illustration of the "Web search" subagent. The upper right window is the control window that contains subagent functions. The left big window is the main window that displays the content of a website page. In this example, the upper part of the main window is the "Web search" subagent interface, and the lower part of the main window shows the search result. The subagent works as a meta-search engine which answers user input with the aid of existing Web search engines.

3.2 Website Browsing Agent for the NTUDLM

In this section we describe an implementation of a website browsing agent for the National Taiwan University Digital Library and Museum (NTUDLM).[3] NTUDLM is a project supported by NTU and the National Science Council of Taiwan for building a digitized repository of historical archives and artifacts concerning the indigenous Taiwanese people and earlier settlements. The goals of the project are to build a system which

1. provides a user-friendly Web-based environment for learning about Taiwanese history,

2. provides a modern research tool for historians and anthropologists of Taiwan,

3. preserves Taiwanese history and artifacts.

Since different types of users may need different kinds of assistance, we have divided the services provided by our website browsing agent into three groups.

- System resources: This group contains six services about system resources. They are:

---

[3]Since most NTUDLM users are Chinese people, we have only implemented a Chinese interface. The website is accessible through the Web at http://ntudlm.ntu.edu.tw (January 28, 1999).

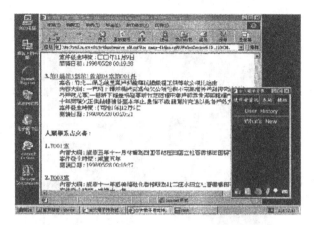

Figure 6: An example of the "user history" subagent. When the user reads a website page, she may invoke the subagent to recall visited pages related to the one currently being read.

1. An introductory page about the content of NTUDLM and about how to use the agent.

2. An FAQ page which answers questions frequently asked by users.

3. A demo subagent which presents selected NTUDLM pages automatically. A user may change the time required to show a webpage and may stop the demo at any time.

4. A page with a list of hot website pages (i.e., most frequented pages).

5. A page which collects webpages or resources related to the NTUDLM.

6. A mailbox which allows a user to ask questions by e-mail. The messages will be answered by the maintainers of NTUDLM.

- Auxiliary tools: This collection contains services to help a user find or read Web pages. It consists of four subagents:

1. A local search engine which helps a user find website pages. It makes use of categories and metadata to improve the retrieval performance [16].

2. A meta-search engine which utilizes existing Web search engines to find (external) webpages which may be relevant to a user query. We illustrate an example in Figure 5.

3. A subagent which uses an existing calendar translator[4] to help a user convert between Chinese and Gregorian calendars.

4. A chatroom which allows users to communicate on line.

---

[4]http://www.sinica.edu.tw/ftms/luso.htm (January 28, 1999).

Figure 7: Control windows for a registered and an unregistered user. There are three groups of agent services for a registered user (the left window); while there are only two groups for an unregistered one (the right window).

- User profile: There are two subagents which offer personalization services for a registered user.

    1. User history: It is often useful to analyze a user's visiting pattern to know her browsing behavior and preference [14]. A "user history" subagent is one which maintains what a user has visited. When a user reads a website page p, she may want to recall visited pages that are relevant to p. The subagent makes use of visiting pattern and category information to present visited pages that may be useful. For instance, a page that is visited more times and are in the same category as p (the page currently being browsed) will be ranked higher. See Figure 6 for a demonstration.

    2. What's new: A subagent which notifies a user whether there is interesting new content in NTUDLM. For an unregistered user, the "what's new" service is moved to the "system resource" group since the subagent does not have a profile about the user (cf. Figure 7).

The NTUDLM browsing agent has two distinctive features on the interface design. First, it offers different services for a registered and an unregistered user. A registered user is allowed to enjoy more sophisticated system services. Secondly, instead of using a *control frame*, the browsing agent has a dedicated *control window* to separate system services and the content of webpages. As pointed out by Nielsen [9], frames are confusing and may cause undesirable results. Since the dedicated window is independent of the browsing window which displays normal page content, a user will not lose agent assistance when visiting an external webpage. See [8] and [16] for more detailed information about the integrated interface.

4 BibTex Agent

The BibTex agent is currently being developed by the NTU agent group. The goal of the project is to see how agent technology can be used to help a user find on-line papers. Unlike the two agents mentioned in the previous sections, this one is not yet completed.

There are several websites offering paper-searching services, including THE COLLECTION OF COMPUTER SCIENCE BIBLIOGRAPHIES[5] (BIBCOLLECTION for short) whose database contains 850,000 references in *BibTex* format. The BIB-COLLECTION provides a search interface and uses conventional text retrieval tools to index and retrieve content from the database. Since it only contains BibTex entries, full texts of papers are not available. Users who wish to find the text of the papers need to get them elsewhere.

Our BibTex agent is built on top of BIBCOLLECTION. Similar to the interface for NTUDLM, it can also be considered as an agent-ware between the user and the BIBCOLLECTION. It is expected to have the following features:

- **Post-retrieval classification for browsing**:
  BibTex is essentially a metadata system. We can use the BibTex attributes to post-classify the retrieved entry list and provide more useful browsing. For example, the retrieved list may be grouped together according to authors, and within each group further sorted chronologically.

- **Categorical term suggestion**:
  We divide the BibTex entries into several categories, and each category also contains a number of popular papers which are accessed most often by users. If a user is registered and the agent has identified the categories that she is interested in, the agent can recommend the popular papers in those categories that the user has not yet requested. Similar to the mechanism described in Section 2.1, the agent may also provide keywords in a category profile to help a user modify her queries.

- **Notification of new entries**
  A user may wish to know whether there are new entries relates to a certain topic. Sometimes one may want to know whether there are new papers written by specific authors. Our agent allows a user to specify criteria about interesting new content. New entries in the database matching the criteria will then be prompted to the user.

- **On-line paper acquisition**:
  In addition to finding just the BibTex information, a user may want to get

---

[5]http://liinwww.ira.uka.de/bibliography/index.html (January 28, 1999).

Figure 8: The BibTex agent. A user may register to acquire personalization services.

the full content of the paper. The BibTex agent contains subagents which utilize Internet resources and facilities to find on-line papers.

Figure 8 illustrates the entry page of our BibTex agent. While most of the features mentioned above are completed, we are still developing the subagent for paper acquisition. Our BibTex agent is, in a sense, another example of an agent for website browsing and navigation. It is different from the one for NTUDLM in that (1) the BibTex entries have a readily available metadata structure and (2) its retrieval and display functions are more important than navigation.

As mentioned before, BibTex can be construed as metadata that describe certain properties of the papers.

As with any metadata systems, BibTex may contain semantic information not easily extractable from the text of a paper. And as with other metadata system, such information can be used to improve retrieval performance.

Metadata information is also useful for browsing purposes. Let M be the set of all possible values for the metadata property author. An element $m \in M$ corresponds to a specific author name. Given a set of BibTex entries E, let $E(m) \subseteq E$ be the entries whose authors include $m \in M$. The agent may display tuples $\langle m, |E(m)| \rangle$ in a separate frame to classify E according to author names. A user may click on a name (from the tuple list) to access $E(m)$, which may be much smaller than E.

BibTex entries are pre-classified into several categories, and techniques discussed in Section 2.1 and Section 2.2 can be used to help a user refine a query. Techniques discussed in Section 3.1 can also be used to notify a user whether interesting new content arrives.

5 Discussion

In [15] we pointed out that a good Web browsing environment should provide the following services:

- *Personalized search and retrieval*: This includes refining a query and post-filtering and classifying returned results, all according to a user's preferences.

- *Navigational guide*: It is easy to get lost when surfing. A good navigational guide should provide a user a sense of orientation.

- *Information auto-notification*: A frequent visitor to a website wants to know if the contents of the site has changed. An experienced user may want to know if there is any new resource related to her interests which has been added to the Web. An auto-notification mechanism can significantly reduce user time and effort in finding such information.

- *Reading-aide*: Reading-aides such as on-line dictionaries, encyclopedia, language translators, calendar converters, and chatroom facilities can provide significant help to a user.

In this paper, we discussed how agent technology can help by describing three Web information retrieval agents developed at the National Taiwan University. The first agent works as an information broker between a user and existing search engines, and makes use of a notion of categories to help formulate user queries and re-rank search results. The second agent offers an integrated interface to help a user navigating through the NTUDLM. Finally, we discuss the BibTex agent project for on-line paper retrieval.

All three agents put emphasis on *personalization*, which is a most important trend in Web technology. Another trend we point out is the concept of *website* browsing and navigation. Content-rich websites are the most useful source of information on the Web. By providing internal browsing and retrieval facilities, they can be even more helpful to the users. Since the information of a content-rich website is usually much better organized than the average Web, internal representation mechanism such as *metadata* can be utilized to provide better services. It is an interesting challenge to build generic website browsing and navigation tools which can be easily adapted by individual websites.

References

[1] Rob Barrett, Paul P. Maglio and Daniel C. Kellem, *How to Personalize the Web*, ACM SIGCHI'97, 1997. Available through
http://www.acm.org/sigchi/chi97/proceedings/paper/rcb-wbi.htm (January 28, 1999).

[2] Abraham Bookstein, *Explanation and Generalization of Vector Models in Information Retrieval*, ACM SIGIR'82, pp. 118-132, 1982.

[3] Chris Buckley and Gerard Salton, *Optimization of Relevance Feedback Weights*, ACM SIGIR'95, pp. 351-357, 1995.

[4] Fah-Chun Cheong, *Internet Agents: Spiders, Wanderers, Brokers, and Bots*, New Riders Publishing, Indianapolis, Indiana, 1996.

[5] Donna Harman, *Relevance Feedback Revisited*, ACM SIGIR'92, pp. 1-10, 1992.

[6] Min-Hung Lee, *Java-based Personal Proxy Server and its Applications*, Master Thesis, National Taiwan University, 1997.

[7] Shu-Hsien Liao, *Personal Category Profiles for WWW Information Retrieval*, Master Thesis, National Taiwan University, 1998.

[8] Michael Li-Wei Lu, *The Design and Implementation of Integrated User Interface for Web Browsing*, Master Thesis, National Taiwan University, 1998.

[9] Jakob Nielsen, *User Interface Design for the WWW*, ACM SIGCHI'97, 1997. Available through
http://www.acm.org/sigchi/chi97/proceedings/tutorial/jn.htm (January 28, 1999).

[10] Stuart J. Russell and Peter Norvig, *Artificial Intelligence: A Modern Approach*, Prentice-Hall International, Inc., 1995.

[11] Gerard Salton, editor, *The SMART Retrieval System: Experiments in Automatic Document Processing*, Prentice-Hall Inc., 1971.

[12] Gerard Salton, *Automatic Text Processing: The Transformation, Analysis, and Retrieval of Information by Computer*, Addison-Wesley, 1989.

[13] Myaeng H. Sung and Robert R. Korfhage, *Integration of User Profiles: Models and Experiments in Information Retrieval*, Information Processing & Management, pp. 719-738, 1990.

[14] Linda Tauscher and Saul Greenberg, *Revisitation Patterns in World Wide Web Navigation*, ACM SIGCHI'97, 1997. Available through
http://www.acm.org/sigchi/chi97/proceedings/paper/sg.htm (January 28, 1999).

[15] Hsieh-Chang Tu and Jieh Hsiang, *An Architecture and Category Knowledge for Intelligent Information Retrieval*, the 31st Hawaii International Conference on System Sciences, HICSS-31, January 1998.

[16] Hsieh-Chang Tu, Michael Li-Wei. Lu and Jieh Hsiang, *Agent technology for website Browsing and Navigation*, the 32nd Hawaii International Conference on System Sciences, HICSS-32, January 1999.

[17] Bienvenido Vélez, Ron Weiss, Mark A. Sheldon and David K. Gifford, *Fast and Effective Query Refinement*, ACM SIGIR'97, pp. 6-15, 1997.

[18] Michael Wooldridge and Nicholas R. Jennings, *Intelligent Agents: Theory and Practice*, Knowledge Engineering Review, Vol. 10, No. 2, June 1995.

[19] C. T. Yu, K. Lam and G. Salton, *Term Weighting in Information Retrieval Using the Term Precision Model*, Journal of the Association for Computing Machinery, JACM Vol. 29, No. 1, pp. 152-170, January 1982.

Single-agent and Multi-agent Approaches to WWW Information Integration

Yasuhiko Kitamura[1], Tomoya Noda[1], and Shoji Tatsumi[1]

Department of Information and Communication Engineering
Faculty of Engineering, Osaka City University
3-3-138 Sugimoto, Sumiyoshi-ku, Osaka 558-8585, Japan
{kitamura, tnoda, tatsumi}@kdel.info.eng.osaka-cu.ac.jp
http://www.kdel.info.eng.osaka-cu.ac.jp

Abstract. The WWW is a most popular service on the Internet and a huge number of WWW information sources are available. Conventionally we access WWW information sources one by one by using a browser, but *WWW information integration* gives a unified view to users by integrating multiple WWW information sources elaborately. In this paper, we introduce our single-agent and multi-agent approaches to WWW information integration.

1 Introduction

As the Internet spreads out over our society, it is becoming one of indispensable social infrastructures which support our daily life. Among various services offered by the Internet, the WWW (World Wide Web) becomes most popular and a huge number of WWW information sources support our research, business, and personal activities. Conventionally we access WWW information sources one by one by using a browser and utilize each of them as an independent information source. On the other hand, *WWW information integration* gives a unified view to users by integrating multiple WWW information sources elaborately.

For instance, the Softbots project led by Oren Etzioni at University of Washington aims at integrating information sources on the Internet to offer more advanced and better quality information services [1]. MetaCrawler[1] is a meta search engine which integrates query results obtained from multiple generic search engines and improves the quality of query results [6]. Ahoy![2] is a special purpose search engine to find a personal homepage by filtering query results from the Metacrawler by using other information sources such as an E-mail database [7].

In academic research fields, WWW information integration plays an important role. In the Human Genome Project, researchers are developing a number of various biological databases, concerning sequences, 3D structures, functions, and bibliography of DNA and protein etc., which are now available through the WWW. These databases will be more useful if they are interoperable. As a first

---

[1] http://www.metacrawler.com/
[2] http://ahoy.cs.washington.edu:6060/

step to information integration, DBGET[3][3] and SRS[4][2] have been developed to make data items interreferable by using hyperlinks.

The above examples are precursors of WWW information integration but have some drawbacks such that they achieve only page-level integration on third-party servers where users cannot specify how to integrate the information. In the future, we need to achieve WWW information integration more easily, freely, and elaborately on our client machine.

In this paper, we introduce our two approaches to WWW information integration. As our first approach, we developed a single-agent system called Meta-Commander. The MetaCommander collects WWW pages, extracts data, and merges them on behalf of a user following a script described by the user. We then, as our second approach, introduce a multi-agent system called Personal WWW Information Integrator (PWII). PWII consists of Information Agents which extract data from WWW servers, Task Agents which synthesize extracted data, and Interface Agents which mediate between the system and users. We combine these agents on a single platform with GUI, hence we can not only integrate WWW information easily and flexibly, but also we can reuse and share the agents among users.

2 MetaCommander

The MetaCommander is an agent with the following features which automatically collects and sorts data from distributed WWW information sources on behalf of its user.

Paragraph-level integration. The purpose of developing MetaCommander is to achieve WWW information integration at paragraph level, while current WWW tools like search engines and bookmarks of WWW browser achieve it at page level. Hence, we can cut and paste paragraphs in various WWW pages at different sites and produce new pages automatically.

Script language. Because current WWW pages (HTML documents) contain little semantic information, cutting and pasting paragraphs in WWW pages is not an easy task for an agent, and its user needs to assist the agent in teaching how to do it precisely. For this purpose, we adopted an easy-to-use script language to represent the user's requirements for integrating information from distributed WWW servers. It is easier to represent the requirement in a script language than a high-level language although it may constrain the functionality. The script should be easy enough for a non-expert of computer, who has a little knowledge of programming, to use. However, for facilitating complicated information integration, the script should have basic functions that ordinary programming languages provide such as local file access, mathematical/logical calculation, control, and so on.

---

[3] http://www.genome.ad.jp/dbget/dbget.html
[4] http://www.embl-heidelberg.de/srs/srsc

Java implementation. The system should run on a client machine like PC. Hence, we implemented the MetaCommander with the Java language, which is platform independent and runs on most of current platforms like UNIX, MacOS, and Windows.

2.1 System Components

We show the MetaCommander components and the data flow in Fig. 1. We give commands to the MetaCommander by describing a script. The MetaCommander interprets the script and executes it. It uses the HTTP (Hyper Text Transfer Protocol) to access WWW servers through the Internet. It also can read and write local data files. Finally, it outputs an HTML text, and we can display it on an ordinary WWW browser.

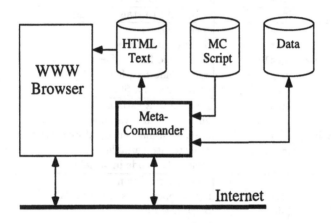

Fig. 1. MetaCommander components.

2.2 MetaCommander Script

We show major functions of MetaCommander script in Table 1.

The style of MetaCommander functions is similar to that of the language C like **function(arg1, arg2, ...)**. The scope where a function is effective is specified by braces('{' and '}'). By adding **else** with braces after the function name, we can specify another scope which is effective when the function fails.

For example,

```
getURL( "http://www.ieice.or.jp/" ) {
    print
} else {
    print( "ERROR" )
}
```

Table 1. Major functions of MetaCommander script.

Group	Name	Description
Page Retrieve	getURL	get a page at URL
	postURL	get a page at URL by posting to CGI
	multipartURL	get a page at URL by posting in MIME format
	fileURL	download a page at URL
	password	set user's name and password
Data Extraction	getAnchor	extract an anchor
	getString	extract text strings
	searchString	extract a paragraph
	searchTag	extract an HTML tag
	cutString	extract text strings by specifying the region
Layout	tag	insert an HTML tag
Print	print	print data to standard output
File Access	open	open a file
	eof	check if end of file
	getline	read a line from a file
	putline	write a line to a file
	fprint	write data to a file
Variable	set	set data to a variable
	unset	unset data in a variable
	calc	evaluate a mathematical expression
	strcat	concatenate variables
	chop	remove CR code in variable
Control	if	jump on condition
	foreach	repeat operations for each data
	while	begin a loop
	exit	halt
	break	break the loop
	continue	jump to the top of loop

outputs the contents of the designated page when the MetaCommander succeeds to access it, otherwise it outputs "ERROR."

Unique functions of the MetaCommander are those for WWW page retrieval, data extraction, and layout. Functions for WWW page retrieval collect HTML documents from WWW servers at the designated URLs. The function getURL is mainly used with a URL as its argument. When we need to send data to a CGI (Common Gateway Interface) through a form, one of getURL, postURL, or multipartURL is chosen depending on the form type. When we need user's authentication to access a secured server, password function is used to specify user's name and password.

Functions for data extraction are used to cut data from and paste them to HTML documents. They are getAnchor that extracts link data, getString that extracts pure text strings without tags, searchTag that extracts a tag, `searchString` and `cutString` that extract text strings by using key strings. For example,

```
cutString("ABC","XYZ") {
    print
}
```

cuts text strings beginning with "ABC" and terminating with "XYZ."

The `tag` is a function for layout, which inserts a tag in an HTML text. The `print` is a function for outputting a specified data into the standard output (a file named "meta.html"). If the function has no argument, the contents in the valid scope become the output.

Furthermore, functions for local file access, variables, calculation, control, and so on, are prepared. Subroutine calls are also available.

2.3 Applications to Scientific Research Domain

The Human Genome Project is an international project to elucidate all the genetic information and mechanism of human body. This project has a big expectation that the genetic information will contribute to the revolutionary progress in biology, medicine, and pharmacy such as elucidation and treatment of genetic diseases. On the other hand, information processing technologies are essential to manage and utilize a huge amount of various data obtained by biological experiments[9]. At present, the WWW is a nucleus technology to share information among genome researchers in the world, and a number of various databases and analysis tools are open to the researchers such as the GenomeNet[5] in Japan.

To integrate databases by hyperlinks however causes an operational problem. For example, it is possible to collect reference information from a nucleic acid database GenBank by sending a query through its CGI, but the operations become repetitive when a user wants to collect related information from a number of entries because each entry is contained in a single WWW page. For this problem, the MetaCommander can automate to follow hyperlinks and cut some parts (ex. reference data) out of GenBank pages, and integrate them into a page. We here show a MetaCommander script to execute the above operations in Fig. 2.

At first, the URL of GenBank server (Line 1), the number of entries to retrieve (Line 2), and keywords (Line 3) are set to variables. Then, a MetaCommander gets access to the GenBank server (Line 4) and obtains a list of links to entries as shown in Fig. 3(a). It extracts the link (Line 6) and outputs it (Line 8). As the URL designated by the link has been set to a system variable $\$_$, it follows the link (Line 10). Since the server returns a page shown in Fig. 3(b), the Meta-Commander cuts reference data between "REFERENCE" and "FEATURES" (Line 11) and outputs them (Line 12). Finally an HTML text shown in Fig. 3(c) is obtained. In Fig. 4, we show an example produced by executing the script in Fig. 2.

---

[5] http://www.genome.ad.jp

```
1:set( url, "http://www.genome.ad.jp/htbin/www_bfind_sub" )
2:set( max_hit, 5 )
3:set( keywords, "hiv human")

4:getURL($url,"dbkey"="genbank-today", "keywords"=$keywords,
  "mode"="bfind", "max_hit"=$max_hit) {
5:  file( "result.html" ) {
6:    getAnchor($max_hit) {
7:      tag("LI")
8:      print
9:      tag("BR")
10:      getURL($_) {
11:        cutString("REFERENCE","FEATURES",1,0){
12:          tag("PRE") { print }}}}}
```

Fig. 2. A MetaCommander script to collect reference information from GenBank.

2.4 Application to Business Domain

Electronic commerce becomes one of most popular applications of the Internet. There are a number of virtual shops which carry various goods. An advantage of electronic commerce for a consumer is that he/she can compare the prices of goods and choose cheapest ones much easier that he/she does in traditional commerce. The MetaCommander makes the comparison shopping more easier.

Fig. 5 shows a collection of price information about a graphic board for PC named "Revolution 3D" from 3 Japanese virtual shops (System Works[6], DOS/V Paradise[7], and TWO TOP[8]).

Collecting price information from virtual shops is not easy. There is no definitive rule to find a catalogue page which contains an item which a customer like to buy because how to build catalogue pages depends on the shop. Normally a customer is required to follow several links to find the page from the top of virtual shop homepage and sometimes he/she has a difficulty to find it. If we describe the above process in a script, it will be a quite complicated and lengthy one. As a remedy, we can incorporate a use of ordinary search engine into the script. In the script which outputs Fig. 5, we consult a search engine with a keyword "Revolution 3D." Although it returns a number of links concerning the keyword, we can sift the output by using the URLs of virtual shops. For example, if http://twotop.exa.co.jp/tuhan/video.html is included in the links from the search engine, we get to know that the TWO TOP (twotop.exa.co.jp) carries "Revolution 3D" and that it is located at http://twotop.exa.co.jp/tuhan/video.html. By incorporating a search engine, we can reduce the length of script to about 200 lines.

---

[6] http://www.systemworks.co.jp

[7] http://www.dospara.co.jp

[8] http://twotop.exa.co.jp

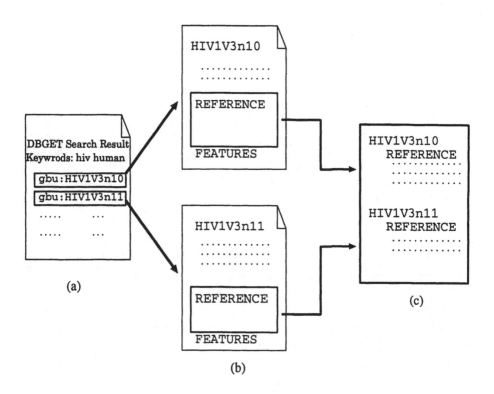

Fig. 3. Collecting reference information from GenBank.

2.5 Future Work

The MetaCommander is now downloadable from our WWW site[9] and has been applied to various purposes. Our future work on the MetaCommander is summarized as follows.

Automatic script generation. The MetaCommander reduces the burden of WWW information integration but developing scripts still remains as a tough work especially for novice users. Now we have interest in automatic script generation based on "demonstration-oriented user interface" (DoUI) [5] which produces a script that mimics the user's operations on a WWW browser.

Sociability. In the future, more automated WWW access tools like the Meta-Commander will be widely used, and this will make the traffic in the Internet increase rapidly. In the current Internet environment, selfish users can use the resource (network bandwidth and servers) as much as they like. For this issue, the sociability of agent would work effectively. For example, by monitoring the load of network and servers, agents can selectively access less-loaded servers, or schedule the access plans cooperating with the servers.

---

[9] http://www.kdel.info.eng.osaka-cu.ac.jp/ mc/

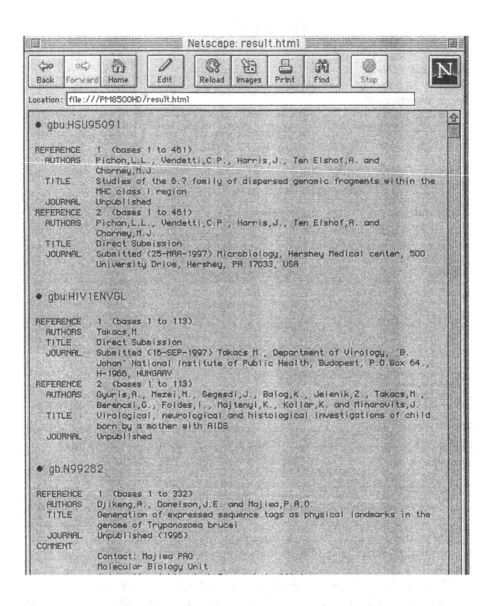

Fig. 4. A WWW page obtained by executing the script in Fig. 2

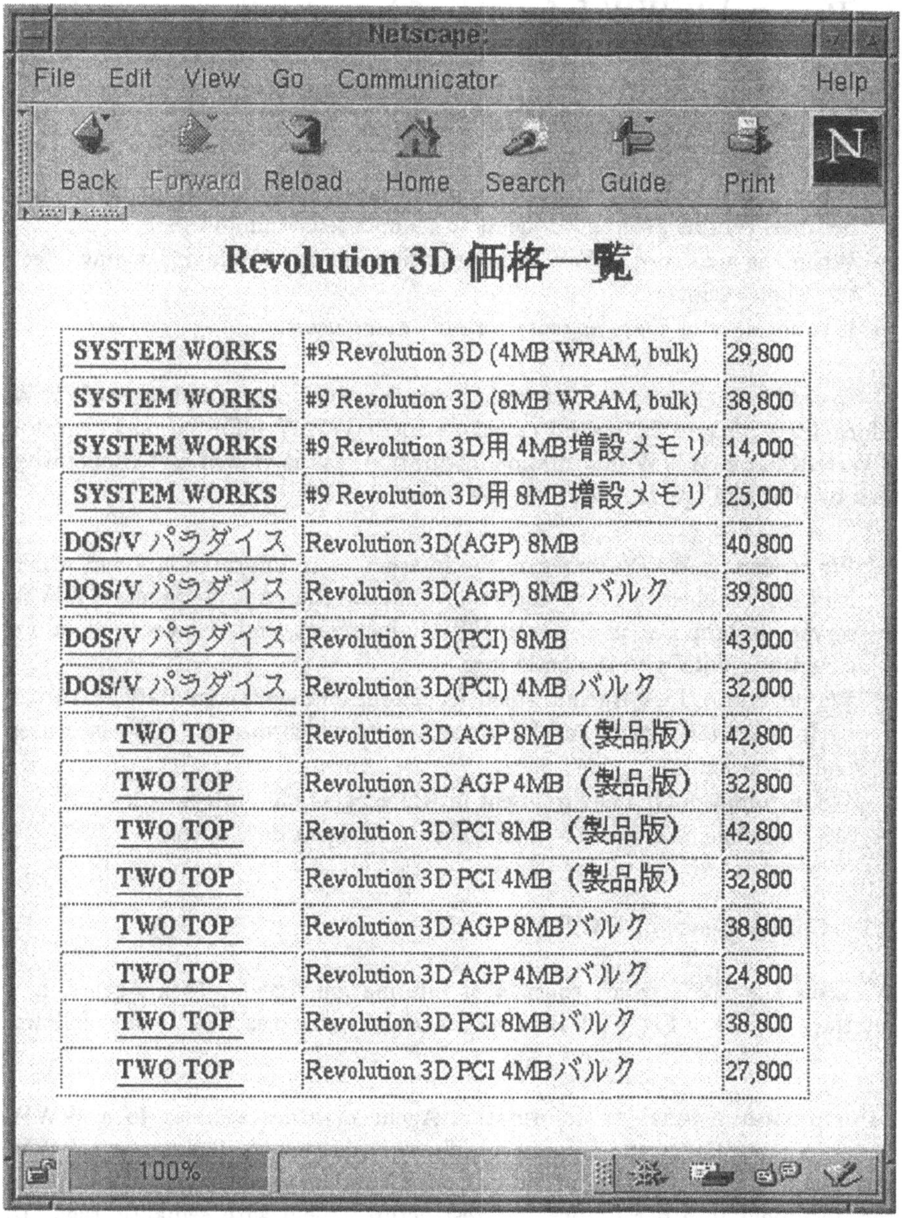

Revolution 3D 価格一覧

SYSTEM WORKS	#9 Revolution 3D (4MB WRAM, bulk)	29,800
SYSTEM WORKS	#9 Revolution 3D (8MB WRAM, bulk)	38,800
SYSTEM WORKS	#9 Revolution 3D用 4MB増設メモリ	14,000
SYSTEM WORKS	#9 Revolution 3D用 8MB増設メモリ	25,000
DOS/V パラダイス	Revolution 3D(AGP) 8MB	40,800
DOS/V パラダイス	Revolution 3D(AGP) 8MB バルク	39,800
DOS/V パラダイス	Revolution 3D(PCI) 8MB	43,000
DOS/V パラダイス	Revolution 3D(PCI) 4MB バルク	32,000
TWO TOP	Revolution 3D AGP 8MB（製品版）	42,800
TWO TOP	Revolution 3D AGP 4MB（製品版）	32,800
TWO TOP	Revolution 3D PCI 8MB（製品版）	42,800
TWO TOP	Revolution 3D PCI 4MB（製品版）	32,800
TWO TOP	Revolution 3D AGP 8MBバルク	38,800
TWO TOP	Revolution 3D AGP 4MBバルク	24,800
TWO TOP	Revolution 3D PCI 8MBバルク	38,800
TWO TOP	Revolution 3D PCI 4MBバルク	27,800

Fig. 5. Collecting price information from virtual shops. The table consists of price information about a PC graphic board "Revolution 3D" collected from three Japanese virtual shops; SYSTEM WORKS, DOS/V Paradise, and TWO TOP, on the Internet. Each line consists of the name of virtual shop, the specification, and the price in Yen.

3   Personal WWW Information Integrator

The MetaCommander, in which a WWW information integration task has to be described as a script, has following shortcomings.

- When a WWW information integration task is complicated, the script also becomes complicated and difficult to be updated or modified.
- When the structure of WWW information source is updated, it may affect the whole script.
- It is not easy to share or reuse scripts among users.

To deal with the above shortcomings, we are developing a multiagent WWW information integration system called Personal WWW Information Integrator (PWII) where a WWW information integration task is viewed as a cooperative task by multiple agents. PWII has the following features.

- We agentize a WWW server on the Internet as an Information Agent which is interoperable on a client machine. An Information Agent accesses a WWW server, decomposes an obtained HTML document, and transforms it into a structured data with semantic tags.
- We introduce Task Agents which transform and synthesize data extracted by Information Agents and Interface Agents which mediate between a user and the system.
- We introduce a GUI environment in which agents are integrated.
- We make agents shareable among users and agent developers.

3.1   Components of PWII

We show the PWII which consists of Information Agents, Task Agents, and Interface Agents in Fig. 6 [8]. Here we concisely describe each of them as follows.

Information Agent   An Information Agent manages accesses to a WWW server on the Internet and gives an interface to other agents. It accesses a WWW server through the HTTP and obtains a HTML document. It then decomposes the document into paragraphs and restructures them with semantic tags. To represent this structured data, we plans to use XML (eXtensible Markup Language). We call the output of Information Agent *message*.

A straight forward method to transform a HTML document to a XML document is by hard coding using script or programming language, but it has drawbacks such that the coding sometimes can be complicated and this method is not robust against the structure change of WWW pages. Hence, we may be able to adopt an approach by [4] which use a template to extract information automatically.

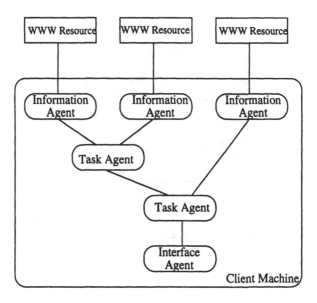

Fig. 6. Components of PWII

Task Agent For WWW information integration to satisfy requests from a user, we need to transform and synthesize messages from Information Agents. Because requests are various and depend on users, a generic task agent, which performs generic data transformation or synthesis such as relational operations of database management system, may be useful since we can satisfy many requests by reusing or replicating the generic agents.

Interface Agent An Interface Agent mediates between its user and other agents. It receives parameters for WWW server access from its user and displays the result to the user or saves it in a file.

3.2 Integration Network

A WWW information integration task is achieved through message exchange among Information Agents, Task Agents, and Interface Agents.

Here we show an integration of search engines as an example scenario of WWW information integration in Fig. 7. We assume query keywords are stored in a file. An Interface Agent (File Input) reads keywords from the file and send them to Information Agents (Search Engines A and B). Search Engine A sends its output to Task Agent (Filtering) for message filtering. The Task Agent passes search results with score of 80% or more to another Task Agent (Union). Search Engine B sends all the results to Union. Union compares both results and takes ones which are included in both results and sends them to another Interface Agent (File Output). The Interface Agent saves the result in a file.

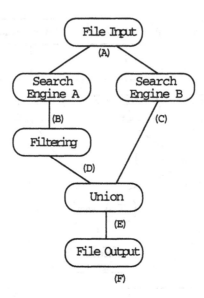

Fig. 7. Integration of Search Engines.

3.3 Agent Integration on GUI

In Fig. 8, we show our GUI system for agent integration. This GUI consists of a canvas and buttons. We locate agents and links on the canvas, and can edit them like a drawing tool. We can use buttons whose functions are shown in Table 2 to manipulate agents and links.

A most common manipulation is as follows. We choose agents from the pull-down menu and locate them on the canvas. We then add links between agents to specify the flow of data among agents. We can change the properties of an agent if needed by using its property window which appears when we click the agent. Fig. 9 shows the property window of search engine called **goo**[10]. The parameters correspond to the original CGI of the search engine and we can change these except KEYWORD which is set by other agent (**input file**) connected by a link because $KEY means outer reference. This **goo** agent outputs the number of hits (**HITS**) and the list of URL (**RESULT**) from the search engine and sends them to **filter** agent.

Once we construct an integration network, we can execute the integration task by pressing "VIEW." The execution starts from root agents of the message flow tree. When an agent receives a message, it processes the message and send result messages to other agents as it is specified in the integration network. When a leaf agent is an Interface Agent for file access, the output is saved in a file in the HTML format, so we can see the result by using a WWW browser.

---

[10] http://www.goo.ne.jp/

When we press "EXPORT," the system generates a MetaCommander script whose operations are the same as that of the integration network on the canvas.

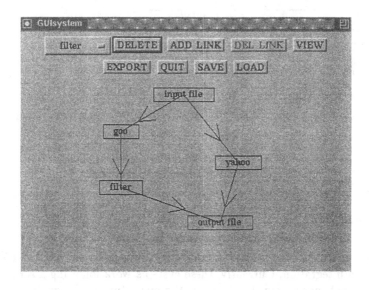

Fig. 8. GUI of Personal WWW Information Integrator.

Table 2. Functions of Buttons

Name	Function
DELETE	delete a specified agent
ADD_LNK	add a link between two spedified agents
DEL_LNK	delete a specified link
VIEW	display the result
EXPORT	output MetaCommander script
QUIT	quit
SAVE	save the integration network
LOAD	load a saved integration network

3.4 Implementation

We developed a PWII prototype as a Java application. In this prototype, an agent is coded as a class, so we can share one among users easily by copying the class from a client machine to another.

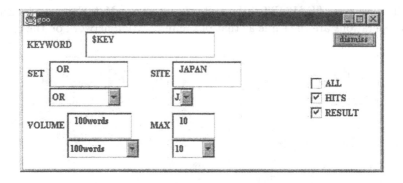

Fig. 9. Property window of **goo** agent.

4 Summary

In this paper, we introduced two systems MetaCommander and PWII for WWW information integration. Currently, these systems work following a script or an integration network specified by a user. For our future study, we have interest in making these agents autonomous and smart.

Acknowledgements

This work is partly supported by a Grant-in-Aid for Scientific Research on Priority Areas, "Genome Science," from the Ministry of Education, Science, Sports and Culture of Japan.

References

1. Etzioni, O.: Moving up the information food chain: deploying softbots on the World Wide Web. Proc. 13th National Conference on Artificial Intelligence (1996) 1322–1326
2. Etzold, T., Argos, P.: SRS – an indexing and retrieval tool for flat file data libraries. CABIOS, **9**(1) (1993) 49–57
3. Fujibuchi, W., Goto, S., Migimatsu, H., Uchiyama, I., Ogiwara, A., Akiyama, Y., Kanehisa, M.: DBGET/LinkDB: an Integrated Database Retrieval System. Pacific Symp. Biocomputing **3** (1997) 683-694
4. Hsu, J. and Yih, W.: Template-based information mining from HTML documents. Proceedings of 14th National Conference on Artificial Intelligence (1997) 256–262
5. Knoblock, C.A. et al.: Modeling web sources for information integration. Proc. 14th National Conference on Artificial Intelligence (1997) 211–218
6. Selberg, E., Etzioni, O.: The MetaCrawler architecture for resource aggregation on the web. IEEE Expert, **12**(1) (1997) 11–14

7. Shakes, J., Langheinrich, M., Etzioni, O.: Dynamic reference sifting: a case study in the homepage domain. Proceedings of 6th International World Wide Web Conference (1997)

8. Sycara, K., Pannu, A., Williamson, M., Zeng, D., Decker, K.: Distributed Intelligent Agents. IEEE Expert, 11(6) (1996) 36–45

9. Takagi, T.: Application of deductive databases to genome informatics. Journal of Japanese Society for Artificial Intelligence 10(1) (1995) 17–23 (in Japanese)

A Multi-agent Framework for Intranet Service Integration

Jane Yung-jen Hsu

yjhsu@csie.ntu.edu.tw

Department of Computer Science and Information Engineering
National Taiwan University
Taipei, Taiwan 106

Abstract. Networked computing has drastically changed the way in which people work and exchange information. Although the standard client-server architecture enables sharing of common resources among multiple users, it is non-trivial to share computational resources over the network. In this paper, we present a *client-agent-server* framework for integrating intranet services in satisfying complex informational tasks. Agents play the key role in linking individual commands into useful plans, and in transforming heterogeneous data into valuable knowledge. The agent-based approach reduces the burden of using distributed services for the end users, and fills the gap between information service providers and clients. In particular, a community of printer agents are presented to demonstrate the advantages of the proposed multi-agent framework.

1 Introduction

The world-wide web has become the most effective means for people to share *data*, i.e. hyper-linked documents, over the Internet. Meanwhile, an intranet, which refers to the application of Internet standards and systems to the management of internal networks, enables people to work and communicate efficiently within an organization. While many computational *services* are available over the intranet, it is non-trivial to integrate and share such resources.

Consider a network consisting of multiple (possibly heterogeneous) servers interconnected with multiple clients. The former offer a variety of data and computational services, while the latter issue a variety of informational requests. Under the standard client-server architecture, utilizing shared server resources often requires sophisticated user manipulation or even programming. For example, suppose that John wants to produce a printed copy of a report, which appears as an attachment `report.tar.gz` to an email from his colleague. First of all, he opens an email application, finds the email message, and saves the attached file to a local hard disk. He then has to unzip and untar the file, only to find that the report is in fact contained in multiple `.tex` and `.ps` files. Undaunted by the fact that `latex` is not readily available on his machine, John proceeds to transfer the files to another machine, processes the files, sets up the printer, and finally generates a printed document. The seemingly simple task of "printing a document" can be laborious for expert users, and challenging or mission-impossible for novices, especially when the utilites and applications are scattered on different machines within a distributed environment.

As is illustrated in the scenario above, there are several problems with how computers are used today.

- Computers and software applications are viewed as tools to be manipulated directly by the users.
- In order to solve a single task, a sequence of software utilities and applications may need to be deployed manually.
- There is no easy way to instruct the computers at an intuitive level. The current generation of graphical user interface are friendly looking, but the mode of interaction is passive in nature.
- With increased functionalities, software are growing in terms of both program size and resource requirement.
- The applications can't communicate to coordinate their functions or data transfer automatically.

In recent years, intelligent agents have emerged as a new software paradigm in which users are able to *delegate* tasks to the computers. There is a wide variety of agents [1]. While the definition of an agent is still a subject of much controversy, we take an agent to be "any program that can be considered by the user to be acting as an assistant or helper, rather than as a tool in the manner of a conventional direct-manipulation interface"[15]. For example, the SoftBots [8, 7] allow a user to specify (incompletely) a task, e.g. send emails to someone, and the computer then carries out the appropriate sequence of commands in order to accomplish the task. For the softbots to work properly, all system utilities are assumed to be at their disposal. Additionally, multi-agent systems offer a modular solution for domains that are particularly complex, large, or unpredictable [18].

Instead of viewing the computer as a desktop with an array of tools, the user should be able to interact with the computer by delegating tasks to the team of agents who manage the intranet services for her. This research attempts to establish a multi-agent framework for the problem of *intranet services integration*. Section 2 starts by formulating the problem. A three-tier *Client-Agent-Server* is introduced in Section 3, and a hierarchy of agents are defined in Section 4. Some important issues in designing such an infrastructure are also discussed. Section 5 presents a case study of AutoPrint agents that assist intranet users in printing documents. This paper concludes by outlining some future research directions.

2 The Service Integration Problem

Manipulating multiple services on distributed machines is problematic. Due to the mismatch between the level of services provided and the level of tasks requested, it takes a lot of skills on the user's part to *coerce* the computer to do the right things. A user has to utilize the shared data and computational resources effectively. This section formulates the problem of *service integration* in such a way that it can be decomposed into more manageable problems. Let us start by defining the basic components.

Definition 1. *A service* $s = \langle c, h, r, f \rangle$ *is any computation that*

- *is invoked by a single command* c,
- *can be executed by a single host* h,
- *requires resource* r, *and*
- *achieves functionality* f.

The first component defines the corresponding command for the service, and the other three components define its operating context.

A service can be any specific command, utility, or application available for execution on a host machine. A service functionality can be defined in terms of changes in the task domain. Services may be similar in their functionalities. For example, all print servers offer the same kind of service, e.g. increasing the number of hardcopies of a given file in the world, while each "lpr -P*pname*" command on a specific host machine is considered a distinct service.

Definition 2. *A service operator* $S = \langle N, F \rangle$ *is a set of services, where* N *is a unique service name and* F *is a distinct service function, such that a service* s *is in* S *if and only if* $f(s)$ *is an instantiation of* $F(S)$.

In a sense, a service is an instantiation of a service operator with the proper operating context, e.g. the host information or resource requirements. Services of a given service operator produce similar state transitions in the problem space. The service operators may be further abstracted into *service operator schemas* by introducing variables in the same spirit of *operator schemas* in standard AI planning. Multiple service operators may be combined into a service script for task achievement.

Definition 3. *Given a set* Σ *of service operators, a* service script σ *is a partially-ordered multi-set over* Σ.

Consider a simplified version of the printing task discussed in the previous section. Given a file f.tar containing two gzipped files f1.ps.gz and f2.tex.gz, together with a LaTeX document f.tex. The document can be printed out using the service script shown in Figure 1. Each node in the script represents a service operator, and an operator o_1 has to be executed before another operator o_2 if there is an arc leading from o_1 into o_2. The shaded operators are optional.

An *instantiated service script* is one in which each service operator has been instantiated by a specific service. Not all service scripts are executable given the current system configuration.

Definition 4. *A service script is* sound *with respect to the current system configuration if there exists at least one instantiated service script such that the operating context for every service in the script is supported. That is, for each service* $\langle c, h, r, f \rangle$ *in the instantiated service script, the following conditions hold when all the preceding services have been completed.*

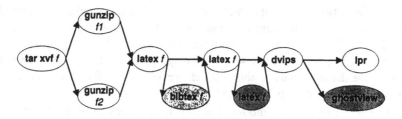

Fig. 1. A Sample Service Script

1. *Host h offers command c.*
2. *Resource r is available.*

We are now ready to define the service integration problem and its solution as follows.

Definition 5. *Given a task specified in terms of a goal G, a set Σ of service operators, a collection of hosts H, each of which offers a subset of services from Σ, and a collection of shared resources R. The solution to the service integration problem ⟨G, Σ, H, R⟩ is to find a service script σ such that the following conditions are satisfied.*

1. *The service script σ is sound.*
2. *Execution of the service script results in goal achievement.*
3. *(Optional) σ requires a minimal amount of resources among all scripts satisfying the first two conditions.*

The benefits of an intranet depend on the effectiveness of service integration that can be supported. While it is indeed possible to program suitable service scripts for specific tasks, it is desirable for the job to be automated. In what follows, a multi-agent framework is proposed as a solution for automatic service integration.

3 The Client-Agent-Server Model

The client-server architecture has provided the cornerstone for distributed computing. In the model, a client program requests a service from a server program by taking the following steps:

1. Create a socket connection with the server.
2. Send a service-request message to the server.
3. Wait for a response from the server.

The server response may indicate further information needed, requested action performed, or provide the data requested. Communications between the server and the client depend on the specific protocol used by the application. It is the responsibility of the programmer to ensure that the types of services provided match the types of requests. Unfortunately, there is a glaring gap between

152

complex informational requests and services provided by individual application servers. A complex client request often has to be satisfied by linking services provided by multiple servers. For example, the client request of "print f.tar" cannot be satisfied by any single server offering lpr alone. Furthermore, a client may not have the information about which server(s) can offer the desired functionality, thus making Step 1 above virtually impossible.

In the client-agent-server model, multiple agents work to bridge the gap due to the mismatch between client requests and server services. The role of agents is two-fold. On the one hand, agents help integrate computational services in order to satisfy the goals of complex tasks. On the other hand, agents help integrate data in order to generate useful information. Figure 2 shows the overall architecture of the proposed three-tier model. Before we describe in detail the

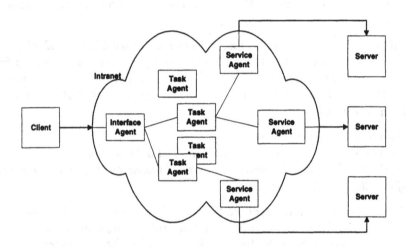

Fig. 2. The Client-Agent-Server Model

functionalities of the various agents, let us examine the information flow in this architecture. A client request is handled by an interface agent, who breaks down the problem into *independent* pieces for a team of task agents. Each task agent computes an appropriate service script for solving the specific sub-problem. The generated script is then handed over to a service agent, who allocates the appropriate resources to carry out the given script. As a result, a user is able to delegate tasks rather than manipulating the services directly. This framework enables the user to utilize with ease any of the networked data or computational services in accomplishing a specific task. Furthermore, the services fulfilling the user tasks can be tailored toward his/her individual needs.

Similar ideas have been explored in the domains of integrating concurrent engineering systems [6], and integrating multiple databases [19]. Client requests are matched up with information sources with the help of a facilitator or broker. Bradshaw et al. [2] proposed a generic agent architecture KAoS that supports reuse, interoperability, and extensibility. Cao and Shi also proposed a Common Agent Request Broker Architecture (CARBA) [3]. Both KAoS and CARBA follow the ideas from the CORBA distributed object architecture. The proposed model is unique in the following ways:

- The framework supports integration of *computational services* in addition to data from multiple servers.
- It avoids the bottleneck of mediating agents using a hierarchical approach, which will be described in more detail in the next section.

4   A Hierarchy of Agents

The community of agents in the proposed client-agent-server model should be designed with care. It is relatively easy to become another *sweep-under-the-rug* model by pushing the hard problems to an "unimportant" black box. This section starts by examining the different styles of software design, defines a hierarchy of abstraction spaces for different agents, and compares their features. The hierarchy of agents are described in Section 4.2.

4.1   Agent-Oriented Software Design

Agent-orientation is becoming a new paradigm in software design. While object-oriented programming has been dominant for the past decade, objects are *passive* in the sense that their actions are initiated by external stimulation, e.g. messages from other objects. In contrast, agents are active objects that can function autonomously and/or pro-actively. Designing software today follows a dramatically different model from designing monolithic computer programs. Several progressively more complex design models are introduced below.

The soloist model In the age of writing monolithic programs, the programmer is responsible for defining all the details of the desired computation. A skilled programmer is like a soloist who knows his instrument and the effects of performing any specific action on it. The programmer is able to carry out complicated computations in the same manner that a soloist is able to perform difficult passages of music.

The conductor model With multiple heterogeneous computers available, the programmer has to understand the features of each in order to coordinate the data or computation properly. A skilled programmer is like a conductor who knows all the instruments and the effects of performing actions on them. The programmer is able to solve complex tasks in the same manner that a conductor is able to direct a symphony orchestra performing a concert. There is little wonder that good programmers for distributed applications are hard to find.

The manager model To manage the increased complexity in large applications, the concept of agents has been introduced. A good manager should delegate tasks, be responsible for setting up reasonable performance goals, understand the characteristics of his team members, and maintain their autonomy. Likewise, a skilled programmer needs to organize her team of agents based on their features and functionalities. A programmer is able to accomplish complex tasks in the same manner that a manager is able to lead his team in meeting project goals. Instead of having to interact with an arbitrary number of agents, a hierarchical organization is used in the proposed model.

The market model For applications involving a large number of agents, but relatively little domain knowledge, the market model may be a good idea. The programmer is responsible for defining the basic architecture of individual agents as well as the protocols governing their interactions. The functionalities of each agent may be simple. Complex behavior of the multi-agent system emerges as dynamic interactions among its constituent agents.

4.2 Abstraction Layers for Multiple Agents

An important feature of the proposed multi-agent framework is its use of a hierarchy of abstraction spaces to manage complexity. The idea is based on *abstraction planning* [17] in which a solution to a goal is found in an abstract space, and the solution is used as a skeleton for a more detailed plan at a less abstract space. As is shown in Figure 3, an interface agent tries to solve a given task by identifying the appropriate team of task agents that should participate in the solution. Each task agent solves his problem in the space of service operators. A candidate service script is generated based on task-specific knowledge about the domain. The service agents attempt to instantiate the service script by allocating a service to each of its service operator. An advantage of this approach is that the interface (service) agents only need to work within the well-defined space of agents (services). Task agents may require varying levels of planning capabilities, depending on the specific task domains.

Interface agents Such an agent operates in the interface, as opposed to in the background or "back end" of an application. In our framework, each interface agent corresponds to a class of client requests, e.g. for a specific user or a specific task. The basic functionalities include:

– Accepting task specification from the user,
– Organizing the team of agents for the specified task,
– Presenting results in response to the task request,
– Logging personal information and user behavior,
– Conducting conversations with the user, and
– Offering user help pro-actively (at the right time).

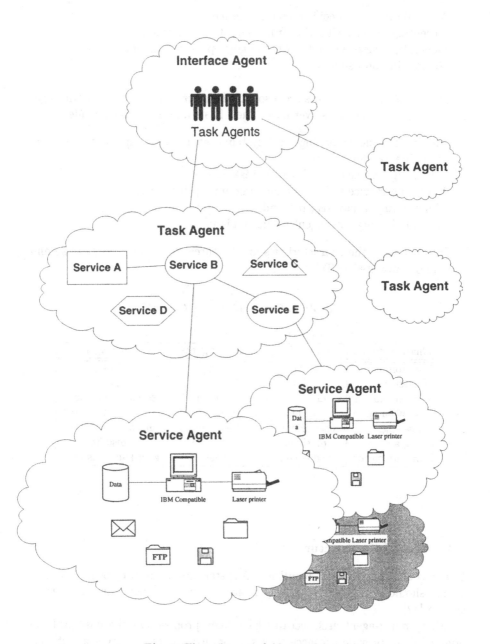

Fig. 3. Three Layers of Abstraction

Task agents Task agents act autonomously, as opposed to having a sequential conversation with the user. Their basic functionalities include:

- Maintaining task-specific domain knowledge,
- Accepting goal specification from the interface agents,
- Generating service script w.r.t. the goal specification, and
- Replanning on demand.

Service agents Service agents are also called *resource* agents. Each service agent corresponds to a specific server host. Their basic functionalities include:

- Monitoring and managing local system resources, e.g. application software or peripheral devices etc.,
- Accepting service script from the task agents,
- Executing service script by allocating appropriate services,
- Maintaining *service registry*, and
- Communicating with agent service registry.

In conclusion, the characteristics for the three classes of agents are summarized and contrasted in Table 1.

Table 1. Characteristics of Agents

Characteristics	Interface Agents	Task Agents	Service Agents
autonomous	Maybe	Yes	Yes
pro-active	Yes	No	No
problem solving	team formation	planning	service allocation
operation space	agents	service operators	services
knowledge	user-oriented	task-oriented	machine-oriented
life span	persistent	episodic	episodic
communication	user+agent	agent	agent+administrator

4.3 Agent Infrastructure

The Huhns-Singh Test for Agenthood: A system containing one or more reputed agents should change substantively if another reputed agent is added to the system [12].

Many multi-agent architectures have been proposed in the past [5, 4], but none of them provide the necessary support for agents operating at different levels of abstraction. To support the hierarchy of agents in this research, an object-oriented architecture called ARBIS (Agent Request Broker InfraStructure) is being developed. In particular, ARBIS is responsible for the following functions:

- Providing agent brokering/naming services,
- Creating and killing agent instances on demand,
- Sustaining life for active agents,
- Maintaining agent registry,
- Maintaining service operator registry,
- Managing user profiles, and
- Interfacing with the underlying communication protocols.

Just as CORBA is a standard for interoperability in heterogeneous computing environments [11, 9], ARBIS intends to provide a standard for interoperability for agents. In the current framework, agents communicate with each other and with ARBIS using a simplified version of KQML [10]. The goal is that any ARBIS-compliant agent can be easily incorporated into an existing multi-agent application.

5 Case Study: AutoPrint Agents

We have experimented with the proposed multi-agent service framework in the domain of intranet printing[13, 14]. Most of us have experienced problems such as printing out the source of a huge postscript file by accident, or fretting over the proper command sequence in preparing a document for printing. With the growth of multimedia applications, there is a greater proliferation of file formats in routine use. Consider a number of interconnected machines, each of which offers any number of services related to printing and file conversion. The experimental environment is as shown in Figure 4, and Table 2 summarizes the host configuration in terms of services registered at each machine.

The AutoPrint interface agent interacts with the users through dialog boxes such as the ones shown in Figure 5. One important principle in our design is that the interface agents should request minimal information from the user in order to simplify task specification. In general, the user only needs to interact with the agent via the dialog box on the left. The interface agent makes decisions about the default values for any unspecified fields as well as the advanced printing options based on statistics collected for each user. The (incompletely specified) print task is passed to AutoPrint task agent, which generates a service script using automatic planning provided by UCPOP [16]. The service scripts are reused when appropriate in an effort to reduce the overhead due to planning [13].

A sample mix of test files were created and the following experimental steps were repeated one thousand times.

1. Register a randomly selected subset of the services for each host.
2. Create a new print job request by randomly selecting a test file and a printer.

Table 3 summarizes the *average time* taken by script planning, service allocation, and service execution. The experiments showed that the AutoPrint agents are able to complete the print tasks successfully under a wide range of randomly

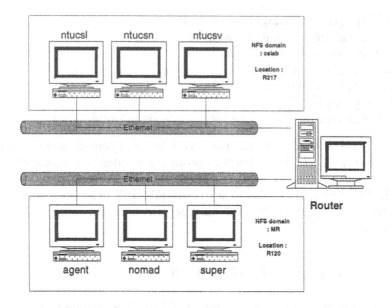

Fig. 4. Host Environment for AutoPrint Agents

Table 2. Host Configuration

(a) Hardware/Software Configuration

Machine	Hardware	OS	A	B	C	D	E	F	G	H
agent	Sparc 20	SunOS 4.1.4	√	√	√	√	√	√	√	
nomad	Sparc 5	SunOS 4.1.4		√	√	√	√	√	√	
super	Sparc 4	Solaris 2.5.1	√		√	√	√	√	√	
ntucsl	Sparc 10	SunOS 4.1.3		√			√	√		
ntucsn	Sparc 5	SunOS 4.1.3		√			√	√		
ntucsv	UltraSparc 1	Solaris 2.5.1		√	√	√	√	√		

(b) Registered Services

Code	Service Operator	Function
A	print2hp3	print postscript file to printer hp3
B	print2hp5	print postscript file to printer hp5
C	tex2dvi	convert tex file into dvi file
D	dvi2ps	convert dvi file into ps file
E	pdf2ps	convert pdf file into ps file
F	uncompress	uncompress .Z files
G	gunzip	uncompress .gz files
H	ucpop	partially-ordered planner

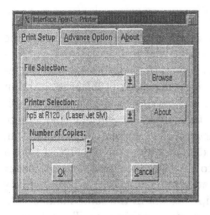

(a) Task Specification (b) Printing Options

Fig. 5. AutoPrint User Interface

Table 3. Experimental Results

File	Size (Bytes)	Planning	Allocation	Execution
test.tex	3214	29.494	3.799	15.041
test.tex.Z	1399	54.318	5.821	9.979
test.tex.gz	885	49.135	7.897	12.555
test.dvi	4004	24.776	0.951	8.033
test.dvi.Z	2339	40.017	4.470	5.267
test.dvi.gz	1633	38.142	3.657	6.417
test.ps	19847	26.951	0.641	0.621
test.ps.Z	11172	29.533	2.163	0.966
test.ps.gz	8385	33.484	3.798	1.084
test.pdf	7088	23.896	2.078	4.470
test.pdf.Z	8540	42.914	2.807	5.215
test.pdf.gz	5979	38.177	5.301	4.336

generated service configurations. A plan library can be used by the AutoPrint agents to reduce the planning time to about 10% of the original time. In addition, the agents are shown to be robust with respect to service break-downs [14].

6 Conclusion

This paper proposed a three-tier *clent-agent-server* architecture to bridge the gap between informational requests and services within a distributed environment. The multi-agent framework provides a powerful and flexible way to integrate arbitrary intranet services. The service integration problem is solved in a hierarchical fashion, with interface, task, and service agents working at different abstraction levels. Agents with user, task, or service-specific competence can be easily incorporated into the framework. The current implementation, which works under the Unix environment, demonstrates the viability of such a multi-agent approach. Work is underway to develop the *Agent Request Broker InfraStructure* for heterogeneous service platforms. The goal is a *plug-and-play* architecture for agents that supports multiple agents in the same manner that CORBA supports distributed objects. The interface problem is still pretty open at this point. Coordinating service scripts among multiple task agents calls for sophisticated inter-agent communication and negotiation schemes, especially if the agents cannot be assumed to be independent. This research has identified the need for personalized information services, and a *profile management* mechanism is being designed. For better cross-platform operation, we also plan to move from the current tcl/tk implementation to a browser-based user interface.

Acknowledgements

The author would like to thank Ming-Wei Jean and Bu-Jian Li for their implementations of the AutoPrint agents. Thanks also go to Toru Ishida, Soe-Tsyr Yuan, and Jieh Hsiang for their helpful comments. Discussions over the last two years among members of the agents project at National Taiwan University have helped shape the ideas presented in this paper. This research was supported in part by grants from the National Science Council of ROC under grant numbers NSC86-2745-E-002-007 and NSC87-2213-E-002-014, and in part by Tjing Ling Industrial Research Institute of National Taiwan University.

References

1. J. Bradshaw, editor. *Software Agents*. AAAI/MIT Press, Menlo Park, CA, 1996.
2. J. M. Bradshaw, S. Dutfield, P. Benoit, and J. D. Woolley. KAoS: Toward an industrial-strength generic agent architecture. In J.M. Bradshaw, editor, *Software Agents*. AAAI/MIT Press, Cambridge, MA, 1996.
3. H. Cao and Z. Shi. CARBA: Common agent request broker architecture. In T. Ishida, editor, *Proceedings of the 1998 Pacific Rim International Workshop on Multi-agents*, November 1998.

4. D. Chess, C. Grosof, B. Harrison, D. Levine, C. Parris, and G. Tsudik. Itinerant agents for mobile computing. In M.N. Huhns and M.P. Singh, editors, *Readings in Agents*, pages 267–282. Morgan Kaufmann, San Francisco, 1998.
5. P.R. Cohen, A. Cheyer, M. Wang, and S.C. Baeg. An open agent architecture. In M.N. Huhns and M.P. Singh, editors, *Readings in Agents*, pages 197–204. Morgan Kaufmann, San Francisco, 1998.
6. M.R. Cutkosky, R. Engelmore, R.E. Fikes, M.R. Genesereth, T.R. Gruber, W.S. Mark, J.M. Tenenbaum, and J.C. Weber. PACT: An experiment in integrating concurrent engineering systems. In M.N. Huhns and M.P. Singh, editors, *Readings in Agents*, pages 46–55. Morgan Kaufmann, San Francisco, 1998.
7. O. Etzioni, H. M. Levy, R. B. Segal, and C. A. Thekkath. Os agents: Using ai techniques in the operating systems environment. Technical Report 93-04-04, University of Washington, Seattle, August 1994.
8. O. Etzioni and D. Weld. A softbot-based interface to the internet. *CACM*, 37(7):72–76, July 1994. http://www.cs.washington.edu/research/softbots.
9. E. Evans and D. Rogers. Using java applets and corba for multi-user distributed applications. *IEEE Internet Computing*, 1(3):43–55, May-June 1997.
10. T. Finin, R. Fritzson, D. McKay, and R. McEntire. KQML as an agent communication language. In *The Proceedings of the Third International Conference on Information and Knowledge Management (CIKM'94)*. ACM Press, 1994.
11. Object Management Group. The common object request broker: Architecture and specification, revision 2.2. OMG 98-07-01, Object Management Group, February 1998. Also available at http://www.omg.org/corba/cortiiop.htm.
12. M.N. Huhns and M.R. Singh. Agents on the web. *IEEE Internet Computing*, 1(5):78–79, September/October 1997.
13. M.W. Jean. Intelligent printer agents for intranet environments. Master's thesis, National Taiwan University, Computer Science and Information Engineering, June 1997.
14. B.J. Li. Task agents and service sharing in local area networks. Master's thesis, National Taiwan University, Computer Science and Information Engineering, June 1998.
15. H. Lieberman. Autonomous interface agents. In *CHI'97*. ACM, 1997. http://www.acm.org/sigchi/chi97/proceedings/paper/hl.html.
16. J. S. Penberthy and D. Weld. UCPOP: A sound, complete, partial order planner for adl. In *Proceedings of KR-92*, pages 103–114, October 1992.
17. E.D. Sacerdoti. Planning in a hierarchy of abstraction spaces. *Artificial Intelligence*, 5:115–135, 1974.
18. K. P. Sycara. Multiagent systems. *AI Magazine*, 19(2):79–92, 1998.
19. G. Wiederhold. Mediators in the architecture of future information systems. In M.N. Huhns and M.P. Singh, editors, *Readings in Agents*, pages 185–196. Morgan Kaufmann, San Francisco, 1998.

Secure Agent-Mediated Mobile Payment

X.F. Wang[1], K. Y. Lam[1] and X.Yi[2]

[1]Department of Information System and Computer Science
Faculty of Science, National University of Singapore
Lower Kent Ridge Road, SINGAPORE 119260
E-mail:{wangxiao,lamky}@iscs.nus.edu.sg
and
[2]School of Information Science
Japan Advanced Institute of Science and Technology, Japan
E-mail: xyi@jaist.ac.jp

Abstract. *Mobile devices usually have too limited and expensive communication capacity to meet consistent connection requirement of online payment protocols such as SET. Mobile agent approaches have been proposed by SET/A and SET/A+ to solve the problem. In this paper, we propose a new secure agent-mediated payment scheme which provides simpler and more compatible solution. Its particular features lie at: (1) the payment procedure is combined with brokering stage during the internet trading. (2) there is no modification to the SET protocol which results in 100 percent compatibility. Moreover, system simplification can be achieved in the proposed scheme without any sacrifice of security.*

1 Introduction

Wireless networks, especially cellular ones, have known explosive growth over the last few years, reflecting a world in which it's important to be active regardless of the location. As the Internet becomes more and more important for business transactions, it is natural that wireless technology be used to connect to this global network. The possibility of having all the resources and benefits offered on the Internet available while being away from home or office is particularly attractive. This provides great flexibility and convenience to facilitate Internet trading under mobile computing scenario.

However, most mobile devices have limited communication capacity. For example, terrestrial wireless network protocols like GSM or satellite-based systems like IRIDIUM[1], typically offer bandwidths in the range of 2,400bps to 9,600bps. Even this kind of connectivity is suffered from low quality with high error rates. On the other hand, using a cellular phone or a satellite-based connection is generally more expensive than through a traditional telephone carrier or ISDN. What is more, the poor connectivity usually raises the costs even farther. These factors make mobile devices difficult to handle long, connected sessions and transferring large amounts of data which, however, is required in SET payment protocol.

The SET protocol is developed by VISA and MasterCard to secure payment card transaction over open networks. It provides important properties like authentication of the participants, non-repudiation, data integrity and confidentiality. Each player knows what is strictly necessary to play its role, for example, the selling company never knows the buyer's credit card information, and the financial institution authorizing the transaction is not aware of the details of the purchase, like the nature of the products, quantities, etc. This feature effectively guarantees the security during credit card payment procedure.

SET protocol, in particular its purchasing phase, is intended for users connected to the Internet during an entire transaction. Just as mentioned above, this requirement can not be easily satisfied in mobile computing environment. In an error-prone environment like GSM or any other used for mobile communications, a user shopping on the Internet and trying to pay using SET compliant software may experience several connectivity problems during the payment operation. Even with recovery mechanisms, it's easy to imagine how frustrating it can be for the cardholder to deal with a series of connection interruptions, let alone the accumulation of state information both in the wallet and in the merchant's server, in order to let the transaction proceed. Even if it eventually succeeds, its overall cost has probably been too high.

To worm out of the dilemma, Artur Romao and Miguel Mira da Silva come up with SET/A[3] which takes up mobile agent paradigm to relieve mobile devices of heavy communication and computational burden. This results in the possibility of executing the transaction while user device is off-line. However, SET/A stakes its security on the tamper-proof environment. It's our opinion that this will complicate the realization and increase the its expense as well.

We proposed a revision to the SET/A, which is called SET/A+. The protocol can successfully solve the problem with the expense of a little modification on the SET protocol. In this paper, we try to provide a solution from a totally new angle. From mobile user's point of view, payment is only one stage of internet trading, and the successor to the commercial information brokering and negotiation. Since mobile agents are well-known as the best medium to conduct internet trading under mobile computing scenario, it is natural and beneficial to combine payment with agent-based brokering and negotiation stages. We propose a new secure agent-mediated payment scheme based on this idea which results in simple system architecture and full compatibility to the SET.

The rest of the paper is organized as follows. Section 2 introduces the SET purchase request transaction and scheme provided by SET/A. In section 3, we describe our agent-mediated mobile payment scheme. Section 3 makes an analysis and evaluation to the security and performance of proposed scheme. Conclusion will be drawn in the last section.

2 SET Purchase Request Transaction and SET/A

SET defines a variety of transaction protocols that use cryptographic technology to securely conduct electronic commerce. These transactions include cardholder registration, merchant registration, purchase request, payment authorization and payment capture. Since most of cardholder(user)'s involvements occur in the purchase request phase, we will give it a brief introduction first.

The major characters involved in purchase request transaction are: cardholder(C), merchant(M) and payment gateway(PG). The payment gateway is a device operated by a financial institution with which the merchant established an account for processing payments with the brand used by the cardholder. Each of these characters possesses two kinds of certificates, one for key-exchange (whose public key is contained in certificate C_k), which is used for encrypting and decrypting operations; the other for creation and verification of digital signatures(its public keys are stored in certificate C_s).

The outline of purchase request transaction is as follows[2]:

Step 1: After cardholder has completed browsing, selection and ordering, he makes a decision on purchase by sending merchant an approved order form including the description of the service of the services or the quantities of the goods, the terms of the order, and the brand of the credit card that will be used for payment.

Step 2: When the merchant receives the request, it assigns a unique transaction identifier to the message. It then transmits its own signature certificate $C_s(M)$ and payment gateway's key-exchange certificate $C_k(PG)$ that correspond to the payment card brand indicated by the cardholder, along with the transaction identifier to the cardholder.

Step 3: The cardholder software verifies the merchant and gateway certificates by traversing the trust chain to the root key, then holds these certificates to use later during the ordering process. After that, it continues to create the order information(OI) and payment instruction(PI). The former contains control information, card brand, bank identification and a digest of the order description. The latter is composed by the amount of the transaction, the card account number and expiration date, instructions for instalment payments(if that's the case) and a couple of secret values to prevent guessing and dictionary attacks on the data. The cardholder software dually signs on the OI and PI, and then generates a random symmetric encryption key and uses it to encrypt the dual signed PI. Next the software encrypts the cardholder account number as well as the random symmetric key used to encrypt the PI into a digital envelope using the payment gateway's key-exchange key. Finally, cardholder transmits a message consisting of the OI and PI to the merchant.

Step 4: The merchant verifies the cardholder certificate and the dual signature on the OI. The order is then processed and the digital envelope is forwarded to the payment gateway for authentication. After that, the merchant software generates and digitally signs a purchase response message which is passed to the cardholder along with merchant's signature certificate. If the authorization response indicates that the transaction was approved, the merchant will deliver the goods or perform the services indicated in the order.

Step 5: When the cardholder receives the purchase response message from the merchant, it verifies the merchant signature certificate by traversing the trust chain to the root key. It uses the merchant public signature key to check the merchant digital signature. Finally, it takes some action based on the contents of the response message, such as displaying message to the cardholder or updating a database with the status of the order.

Following figure shows the process:

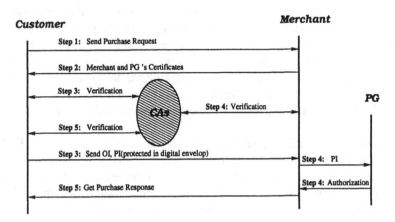

Fig. 1. SET Purchase Request Transaction

The software responsible for the cardholder's side of the protocol manages a data structure called a digital wallet[3], where sensitive data like certificates, private keys and payment card information are kept, usually in encrypted files.

SET requires cardholder to connect to the Internet during the purchase request transaction. This is very costly under low bandwidth, error-prone and high cost mobile computing scenario. The problem is exacerbated for the online retail commerce. For example, suppose a mobile cardholder wants to buy an umbrella. He must connect to the Internet through his wireless device first, and then, send out his purchase requirements to the potential retailer. After that, he has to wait for the vendor's certificates to compose his OI and PI. All these information will be returned to vendor's server. Even during the vendor processes information with the PG and authenticates signatures to CAs, cardholder is still required to be online to monitor vendor's reply. Thus, when cardholder finally completes the transaction, he may sadly find that the communication expense to conduct transaction even exceeds the price of the umbrella!

A solution to this problem is to take up some kinds of asynchronous mode of operation, in which the cardholder can send the request, disconnect and later re-connect to receive the response from the merchant. The idea brings in the mobile agent based SET,i.e. SET/A[3].

SET/A is meant to implement the purchase request phase of SET using mobile agent. A mobile agent can be defined as a software, owned by a user, capable of migrating from one computer to another, to execute a set of tasks on behalf of its owner. Mobile agents are said to be autonomous, in the sense that they can make their own decisions while away from their original hosts. This implies that a mobile agent is not just a piece of data being transferred between systems, but also carries some logic and state, which enables it to perform parts of its tasks in one system, migrate to another and continue its work there.

In the SET/A, after cardholder chooses a merchant and builds a request with the same elements as in the original SET request, he will send out a payment agent to merchant server with all the necessary materials. The agent will conduct step 2 to step 5 of SET request transaction on merchant's machine, including composing OI, PI and dual signatures, generating random symmetric keys and digital envelop, and verifying merchant's signatures and certificates. Finally, the agent will bring merchant's purchase response message back to the cardholder's computer.

It is obvious that SET/A provides effective support to performing SET in mobile environment. During the transaction, cardholder only needs to connect to the Internet twice, one for sending agent out, the other for accepting the agent back. The connectivity is kept to minimal and the purchase request procedure is also benefited by the local interaction(most of communication will occur within the merchant's host). Mobile cardholder therefore can expect low expense and high efficiency services from the new protocol.

The problems, however, come from security concern. To execute the purchase request transaction, payment agent has to bring confidential materials like digital wallet with it. What is more, a random symmetric key used to encrypt PI will be generated in merchant host. The divulgement of any of these confidential information will cause disaster and give edge to the malicious breeders. For the time being, there is no effective way to protect mobile codes and data from the scaning of the hosts in which they are executed. Thus, it is a great risk to let mobile agents run with confidential data in malicious environments. Protective measures SET/A suggested are to make use of tamper-proof environment[4] or a secure coprocessor[5]. Nevertheless, all these technologies need further development and expense is high. Therefore, an improvement is needed to make SET/A applicable.

3 Secure Agent-Mediated Mobile Payment Scheme

In this section we introduce our scheme to conduct SET in mobile computing environment. Different from traditional approaches to the payment protocol, we suggest a new angle to consider the problem, that is regarding payment as a part of general marketing model rather than a separated process. The advantage of such approach lies in its practicability. In real world, no one starts payment in the isolated context. The payment is only the successor to the other commercial activities.

3.1 Consumer Buying Behaviour Model in Mobile Environment

Consumer Buying Behavior (CBB) marketing research builds descriptive theories and models for analyzing consumers' actions and decisions involved in buying and using goods and services[6]. It divides the purchase procedure into six stages:

1. Need Identification. This stage characterizes the consumer becoming aware of some unmet need.
2. Product Brokering. This stage comprises the retrieval of information to help determine what to buy.
3. Merchant Brokering. This stage combines the "consideration set" from the previous stage with merchant-specific information to help determine who to buy from.
4. Negotiation. This stage is about how to determine the terms of the transaction.
5. Purchase and Delivery. This stage concerns the payment for and delivery of the product.
6. Service and Evaluation. This post-purchase stage involves product service, customer service, and an evaluation of the satisfaction of the overall buying experience and decision.

Obviously, the payment (purchase and delivery stage) is the subsequence of brokering and/or negotiation behaviors. In real world, most of commercial payments come from previous actions on the information gathering and negotiation. For instance, a buyer must first spend time to find the retailer selling umbrella and settle down the price issue with him. Then, he can pay the money for the purchase. Under mobile computing scenario, similarly, the payment has inevitable relation to its foregoing commercial activities.

It's well-known that mobile agents can provide better support for mobile clients. In the low-bandwidth, error-prone, expensive connectivity and limited local processing capacity environment, agents have advantage to conduct asynchronous interaction, remote searching and filtering, etc.[7],. In Internet trading, sending trading agent out and waiting for product information it brings back are much more attractive and efficient than traditional brokering scheme such as spending long time to retrieve online catalogs. Thus it is natural to take mobile agent as the best candidate to carry out CBB model in mobile computing, especially for the brokering and negotiation stages. Remember the person interested in umbrella, let us consider his behavior before the payment. Obviously, he must know first where to buy the item and the price. Under the mobile environment, using wireless channel to browse online catalogue is a crazy idea since the expense will be too high to be reasonable for the umbrella. However, if the person take mobile agent as the broker and negotiator, he just needs to send agents out and wait for results. All the process can be carried out in asychronous way. Therefore, mobile agent is the best soluation to get information in this case. In fact, agent application in mobile computing has been a major research topics for long and practical product is expected soon.

Once agent-based brokering and negotiation scheme is taken, mobile payment transaction can be effectively improved by assigning partial payment tasks to the information gathering and negotiation agent(INA). Our scheme is to let INA execute step 1,2,3 of original SET purchase request transaction and payment agent(PA) deal with the step 4,5. So the security features of SET can be fully preserved while the connectivity requirements are minimized.

The new problems brought in by the proposed scheme are how to guarantee the security of INAs. We have proposed several models to protect information gathering agent and negotiation agent from malicious hosts under Internet trading scenario[8][9]. All these methods can be applied to mobile computing. Since the details of these scheme are beyond the scope of payment, we will not discuss them further now.

3.2 Purchase Request Procedure

Since we consider the payment from cardholder's entire commercial behaviors, the purchase request of proposed scheme starts from brokering stages rather than purchase and delivery stage. Our purpose is, by assigning INAs some extra payment tasks, to reduce the connectivities needed during the trading procedure. In view of that we just use agent to execute SET, the protocol itself is kept unchanged. The procedure is described below.

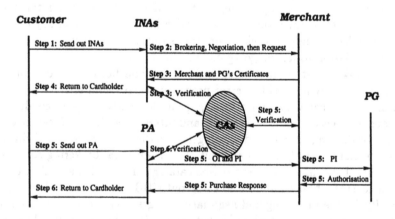

Fig. 2. Secure Agent-mediated SET Purchase Request Transaction

Step 1: A cardholder, with intention of purchase, sends INA out to conduct brokering and negotiation. The INA must have cardholder's profile and understand about his requirement and preference.

Step 2: The INA mobiles through the online merchants, gathers commercial information and negotiates over transaction terms with them to make comparison. Once potential vendor is selected, the INA composes a request with the same elements as indicated in step 1 of original SET and sends it to the merchant.

Step 3: The merchant responses to the request with

$$C_s(M), C_k(PG), I_t, M_s(NegotiationResult) \tag{1}$$

where I_t is the unique transaction identifier assigned by the merchant and M_s is the secret key of the merchant. The INA then verifies the certificates by traversing the trust chain to the root key to get the following certificates chain:

$$CertChain_y(X) = CA_1(Cert_y(X)) \| CA_2(Cert_{CA_1}) \| \tag{2}$$
$$\cdots \| CA_r(Cert_{CA_{r-1}}) \| CA_r(Cert_{CA_r})$$

Where entity X's certificate $(Cert_y(X))$ is ensured by the certificate authority CA_1, CA_1's certificate $(Cert_{CA_1})$ is ensured by CA_2, $\cdots$, CA_r's certificate $(Cert_{CA_r})$ is ensured by its own public key, which is the root key and is known to all participants. X can be replaced by M or PG and y by s or k respectively. After that, the INA finishes all the trading procedure and is ready to return to cardholder's computer.

Step 4: The cardholder connects to the Internet and takes in the INA. As to how to take in the INA, one possible approach is to use a mechanism similar to the one used by cellular phone operators to deliver SMS messages when the user re-connects.

Using the root key, the cardholder's software checks the validity of the $CertChain_s(M)$ and $CertChain_k(PG)$.

If no problem is found, on basis of the negotiation result, local software will continue to compose OI, PI and symmetric key etc., just as described in step 3 of original SET. All the information will be furnished to a payment agent(PA) to finish the rest of payment procedure.

Step 5: The cardholder gets access to the Internet again and send the PA to the merchant server. The merchant fulfils the step 4 of the SET purchase request, sending a signed response along with its signature certificate $C_s(M)$ to the PA. PA verify the signature to hierarchical CAs until the root key is found. A certificate chain is preserved. Then, the PA waits in the merchant server until the cardholder online again.

Step 6: The cardholder connects to the Internet and accepts the PA. Then on basis of the certificate chain, the PA verifies the $C_s(M)$ and checks the signature of the merchant. If no problem is found, the cardholder's software will take appropriate actions based on the content of purchase response.

Remember the example in the section 2. If the mobile cardholder takes the proposed protocol to buy an umbrella, the story starts from the information brokering stage. In this case, the cardholder has no knowledge about the umbrella sellers and thus he connects to the Internet to send out INAs to look for such retailers. After that, the cardholer can disconnect from the Internet. The INAs autonomously gather retailer information from online catalogues to locate potential vendors. After negotiation, the INAs select the optimal umbrella seller and obtain his certificates. The validation of these information the seller provided can be verified by the agents through CAs. Once the mobile user appears online again, the INAs bring back all the information to his mobile devices. In the offline state, the cardholer composes OI, PI and symmetric key. A PA is sent to the selected retailer with all these protected confidential data. The PA then completes the rest of payment steps and returns to the cardholer's device once he connects to the Internet again. Therefore, during the whole trading process, the cardholder needs only four connectivities to cover the brokering, negotiation and payment stages of CBB model.

4 Analysis and Evaluation

The purpose of our research is trying to improve SET to meet requirements of mobile computing while preserve its security features. So security and performance will be our focus. In this section we will discuss the advantages of the proposed scheme from these two aspects and point out some potential problems.

4.1 Security Issues

In SET/A, mobile agent has to compose OI, PI and generate random symmetric key in merchant server. This is very risky action, because agent need brings electronic wallet to the foreign host. Whereas, up to now, there is no effective way to protect mobile agent from malicious hosts. If any confidential information in the wallet or the symmetric key is leaked out, cardholder will get into great trouble and be vulnerable to attacks. Although SET/A tries to rely on the tamper-proof hardware to securely execute agent codes, this solution is not only expensive and premature, but far from practice, because even provided trusted environment, some information, such as secret key, is still too confidential to be brought outside of cardholder's control.

By comparison, the proposed scheme provides a more secure alternative. In the scheme, all the confidential actions such as signing, authentication, key generation and encryption are performed in cardholder's computer. The only exception is that certificate authentications are carried out by agent in the remote server. However, cardholder still takes control of these actions by checking the certificate chains which can not be forged. Therefore, there is no possibility of divulgement of any confidential information in the scheme, and the security features of original SET are fully preserved.

The problems, however, come from another aspect. Since the payment procedure is merged into brokering and negotiation stages in the proposed scheme, thus their security problems will influence the payment transaction to some extent. For example, in the scheme, INAs is in charge of issuing initial request, so it is possible that the agents are forced to start payment procedure with malicious merchants and directly sent back after that. This can be avoided by well designed security mechanism for agent-mediated brokering and negotiation. We have proposed "detection and investigation" schemes to protect INAs from malicious hosts. To start trading, mobile users must connect to an online Agent Service Center(ASC) which can provide security service to users' mobile agents. During the trading procedure, all the servers INAs passed by must preserve some nonrepudiation evidence from agents' body. After agents return, the ASC checks the validation and integration of the INAs. Once the agents are suspected to be tampered with, an investigation process will be activated to dig out the malicious breeders through the nonrepudiation chain. The detailed discussion on above schemes can be found in [8][9].

4.2 Performance and Practicability

The main obstacle to mobile payment application is limited, error-prone and expensive communication capacity of mobile devices. How to reduce communication requirements becomes the crux of adapting SET to mobile environment. SET/A proposes a two-time connectivity scheme, that is, sending agent out for the purchase request transaction and then accepting the return agent. This effectively minimizes the communication expense during the transaction.

In the proposed scheme, we bring agent-mediated payment to a much bigger scenario where the purchase request transaction is combined with other CBB stages, i.e. brokering and negotiation. Although, seemingly there will be four connectivities needed for completion of a SET purchase request, since the first two connectivities are also the requirements of brokering and negotiation, it is only the rest two connectivities that are specialized for payment purpose. On the other hand, though cardholder can choose various ways of electronic brokering and negotiation such as retrieval of online catalogs and bidding in the Internet auction room, it is obvious that mobile agent will be the optimal medium for all these activities. In fact, the limited communication capacity usually makes agent-mediated approach as the only practical and economic solution to the electronic commerce in mobile computing environment. Therefore, from the viewpoint of general consumer buying behavior, the proposed scheme also realizes the optimization of communication requirements under mobile computing scenario.

In addition, the proposed scheme is fully compatible to the original SET. From merchant's point of view, he need not make any modification to his SET related software except providing an agent execution environment which, actually, is also required in brokering and negotiation stages. This feature enables merchant to provide uniform payment service to both online and mobile users with little extra expense, thus improves the practicability of proposed scheme.

4.3 Limitations

The major limitation of the proposed scheme comes from the interruption of SET purchase request transaction. After INAs issued initial purchase request, they have to wait for the cardholder returning to the Internet to continue the rest of the transaction steps. Since the cardholder may be disconnected for an arbitrary long period after sending the INAs out, the whole transaction would be significantly delayed.

To deal with the above problem, a further improvement of the proposed scheme can be achieved through compromising the duties of INAs and PA. Instead of starting purchase request transaction, the INAs simply ask the retailers for the certificates of their PG for the cardholer's card brand. The PA, equiped with all the protected confidential data i.e., OI, PI and symmetric key, mobiles to the retailer's server to start the purchase request transaction. Thus, the whole transaction can be executed continuously and securely.

Another problem of the proposed scheme is unable to provide optimal payment service to the cardholders who get the product information from the resources other than Internet. For example, they may refer to the newspaper, CD and other advertising resources for production information. In these cases, the proposed scheme needs up to four connectivities specialized for the purchase request. We believe, however, since the Internet is becoming the backbone of commercial information exchange, it is also for cardholder's benefit to make full use of the web-attached feature of mobile devices to conduct brokering and negotiation process.

5 Conclusion

With the combination of the credit card payment method with an elaborate security protocol, SET is expected to gain wide acceptance as a secure Internet payment protocol. It is aimed at providing the necessary security through the authentication of the participants in a commercial transaction, as well as confidentiality of financial information. The fact that SET was developed by the major credit card companies is yet another factor contributing to its acceptance [3].

To guaratee the security, SET adopts very complex transaction procedure. Under mobile environment which is characted by low bandwidth and high connection costs, this becomes an obstacle for cardholders to conduct Internet payment. An attempt to solve this problem is suggested by SET/A which tries to make use of mobile agents to execute the transaction. However, its scheme to protect confidential data during the transaction is still far from practice.

In this paper, we discussed an alternative to the SET/A. Based on mobile agent technologies, we propose a scheme which fully preserves the security features of SET while realizes the communication optimization objective of SET/A. The features of the proposed scheme lie in:(1) the payment procedure is combined with brokering and negotiation stage during the Internet trading.(2) there is no modification to the SET protocol which results in 100 percent compatibility.

Payment is an important stage of CBB model and also a field which can be promoted by mobile agent. In fact, consumer buying behavior under Internet trading scenario can be greatly facilitated by agent technologies. We are working towards establishing an integrate, agent-mediated secure Internet trading architecture based on CBB model and some prototype systems are expected soon.

References

1. IRIDUM LLC.The IRIDIUM System.http://www.iridium.com/systm/systm.html
2. VISA INTERNATIONAL, and MASTERCARD INTERNATIONAL. Secure Electronic Transaction (SET) Specification. Version 1.0, May 1997.
3. Artur Romao and Miguel Mira da Silva. An Agent-Based Secure Internet Payment System for Mobile Computing, Trends in Distributed Systems'98: Electronic Commerce, Hamburg, Germany, LNCS, Springer-Verlag, June 3-5 1998
4. U.Wilhelm, and X. Defago. Objets Proteges Cryptographiquement. In Proceedings of RenPar'9, Lausanne, Switzerland, May 1997.
5. B.Yee. A Sanctuary for Mobile Agents. In Proceedings of the DARPA Workshop on Foundations for Secure Mobile Code, Monterey CA, USA, March 1997.
6. R.Guttman and P.Maes. Agent-mediated Integrative Negotiation for Retail Electronic Commerce. Proceedings of the Workshop on Agent Mediated Electronic Trading(AMET'98). May1998.
7. Colin G.Harrison, David M.Chess and Aaron Kershenbaurn. Mobile Agents: Are they a good idea? IBM Research Report.
8. X.F.Wang, X.Yi, K.Y.Lam and E.Okamoto. Secure Information Gathering Agent for Internet Trading. 11th Australian Joint Conference on Artificial Intelligence(AI'98), Brisbane, Australia, 13 July 1998, Springer-Verlag Lecture Notes in Artivicial Intelligence.
9. X.Yi, X.F.Wang and K.Y.Lam. "A Secure Auction-like Negotiation Protocol for Agent-based Internet Trading", 17th IEEE Symposium on Reliable Distributed Systems. Purdue University 20-23 October 1998.

A Secure Communication Scheme
for
Multiagent Systems

Hongxue Wang[1], Vijay Varadharajan[2], Yan Zhang[2]

[1] Department of Computer Science
Australian National University
Canberra, ACT 0200, AUSTRALIA
hongxue@cs.anu.edu.au

[2] School of Computing and Information Technology
University of Western Sydney, Nepean
Kingswood, NSW 2747, AUSTRALIA
{vijay, yan}@cit.nepean.uws.edu.au

Abstract. In this paper we present a secure communication scheme for multiagent systems. First, we briefly introduce an architecture for multiagent systems, and discuss security problems with such systems. We then present the communication scheme in detail, including the mathematical principle and the cryptographic protocol. To further demonstrate how our communication scheme works, we present an example with which we show how a piece of plaintext message is encrypted and decrypted between two agents within a multiagent system in accordance with our communication scheme. In evaluation we show that, compared with other encryption systems such as RSA, our scheme is more simple and suitable for implementation on computers used in multiagent systems. Importantly, it remains as secure as other systems as long as the plaintext is not too short. In conclusion, we discuss issues about the management of secret keys and the suitability of the communication scheme.

Key words: Multiagent, cooperation, communication, security,
encryption, cryptography

1   Introduction

The development of modern technology often brings positive impacts on the society. In this century, people have been benefited a lot from a variety of modern science and technology. Unfortunately however, modern technology also can be harmful to the society if it is misused, such as in the case of nuclear science. The rapid development and wide application of computer systems, networked ones in particular, are undoubtedly revolutionising our industries, educations, scientific research and even our everyday life, by offering us a convenient way to access information and other computing resources. On the other hand however, networked computer systems also give amateurs, crackers and career criminals similar convenience to access and misuse resources on computer networks. To protect our networked computer systems from unauthorised access, attacks of these malicious people in particular has therefore become a serious issue [1].

Amongst various computer systems, multiagent ones are of important kind, where more than one agent acts in a system. During the last few years, multi-agent systems have become increasingly popular not only in theory, but also in practice [7, 3, 6]. Particularly, the wide application of the Internet makes multi-agent systems more famous and important.

1.1 Multiagent systems

As implied by its name, a multiagent system is such an agent system in which at least two agents exist and act together in the system. According to the generic theory of intelligent systems proposed in [10, 12, 15], an agent system is generally made of some agents and their worlds, including necessary tools, resources and other entities in the designated environment that are relevant to the tasks that the agents should carry out [13]. Each of these agents must be equipped with a model of its world from which necessary knowledge or information for the agent to act can be accessed or acquired. Fig. 1 is an illustration of the architecture of such multiagent systems.

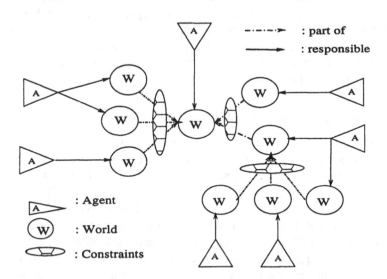

Fig. 1. An illustration of a multiagent system

In Fig. 1, there are nine sub worlds which are hierarchically organised. Other relationships amongst sub worlds and other entities are formalised as constraints. In such a multiagent system, an agent could be responsible for fulfilling duties in some different worlds. From this point of view, many human organisations such as companies, governments and universities can be considered as (multi)agent systems where each human involved is an agent. Examples of artificial agent systems are teams of robots that can play football or do other fancy jobs [8], and information retrieval agents over the World Wide Web [14].

1.2 Communication and its importance

Though multiagent systems, such as BDI-based systems proposed in [3, 4], may have different architectures from what is shown in Fig. 1, one important feature that is common to different multiagent systems is cooperation and coordination among the agents.

Cooperations and coordinations can be implemented at different levels. There have been some researches on mechanisms for agents to cooperate without exploiting communication, such as [9] on social structures for agents' cooperation, [11] on exploration and adaptation of other agents for better cooperation. We consider those cooperations without communication as lower-level cooperations, because they are mainly based on instinct or nature.

To achieve higher-level cooperations, the agents need to communicate with each other to allocate tasks, inform their states, pass results and so forth. All these information can be composed as messages. Communication between agents is to pass such messages through available communication channels. Without communication, it would be impossible for the agents to conduct higher level cooperations with each other, even though such an agent system could still be usable. Examples are some multiple-CPU machines in which CPUs' activities are scheduled within specific timeslots so that the CPUs can purposely act together without complex communications.

1.3 Security problems and strategies of defence

As with other computer-based systems, there are some security issues associated with multiagent systems [5], with respect to secrecy, integrity and availability. Amongst many of these security issues, our first concern is to ensure that all the agents within a system can communicate with each other securely. We usually mean two things by saying "communicate with each other securely". First of all, genuine communication parties must be able to authenticate one another, which raises the issue of authenticity. Secondly, communication amongst genuine parties must not be bugged by other unauthorised parties, which attracts concerns about secrecy. That is, how to ensure that messages can only be sent by desired agents, and can only be accessed and understood by designated parties. If these cannot be assured, amateurs, crackers and career criminals will be able to access and misuse the messages, which could lead to some fatal damage to the system and the interests of the agents.

As usual, there are mainly four types of attacks on multiagent systems, interruption, interception, modification and fabrication [2]. To protect a multiagent system from these attacks, one may utilise several strategies, such as encryption, physical protection, security policies and so forth. Amongst different security strategies, encryption has been recognised to be the central to secure communications amongst the agents within multiagent systems. That is, we need an encryption algorithm in our secure communication scheme for multiagent systems. In other words, a plaintext message P needs to be encrypted into a ciphertext with secret key(s) K_e, using some encryption algorithm E such that $C = E(K_e, P)$. The agent who wants to send the message out to other agent(s) actually sends encrypted message C instead of the plaintext P. The receiver of the C can only reveal the plaintext message after decrypting C using appropriate secret key(s) K_d and algorithm D, such that $P = D(K_d, C)$.

2 The secure communication scheme

There are two kinds of communications within a multiagent system: peer to peer communication as illustrated in Fig. 2, in which only two agents are involved in a communication, and broadcasting communication as illustrated in Fig. 3, in which the same messages are sent to more than one agent. In broadcasting, there are two ways to use the secret keys. One is to allow all agents involved in a broadcast share the same secret keys. The other is to have each pair of communication parties use different secret keys. In either case, however, a broadcasting communication can be considered as several peer to peer communications, although in a broadcasting case key management appears to be more difficult[1]. Therefore, in this paper we are concerned with only peer to peer communications, without any loss of generality.

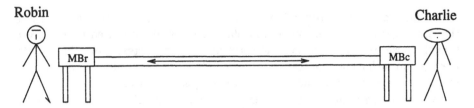

Fig. 2. A peer-to-peer communication channel

In our secure communication scheme, any two agents are assumed to be able to communicate with one another in the following simple way:

---

[1] In a situation where all agents involved share the same secret keys, it would be difficult to tell who is responsible for a leakage of secret keys once that happens; In the other situation, where each pair of agents have different secret keys from the others, key production, distribution and management will become a heavy and essential task for the responsible agents.

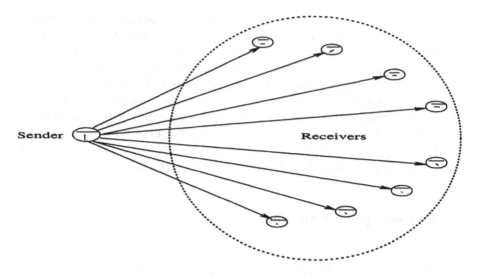

Fig. 3. Broadcast communication channels

There is an existing communication channel in which a message can be passed in either direction. To each side of the channel, there is a mailbox attached for the corresponding agent, as shown in Fig. 2.

Either of the agents can send a message, either encrypted or plain one, to the other by simply putting it into the communication channel, it then will get into the mailbox at the other end automatically. The agent at the other end can retrieve the message from the mailbox, and manage to read it.

As mentioned in Introduction, to secure such communication is to ensure that messages must not be sighted in plain form by unauthorised parties, even though those parties might get the corresponding ciphertexts. In other words, messages in such a communication must be well encrypted. This gives a complete picture of our secure communication system, as shown in Fig. 4.

As can be seen from Fig. 4, encryption and decryption process is needed respectively by the sender and the receiver within a communication.

2.1 The mathematical principle of the encryption

The mathematical principle for encryption and decryption used in our secure communication scheme can be simply described as follows.

Suppose each agent involved in a peer-to-peer communication is given a secret code file. These secret code files contain many random codes such as 4587, 6459 and so on. what is required for such a communication is to let two agents involved in a peer-to-peer communication have and use the same secret code file at each time of communication, and know where to start to use the secret codes in the

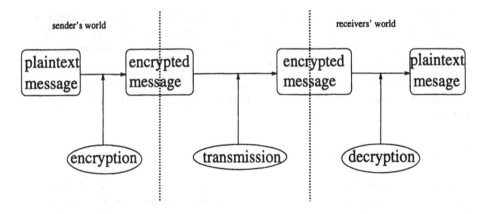

Fig. 4. A complete picture of the communication system

file. Under such condition, encryption and decryption process can be explained with the following example.

Suppose both agent A and B have the required secret code book, and they know they should use the secret codes from the first on a specific page such as page 88, say it is 7725, in the next communication. Now agent A wants to send message 4679 to B. What A does is to do $4679 - 7725$ discarding any borrow. In this case, the result is 7954, which is the encrypted code of 4679. On the receiver side, B does 7954+7725, discarding any carry. In this case, the result is 4679, it is thus decrypted.

These arithmetic operations can also be done directly on binary numbers. Suppose we want to use 2^N as the base to carry out the above operations on X and Y. One can simply do $X \oplus Y \bmod 2^N$ to get either the ciphertext if X is initially a plaintext, or the plaintext if X initially a ciphertext.

2.2 On the sender side

The sending process on the sender side can be generally depicted with Fig. 5.

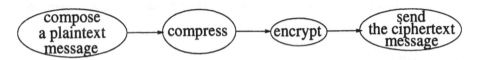

Fig. 5. Sending process at sender side

With regard to the above figure, there is no need to discuss how a plain message should be composed, and how an encrypted message should be sent into the communication channel. Let us now pay particular attention to other two modules.

An obvious role of the compress module is to reduced the size of a message. As shall be explained later, however, the most important role that the compress module could play in this secure communication scheme is to increase the difficulty in breaking ciphertexts in this scheme.

The encryption module does the concrete encryption job on a compressed message. We shall discuss the encryption process in detail in the following subsection.

The encryption algorithm

The encryption module treats a compressed message as a binary file. In theory, additions and subtractions can be done in any base such as 10. In order to make the whole communication scheme to be understood and implemented easily, we assume that the base used in both encryption and decryption is equal to 2^N, where N is a natural number. N should be kept secret as well, because without knowing N, malicious people will have to try to group the binary numbers in a ciphertext in different size.

Thus, the encryption process for a given plaintext message can be depicted in detail as follows:

The encryption algorithm

(1) **Compressing**
To compress the message into a binary file.

(2) **N-bit grouping**
Starting from the first bit of the binary file, to put every N bits into a group, and treat it as a single number in base 2^N;

(3) **2^N-base encrypting**
Using the right secret codes in the right secret code file to subtract numbers produced from step (2) one by one. As indicated before, this can be done in a fairly simple way using only logical operation $\oplus$ and arithmetic operation *mod*.

(4) **Ungrouping**
To ungroup the file into a stream of binary numbers.

(5) **written the ciphertext back into a binary file.**

Following these five steps, a plaintext message can be then encrypted into a binary ciphertext.

2.3 On the receiver side

Not only the addition and subtraction used as core operation in encryption and decryption respectively are symmetric, the whole encryption process and the whole decryption process are also symmetric. Thus, corresponding to Fig. 5, receiving process on the receiver side can be depicted with Fig. 6.

Fig. 6. Receiving process at receiver side

About this figure, we need only to spend little effort to explain the decryption algorithm, because of the symmetric feature of the communication scheme.

The decryption algorithm

Based on the decryption mechanism described above and the symmetric feature of the scheme, the decryption algorithm can be depicted in detail as follows:

The decryption algorithm

(1) **N-unit grouping**
Starting from the first bit of the binary file, to put every N bits into a group, and treat it as a single number in base 2^N;

(2) **2^N-base decrypting**
Using the right secret codes in the right secret code file to do additions with binary numbers in the ciphertext file.

(3) **Ungrouping**
Ungroup numbers in the file produced from step (2), so the compressed file is recovered.

(4) **Uncompressing**
Uncompress recovered the file produced from step (3). Consequently, the plain message file is recovered.

---

3 Evaluation of the scheme

Messages encrypted and transmitted in accordance with the communication scheme presented above are fairly safe from amateurs, crackers and career criminals who do not actually have the right secret code file. The reason is that, as with other encryption algorithms, they have to face combinatorial explosion problems if they try to break such an encrypted message by guessing the secret codes needed for decryption. Moreover, the compressing operation not only reduces the size of a message, but also make it more difficult for attackers to guess the content of the message. The trick is, we can deliberately compress the plaintext file so that the compressed file can not be uncompressed in part. As a result, even though the attackers have worked out some of the secret codes needed for decryption and conducted additions on the numbers, they still cannot reveal the corresponding part of the message. This makes our encryption scheme different from other encryption algorithms based on transposition or substitution.

Unlike the public key encryption scheme and others, this encryption scheme is not suitable for very short messages such as those occur in electronic fund transactions. A very short message encrypted in this scheme can be broken more easily than in other encryption schemes such as RSA or DES. The reason is, although we use different secret keys for different groups of compressed plaintext message, each key is small ($< 2^N$, such as 16). In contrast, other encryption systems such Merkle-Hellman and RSA algorithms use only a single secret key but very large (2^{200} or 2^{400} in some RSA encryption systems), and apply the same key repeatedly to every plaintext block. Thus, the difficulty in breaking a ciphertext in these encryption systems does not vary with the size of the text.

Compared with other encryption algorithms, the big advantage of our encryption scheme is that, it is simple and straightforward, but remain secure on messages that have reasonable length. In addition, it will be more secure if the size of a message increases. For example, given that a plaintext message has a length of 512 in bit, a cracker would have to try 2^{512} times to break the code in the worst case. This would make our scheme securer than some RSA algorithms using 400 bits keys.

Because it is simple, and does not requires expensive computation for either encryption or decryption, it can be implemented easily in software on most current computers, and in electronic devices as well. It is thus suitable for use in multiagent systems, where only limited computation resources are available for each agent. 100-or 200-digit binary numbers used as keys in Merkle-Hellman and RSA algorithms are far larger than most micro processor instructions could handle as a single quantity.

4 An example

In this section, we shall use an example to further explain how the communication scheme works. The compressing/uncompressing program we refer to in the example is *gzip*.

Suppose Robin wants to send the following message to Charlie through the Internet, which is in file **bet.msg**.

Dear Charlie,
I have decided to financially support you to buy the universe. Please withdraw the required fund from account 6969 87654321, which I have

opened on your name. You need to use 866788 as password to access the account.

Yours sincerely,

Robin,
21/12/2000

After compressing the file using *gzip*, we shall have file `bet.msg.gz` containing the following Hex numbers[2]:

```
1f8b0808066e303600036265742e6d7367002d8fb16ec3300c44777dc56d5d8c
c4765bc799d3255bd1ad2323339000877249cb86ffbe72da85cbc3dd3b7e3029
2e81748c5c39777d591803fb38f08039e11e85c4471ac70d96a729e98c2de51d
ddf2863930b2c485d5f880cf91c9d8ad710e1894d62756fec9514bdb3d4b399a
1e20ef539619ddb93ba33f75ef6faf6d53610dd1075c116861972696124ab2eb
14428f22f82e66e1bf65d9187dd79dfa1e6498c86c4dfa24a59ecd76b9fb371d
9c2b51355814cfcae3565efd4ab728956b9b63d31edbbaaedd2f59a1f1fa0c01
000000
```

Given that both Charlie and Robin have a copy of the same secret code file unknow.enc containing the following Hex numbers:

```
1f8b0808a46f30360003756e6b6e6f772e656e63004590c18e03210886efbec8
5e2633b75e7c1a77c711c43a5d84b6f4e98bd9a49b8084df1ff361dad39ec63e
d27f781b3c3f6a481fcf91f672dcf72cdf7030748690c1b882282d862d001b55
6f501b61d88f02ec8a920aa168684b9639608476ea7a6adbd65bdcbcfa65167e
985cd42e8df4c4165d2683c106accded511486942c64b846430a8381c9e2897a
fb8a1bcec3b4c29e8b838d921da5e919ffa219a28fb396c29c7f19d11a92ad8b
682ae2de5ee0f52cf76ea24ae1f902a7f4a1b89e8e82f3fd68e4fb85571e5c04
e6a2be984cb8b699b04d321af79f4edafc3796ab78d44953204bed6cf51ab867
2e0f4f97ac76b9be01c72d69ac8301000000
```

Using our encryption algorithm, the following encrypted code can be produced:

```
0000000620000000000f20114c0000041a0c12cb12a3370804456754180a1c47
0502810416315e8109c63f1e210509392c0f2e2643ef20070d8620568e070f15c
1004742000153540507209c820901110ae5550c18a065514870069602dd4c870a
274d86030c4a15568802e3161901940ae9820f4b5f424f900732345ea292086d0
1b31122919a9e281bcb4e9c3e28002518941e3f861282095a4165268327124c07
460387aa45134e450886032b4e220c48028e09c68641120b4a6a1699294340171
610034daa2f0f0bcb56ac628f07bfab3419059c8b2754b6020a0e0b001206050
```

On the receiver side, Charlie can easily decrypt the code into plain message using the decryption algorithm described in subsection 2.3.

---

[2] To be included in the paper, newlines have been added here. Also, as can be seen, we use 2^4 as the base of numbers in both encryption and decryption.

5 Discussions

We have reported in this paper a secure communication scheme for multiagent systems, including its mathematical principles. It is simple yet secure, as long as the secret codes are kept securely on both sides of the communication channel, and the plaintext messages are enough longer.

Compared with other encryption schemes such as DES and RSA, it has advantages of simplicity, less expensive in computation on both encryption and decryption. A disadvantage might be some inconvenience in producing, transporting and keeping many large secret code files. One way to solve this problem is to use a block of secret keys repeatedly on a plaintext message. The encryption will remain secure if the block is enough big, say containing at least some hundreds of bits.

In addition to using blocks of secret keys repeatedly, a variety of other changes could be made to the scheme. For example, we may use a different pair of encryption function, denoted as $E(K_e, P)$, and decryption function, denoted as $D(K_d, C)$, in the communication scheme, instead of the simple one presented. We may also utilise different secret keys for encryption and decryption, if a pair of suitable functions $C = E(K_e, P)$ and $P = D(K_d, C)$ could be carefully designed. These are remaining questions for us to look at next.

Note: In preparing this paper, some small programs have been written for test and evaluation purpose. They are available free of charge on request for non-commercial parties.

References

1. James A. Cooper, *Computer & Communications Security– Strategies for the 1990s*, pages 310-331, McGraw-Hill, 1989.
2. Pfleeger, Charles P., *Security in Computing*, pages 4-6, Prentice Hall, 1997.
3. Kinny D. and Georgeff, Modelling and Designing of Multi-Agent System, in Jörg P. Müller et al. (eds.) *Intelligent Agent III*, Springer-Verlag, LNAI 1193, pages 1-20, 1993.
4. Rao A.S., Georgeff M. P.(1991), Modelling rational agents within a BDI architecture, in *Proceedings of KR'91 Conference*, Cambridge, Mass, pages 473-384.
5. Kaynak, O., Honderd, G. and Edward G., *Intelligent systems : safety, reliability and maintainability issues*, NATO Advanced Research Workshop on Intelligent Systems: Safety, Reliability, and Maintainability Issues (1992 : Kusadasi, Izmir, Turkey), Springer Verlag, 1993.
6. Boutilier C., Shoham Y. and Wellman M., Economic principles of multi-agent systems, *Artificial Intelligence* 94(1997), pages 1-6, Elsevier, 1997.
7. Wilfred C. Jamison, ACACIA: An agency based collaboration framework for heterogeneous multiagent systems, in Chengqi Z and Lukose D. (eds.) *Multi-Agent Systems – Methodologies and Applications*, Lecture Notes in Artificial Intelligence (LNAI-1286), Springer Verlag Publishers, 1997.

8. T. Balch and R.C Arkin, Motor schema-based formation control for multiagent robot teams, in *Proceedings of 1st International Conference on Multiagent Systems*, pages 10-16, 1995.

9. Mark d'Inverno, Michael Luck and Michael Wooldridge, Cooperation Structures, in *Proceedings of Fifteenth International Joint Conference on Artificial Intelligence*, Morgan Kaufmann Publishers, pp600-605, 1997.

10. Wang H., Constrained Object Hierarchies – An Architecture for Intelligent Systems, doctoral consortium abstract, in *Proceedings of Fifteenth International Joint Conference on Artificial Intelligence*, Morgan Kaufmann Publishers, pp1546, 1997.

11. David Carmel and Shaul Markovitch, Exploration and adaptation in multiagent systems: a model-based approach,in *Proceedings of Fifteenth International Joint Conference on Artificial Intelligence*, Morgan Kaufmann Publishers, pp606-611, 1997.

12. Wang H. and John K. Slaney, On Generalities of Intelligent Systems, *Technical Report* TR-ARP-05-98, Automated Reasoning Project, The Australian National University, 1998.

13. Wang H. and John K. Slaney, The Design of an intelligent system for retrieving and compiling information over the World Wide Web, in *Proceedings of Asian Pacific Web Conference (APWeb98)*, Beijing, 1998.

14. Wang H. , *GISM*: A Language for modelling and developing agent-based intelligent systems, in *Proceedings of the Fourth Australian Workshop On Distributed Artificial Intelligence*, Brisbane, also in LNAI volume 1544, Springer Verlag Publishers, 1998.

15. Wang H., *Constrained object hierarchies—an ontology of intelligent systems*, PhD thesis(under examination), The Australia National University, 1999.

Author Index

Springer
and the
environment

At Springer we firmly believe that an
international science publisher has a
special obligation to the environment,
and our corporate policies consistently
reflect this conviction.
We also expect our business partners –
paper mills, printers, packaging
manufacturers, etc. – to commit
themselves to using materials and
production processes that do not harm
the environment. The paper in this
book is made from low- or no-chlorine
pulp and is acid free, in conformance
with international standards for paper
permanency.

Springer

Lecture Notes in Artificial Intelligence (LNAI)

Lecture Notes in Computer Science